MARCH

THE GRAND PRIX & INDY CARS by ALAN HENRY

MAR

THE GRAND PRIX & INDY CARS

by ALAN HENRY

CH

PUBLISHER
Richard Poulter

EXECUTIVE PUBLISHER
Elizabeth Le Breton

ART EDITOR
Steve Small

EXECUTIVE PRODUCTION MANAGER
George Greenfield

HOUSE EDITOR
Peter Lovering

PRODUCTION ASSISTANT
Deirdre Fenney

Colour photography by:

Pages 81-96	–	David Phipps
Pages 161, 162-3, 164-5	–	David Phipps/Phipps Photographic
Pages 166-7, 168-9	–	Allsport/Pascal Rondeau
Pages 170-1, 172-3, 174, 176	–	David Hutson
Page 175	–	Rick Miller

Black and white photographs contributed by:
Allsport/Pascal Rondeau, Jutta Fausel, Alan Henry, David Hutson, International Press Agency/Jad Sherif, Lisa B. Newsome, Robert B. Newsome, David Phipps/Phipps Photographic and Mark Sproule.

Acknowledgements

In preparing this book I have benefited from a great deal of assistance from a wide variety of sources. While it may seem invidious to select some people for special thanks, I would like to record my appreciation of the care and attention to detail with which Max Mosley and Gordon Kirby checked the draft manuscript of the F1 and Indy car sections respectively.

Thanks are also due to Robin Herd, Alan Rees, Dave Reeves, Peter Briggs, Bob Dance, James Gresham, Gordon Coppuck, Ian Phillips, Adrian Newey, Alan Mertens, Les McTaggert, Teddy Mayer, Tyler Alexander, Alan Jenkins and Richard Seth-Smith.

Alan Henry
June 1989

This first edition published in 1989 by
Hazleton Publishing, 3 Richmond Hill, Richmond,
Surrey TW10 6RE.

ISBN: 0-905138-65-1

Printed in England by Butler & Tanner Ltd, Frome, Somerset.

Typesetting by First Impression Graphics Ltd, Richmond, Surrey.

DISTRIBUTORS

USA
Motorbooks International
PO Box 2, 729 Prospect Av.
Osceola, Wisconsin 54020

Paul Oxman Publishing
17165 Newhope
Unit M
Fountain Valley
CA 92708

Australia
Technical Book & Magazine Co.
289-299 Swanston Street
Melbourne, Victoria 3000

New Zealand
David Bateman Ltd
PO Box 65062
Mairangi Bay
Auckland 10

UK and Other Markets
Osprey Publishing Ltd
59 Grosvenor Street
London W1X 9DA

Contents

Foreword by
MAX MOSLEY

When I told my father I intended to give up the Bar and join Robin and the others in starting March, he said, 'You'll almost certainly go bankrupt, but it will be very good training for something serious later on.' He may or may not have been right about the training, but he was certainly near the mark on the bankruptcy.

March was started just as the big motor industry spending of the Sixties was coming to an end, but before the advent of the pure advertising sponsor. There was never enough income, nor did we have anything approaching the amount of capital needed. The business was a financial puzzle from day one.

Everything we did has to be seen in the context of this acute lack of cash. Probably the worst aspect was that we never found out what Robin might have done in the early Seventies had he been given the financial resources to develop his ideas fully.

We did, however, begin the process which led to the development of modern Grand Prix racing. Some rounds of the 1969 World Championship had only 13 cars. All this changed in 1970 with ten March Formula 1 cars built and usually five or six of them on the grid. In addition, everyone could see there was nothing magic about Formula 1 – if we could start in September with an empty shed and no money yet be on the front row of the grid the following March, so could they.

Of course, this was only possible because we were fortunate enough to assemble an extraordinarily able group of helpers. They achieved an astonishing amount in the early days, working day and night under great pressure. Most of them are still in the motor racing business and now occupy very senior positions.

If anyone wants some good examples of what not to do in business and at the same time an insight into an activity which fascinates millions and is now shown on television in every major country (even China), they should read this book. For my part, I find it difficult to believe that 20 years have gone by and the early days of March are now part of motor racing history.

Max Mosley
London
June 1989

Introduction

March Engineering started by building a Formula 3 special in a Twyford garage – and ended up, 20 years later, as easily the most prolific manufacturer of production racing cars in the world. This book deals with the company's two most prestigious projects, fielding Grand Prix machines and building the Indy cars which took the North American CART racing scene by storm in the mid-1980s.

When the story began, it revolved round four people: Max Mosley, Robin Herd, Alan Rees and Graham Coaker. Although Coaker's tenure with the company was brief, as he died in 1971, the other three are still deeply involved in motor racing. Mosley, having finally convinced himself that a political career would almost certainly be forever haunted by the ghost of his father, Sir Oswald, fulfils a crucial role representing the interests of the major motor manufacturers within the sport's governing body, FISA. Rees is manager of the Arrows Grand Prix team. Only Herd remains involved with the company he helped establish almost exactly 20 years ago.

While the timing of the company's Indy car onslaught could hardly have been more successful from a business standpoint, I think Robin would accept that he never unlocked his true potential as an F1 designer. Many of March's F1 designs were the product of financial and commercial expediency rather than an unfettered commitment to engineering excellence. That was largely because the company always had to keep an eye on its wider interests as a builder of 'proprietary' racing cars on a commercial basis, although it is also true that it never really had the sponsorship budget to get the job done.

Herd was described to me by one old confederate as 'absolutely brilliant. So brilliant, in fact, that he never really had to try if he wanted to do something...but also rather lazy'. Max Mosley, who knew Robin at university, emphatically rejects such a contention. 'Robin may have given the impression of taking a relaxed view of everything, but you don't achieve what he has without considerable effort.'

In terms of business success, it has to be recorded that March has had its fair share of ups and downs – probably rather more of the latter, on balance. You will read within these pages how the company obtained a Stock Exchange listing, then turned in such appalling losses that a major restructuring – including the sale of its F1 team – had to be effected in the early months of 1989.

As I write these words, the company is entering a period of consolidation, taking the first steps to regain the share of the lucrative customer Indy car market which it has lost through a combination of technical complacency and misjudgement over the last few years. Whether Herd and his colleagues climb back onto the commercial high wire once more remains to be seen. Either way, the rest of us will have a lot of fun watching their efforts.

Alan Henry
Montreal
June 1989

In the beginning. Cadwell Park, September 1969: Ronnie Peterson starts the prototype March 693 (no.2) from the outside of the front row in its maiden race. In pole position is Tim Schenken's Brabham BT28, with the Tecno of Jean-Pierre Jaussaud in the middle.

Section 1: The Grand Prix Cars

Chapter 1

In the beginning

Viewed from a distance of two decades, the foundation of March Engineering towards the end of 1969 seems nothing particularly out of the ordinary. A new racing car manufacturer – so what was all the fuss about? There are, and were, plenty of those around. But to appreciate the impact on the sport resulting from the formation of the new company, it is necessary to understand the character of the English motor racing scene in the late 1960s.

Britain was, and remains, the home of the proprietary racing car, built by a number of small companies for the junior single-seater and sports car formulae. Twenty years ago the best-known names in that specialised area were Lotus, Brabham and Lola. Cooper, which had made its mark in the early 1950s, particularly in the world of 500 cc Formula 3 racing, had gradually faltered and finally closed its doors at the end of 1968. As if to take its place, the Bolton-based Chevron company started to make competitive inroads into the huge one-litre Formula 3 market.

Lotus, of course, was at that time riding high on the Grand Prix scene, but its commercial racing car manufacturing operation proved a profitable sideline for Colin Chapman's organisation. Eric Broadley's Lolas had carved themselves an individualistic niche. Most successful by far, however, was the Brabham marque. Throughout the Sixties a whole succession of Brabham Formulae 2 and 3 cars earned designer Ron Tauranac a reputation for producing sturdy, practical, good-handling and easy to set up chassis which proved enormously popular with amateur and professional alike.

Moreover the European Formula 3 market was simply huge, soaking up between 80 and 100 customer cars a year in the late 1960s. Granted, similar production outputs are achieved today by Ralt and Reynard, but the difference in those days was that the cost was manageable. In 1966, for example, English private owner John Fenning (whose company, based in Stockbridge, Hampshire, today produces the Willans seat harnesses used by many Grand Prix teams) undertook a programme of British and selected European Formula 3 races – a total of 15 events – with a Brabham BT15 at an overall cost, after selling the car at the end of the season, of £5243. That figure includes the purchase of the Brabham (price £2275), and operating costs such as spares, fuel and tyres.

Contrast that with the outlay involved on a 1989 Ralt or Reynard F3 chassis, together with a Volkswagen or Toyota engine, and the modern situation compares quite unfavourably from the standpoint of the independent driver wanting to have a crack at an international single-seater category. Typical budgets for the 17-race Lucas British F3 Championship in 1989 are in the region of £180,000. Inflation has not increased prices thirty-fold in the last 23 years, so the junior categories are overwhelmingly more expensive in real terms than they were when March Engineering contemplated its first hesitant steps onto the motor racing scene.

This becomes even more apparent if we consider that, when Max Mosley embarked on a season of international Formula 2 at the wheel of a private Brabham BT23C in the spring of 1968, the whole project cost him about £5000, allowing for the resale of his car at the end of the year. In 1989 a corresponding season in the International Formula 3000 series would set you back an absolute minimum of £300,000. And that sort of budget would be regarded as distinctly modest, sufficient to get you into the field but unlikely to offer much chance of significant success.

The reader may correctly conclude that the foregoing is not directly relevant to the foundation of March Engineering. It is offered merely to set the scene, to provide a flavour of the times, to reflect the prevailing situation in the motor racing business. In order to comprehend how the partners who created the company came together – and established their aims – one really needs to be an expert in contemporary motor racing genealogy.

March Engineering was the product of four enthusiastic individuals, all of whom had subtly

Firestone
STP
STP
STP
STP

different ambitions and aspirations for their joint project, the name of which was an acronym produced from their initials (Mosley, Alan Rees, Coaker, Herd). That is probably the only straightforward aspect of the company's early days.

Robin Herd, the man charged with the task of penning the first March racing cars, was as highly qualified as any designer on the contemporary motor racing scene. Hailing from near Ross-on-Wye, he was educated at Monmouth School before going up to Oxford, where he was to graduate from St Peter's College with a double First in Physics and Engineering, with the second-highest marks of all time, a monumental achievement on the subject of which he has always retained an air of disarming modesty. Joining the Royal Aircraft Establishment at Farnborough in 1961, Robin quickly progressed to the status of Senior Scientific Officer at the remarkably early age of 24.

This is where the 'family tree' element of the story becomes entangled. In 1953, while at Monmouth School, Herd had regularly occupied the back row of the Headmaster's Divinity classes with a fellow pupil called Alan Rees who shared his burgeoning enthusiasm for motor racing. The son of a haulage contractor from Langstone near Newport, Rees confided to Herd that he was going to become a racing driver. It was a view about which Herd had his reservations. Predictably, Rees and Herd concentrated not on the Testaments, but on crumpled copies of motor sporting magazines, as they sat together whispering about their future. History has variously related that the magazines concerned were *Motor Sport* and/or *Autosport* but, reflecting on those heady days of youth, Rees is quite firm on the matter: 'No, it was that one with the bright yellow cover which isn't printed any longer – *Motor Racing*.'

Rees went on to obtain an Economics degree from the University of Wales before pursuing his motor racing career to considerable effect during the late 1950s and early '60s. Meanwhile Herd was to meet another personality during his time at Oxford who would eventually take a central role in the story of March Engineering. This was Max Mosley, the youngest child, born in 1940, of the gifted and controversial pre-war British Fascist leader, Sir Oswald Mosley, and his second wife, the former Diana Guinness, one of the famous Mitford sisters.

Diana Mosley referred to Max when he was still a baby as the *'Entschlossener'* – the determined one. It was a supremely appropriate label for a child who seemed to have inherited the charisma of his mother and the steel and persuasiveness of his father. He admits he wasn't a terribly adroit student, receiving a cosmopolitan education in France and Germany after his father left England in 1950. 'I also got myself expelled from one school following a slight misunderstanding with a teacher who found me in the girls' dormitory,' he recalls.

None the less, with the benefit of private tuition, Max caught up in time to gain a place at Oxford. He studied Physics and Law at Christ Church and seemed on course for the Presidency of the Oxford Union, getting as far as Secretary before the spectre of his father's somewhat extreme political views cast a troublesome shadow across his path.

He went on to become a barrister, being called to the Bar in 1964 and later specialising in the complexities of patent and trade mark law. He also realised an ambition to go motor racing which had originally been fired by a visit to Silverstone while he was still up at Oxford, trying his hand at Clubmans racing at the wheel of a U2 sports car in 1966 and '67 and scoring lots of wins and lap records. He graduated ambitiously to Formula 2 a couple of seasons later but then retired in 1969 after crashing his Lotus 59 when its suspension broke at the Nürburgring during practice for the Eifelrennen. It had suddenly dawned on him that he wasn't on course to become World Champion. Friends say it was absolutely typical of Max that, if he couldn't be good at any given task, then he didn't want to know.

As far as the legal profession was concerned, Max decided there must be more obviously exciting things to do with his life. 'One day, walking through the Middle Temple, it struck me that, if I could stick this out for forty years, I might become a senior, respected barrister. I might even become a judge. But I'd be stuck in court on hot summer days having to wear a suit. I reckoned there had to be something better to do.'

Herd recalls thinking Mosley was 'a rather arrogant piece of work' on first acquaintance, but later warmed to his personality, which was to soften appreciably in the years before March Engineering set up shop. Alan Rees met Mosley through F2 racing, Max's Brabham being kept at Frank Williams's premises, not far from the base of Winkelmann Racing who ran the Brabhams to beat for Alan and Jochen Rindt. 'I got my mechanic, Jon Redgrave, to get Rindt's chassis settings from his mechanic, Pete Kerr,' recalls Max with relish. Incidentally, Jochen never believed Max was a lawyer because he looked too young...

Alan, knowing that Robin was keen to pursue a career in motor racing design, tipped him

Dawn of a bright new future! The March founders (left to right) ***Robin Herd, Alan Rees, Graham Coaker and Max Mosley pose with one of the brand new March 701s outside the Bicester factory, early February 1970.***

When the world was young. Robin Herd in his short-back-and-sides phase, 1970-guise. The years have been easy on him...

...but not as easy as they have on Max Mosley. Looking positively schoolboyish, the March director makes a point with all the demonstrative poise one would expect from a barrister.

Graham Coaker works on an F3 spaceframe in 1970. His knowledge of organisational methods was invaluable in March's first year as the production side of the business gradually took off.

off in 1965 that Bruce McLaren was casting about for a designer to work on his forthcoming 3-litre F1 project. Contact was made with Bruce via Johnny Muller (later to become one of the best F1 mechanics in the business), fellow Kiwi Howden Ganley (then working at McLaren) and Bruce's co-director Teddy Mayer. A deal was duly done which saw Robin installed behind a drawing board at McLaren's Colnbrook factory, where he penned the ultra-strong, but very heavy, Mallite-monocoque M2 which was raced with both Ford stock-block and Serenissima V8 engines during 1966.

Robin's spell with Bruce's company lasted through to the end of 1967, by which time he had produced the one-off M5 (to take a V12 BRM engine), the unbelievably successful M6 Can-Am challenger and the first Cosworth-engined McLaren, the M7. He then left, much to Bruce McLaren's dismay, to join Cosworth Engineering, where his new brief was to produce the Northampton firm's four-wheel drive contender.

Cosworth boss Keith Duckworth had concluded that four-wheel drive was the answer for Grand Prix cars in the DFV era, having witnessed the surplus of power over adhesion produced by his V8 engine when installed in the back of Colin Chapman's Lotus 49. Of course the development of aerofoils over the next couple of seasons spiked this project before it ever had the opportunity to race, but Herd's concept was undeniably a striking and imaginative piece of design engineering.

'It was possibly rather shallow thinking,' Robin now concedes. 'If we'd all dwelt on it a little bit longer, we would probably have appreciated that, with trends going the way they were, four-wheel drive wasn't really practical.' Herd regarded the disappointment of the Cosworth F1 car as signalling the end of his period with the company, although Duckworth did ask him to stay on and work on the engine side. But Robin knew that chassis development was the area which really interested him and in 1970 he commented: 'March really dates back to the day when Keith decided there would not be another Cosworth car after the four-wheel drive. After working for McLaren and Cosworth, at the peak of chassis and engine development respectively, working for anybody else would have been something of a letdown. The only thing left was to go out and create one's own folly.'

By the end of 1968 Rees had also reached a turning point, having concluded that he wasn't going to win a World Championship after all. Despite demonstrating considerable talent in F2, where he frequently proved capable of matching Rindt's speed, his sole F1 outing came at the wheel of an uncompetitive Cooper-Maserati in the 1967 British Grand Prix at Silverstone. He admits that he sensed his entry wasn't regarded too seriously by the fact that his car was left out in the rain at the scrutineering bay the night prior to the race...

At the end of 1968 the spark of Rees's racing ambition had gone out and he quit the cockpit, but he was keen to sustain and expand a management role and the challenge of running another team was something he relished.

Graham Coaker, at 37, was the oldest of the March founders. An amateur F3 driver, he had previously been Production Controller of Components at Hawker Siddeley and came to March from Serck radiators at Slough. His expertise was to help establish the production car aspect of the business, although his tenure at Bicester proved tragically brief. 'He was to make an extremely significant contribution to March in our early days,' says Rees firmly. 'I think a lot of people tend seriously to underestimate the importance of his role. He knew a lot about motor racing and the problems of production.'

However, before the new company finally got off the ground, there was another development bubbling away behind the scenes, involving the mercurial Austrian driver Jochen Rindt. Jochen's Grand Prix aspirations had continually been thwarted ever since his F1 debut in 1965, neither the Cooper nor Brabham teams being in a position to offer him machinery that would do justice to his enormous talent. At the start of the 1969 season he signed with Team Lotus, but it wasn't really the most comfortable of marriages. Chapman, who'd built up a near-telepathic relationship with the great Jim Clark, had been desolated after the Scot was killed in a Hockenheim Formula 2 accident early in 1968. He signed Rindt because he was the man most likely to get on terms with F1's new pacesetting combination, Jackie Stewart and the Tyrrell Matra.

There was no doubting Rindt's raw talent. Throughout his years of F1 disappointment his speed in Formula 2 was simply electrifying. By the end of the 1968 season he had gained no fewer than 19 victories in the three years since he had joined the private F2 team owned by entrepreneur Roy Winkelmann, which was managed by Rees (who drove the other car) and supported by both BP and Firestone. In 1968 Winkelmann had attempted to raise support for an F1 team which would, he hoped, provide Rindt with a winning car. 'It had some possibilities, but it wasn't really a proposition which went very far,' Rees allows.

Far more serious were Jochen's 1969 plans to establish his own F1 team. Moreover he wanted Robin Herd to come aboard as chief designer. What followed was a rather complex sequence of events, just at the time that March Engineering was on the verge of flickering into life. Robin recalls being entertained to dinner at an expensive restaurant off London's Berkeley Square by Jochen's business manager Bernie Ecclestone. The proposition put to him was that a new company should be set up, with Rindt and Herd each taking 45 per cent of the shareholding, the remaining ten per cent going to Ecclestone, but it never quite came off.

It is tantalising to speculate how things would have developed had the Rindt/Herd/Ecclestone F1 triumvirate got off the ground. Bernie's savvy and commercial expertise would almost certainly have developed about four years earlier than they did, to the unquestionable benefit of Grand Prix racing as a whole.

Herd has always remained slightly reflective about the potential of the proposed Rindt deal. In 1973 he told the author: 'For certain obvious reasons I'd have loved to do it, because I'd simply have been the designer, not obliged to take on a business role as well. I like to think that some of March's designs have suffered because of this.'

In the event, after wavering, Robin threw in his lot with Mosley, Rees and Coaker. Max, with characteristic eloquence and diplomacy, tried to turn the whole thing round, visiting Rindt and asking him whether he might consider driving for March.

At this stage of the game, the first March Formula 3 prototype was being finished off in a shed at the bottom of Graham Coaker's garden near Twyford. Rindt's response has echoed down the years. 'That's just something that's being cobbled together in Graham's shack,' he said disparagingly. In his clipped Austrian accent, it came over as 'Grem's shek'. Suitably amused, Max duly registered it as a business name: Gremshek Ltd. 'Absolutely typical Jochen,' laughed Rees. 'If he couldn't control the whole deal, then he just didn't want to know.'

The first March 693 prototype crept onto the motor racing stage almost unannounced, taking part in a handful of F3 races towards the end of 1969. Built round a sturdy square-tube spaceframe, the prototype used specially fabricated front uprights, and Brabham rear uprights, with Lotus front and Brabham rear wheel rims. It was very conventional, with double wishbone suspension all round and outboard coil-spring/dampers.

The driver selected to debut the first March would not only become a celebrated Grand Prix driver in his own right, but also March's personal baby, a man who is remembered with high esteem and great affection by Herd, Mosley and Rees to this day. He was Ronnie Peterson.

Rees had been keeping tabs on the blond Swede from Orebro ever since he had won a sensational victory in the 1969 Monaco Grand Prix supporting race. Rindt's move to the Lotus Grand Prix team meant that Winkelmann Racing had switched from Brabham BT23Cs to Lotus 59s in order to sustain Jochen's F2 challenge. Mosley and Rees collaborated to get Peterson into Max's Lotus 59, now surplus to requirements, to race at Albi in southern France.

'By then we'd given up trying to get a Stewart or a Rindt on board, so it was a case of looking elsewhere,' said Rees. But he was soon convinced that Ronnie was the answer, purely on the strength of what he saw at Albi.

'During practice, Ronnie happened to go out of the pits during a rain shower and came up onto the tail of Jackie Stewart's Matra. He kept up with him for five laps on a soaking track. You could see Jackie glancing in his mirrors trying to work out who it was chasing him. He could see it was one of our Lotuses, but it clearly wasn't Jochen or Graham Hill behind the wheel. Eventually Stewart came into the pits to get rid of him. On the strength of those few laps I was absolutely certain that Ronnie would win Grands Prix. To my mind it was utterly obvious.'

After Albi Ronnie signed on with March, who promised him a Grand Prix drive in 1970 as well as a full season of European Formula 2. In fact, the week prior to the race debut of the March 693, the company's ambitious plans exploded across the pages of Europe's motor racing magazines. March was going to build cars for F1, F2, F3, Formula Ford, Can-Am and the American Formula B series. Moreover it was going to field factory teams in the first four of those categories and, as events were soon to prove, this was only the start. Recalls Robin, 'Our optimism was incredible.'

The four March directors had strictly divided areas of responsibility. Robin was to concentrate on design; sales and marketing would be Max's sphere; Alan devoted himself to team management and Graham took on the task of building up a production facility for customer cars. Backing them up were three key technicians. They were Pete Kerr, formerly Rindt's mechanic at Winkelmann Racing, John Thompson, who had done all the sheet metal work on Herd's Cosworth and McLaren designs, and Ray Wardell, previously responsible for Church Farm Racing's semi-works McLaren, which had won the inaugural British Formula 5000 Championship in the hands of Peter Gethin.

March Engineering's first factory was established on the Launton Road Industrial Estate at Bicester, where it remains in much-expanded form to this day. The first 3000 sq. ft facility, from which the innocently prying author remembers being summarily ejected by Mosley in the summer of 1970 after trying to sneak a glimpse of the first March 712 monocoque, today houses the March/Porsche Indy car chassis development project, just one constituent part of the March Group's diverse business projects. In the early autumn of 1969 it contained a telephone on the floor and not much else.

The news of March Engineering's ambitious plans was met with a mixture of fascination and disbelief by the British motor racing community, many of whom reckoned the new concern was trying to be too clever by half. Unkindly, they would soon become dubbed 'the Bullshit Racers', while a cruel alternative interpretation of the company acronym ('Much-Advertised Racing Car Hoax') was repeated with glee wherever racing people met. Rather unfairly, some critics thought Robin a little smug and Max's saturnine gloss a bit too rich for the pudding.

Meanwhile friends close to March in those backs-to-the-wall formative months recall a sense of almost mischievous amusement on the part of the directors. The more the project was written off as impossibly ambitious, the more confident and expansive they seemed to become. If people wanted to regard the 1970 season as March versus the Rest of the World, then so be it.

The company was funded by an investment of £2500 each on the part of the four founders, so they were obviously anxious to see how their new F3 prototype would fare in the Cadwell Park F3 international at the end of September. By that point both Rees and Herd had shrewdly offset the cost by collecting on a stake of £500 each, at 2-1, that Jackie Stewart would win the 1969 World Championship.

Peterson finished third at Cadwell and, but for a puncture, would probably have won. A week later, at the Montlhéry circuit near Paris, he upended the 693 after clipping a straw bale and the car caught fire. Only thanks to the prompt action of some marshals, aided by Ray Wardell who sprinted from the nearby pits, did Ronnie escape with superficial burns on his arms and wrist. He didn't race again that season and the rebuilt March 693 had its final outing in the Brands Hatch Motor Show 200 meeting, where the virtually unknown James Hunt brought it home eighth.

That was the easy bit. More challenging was the prospect of getting the Grand Prix team off the ground. Peterson was a good long-term bet to grow up hand-in-hand with the new organisation, but the March works effort really needed a top-line runner from day one. Stewart, Rindt and Jack Brabham all seemed to be out of bounds for a variety of reasons, so attention then turned to the 'number four' choice on Alan Rees's list. This was Chris Amon, the talented New Zealander who had spent the previous three seasons wrestling with a succession of promising, but horrifyingly unreliable, Ferraris. Chris, whose capacity for going to the wrong team at the wrong time was becoming something of a legend in motor racing circles, stood poised to quit Maranello just as the Italian team came good. As Mario Andretti once put it: 'I figure if Chris ever became an undertaker, people would stop dying.'

While Amon considered and evaluated his options, March, just like Topsy, 'growed and growed'. Andy Granatelli's STP oil additive company came in as 'major sponsor', contributing £25,000 to the works team's 1970 budget. But this wasn't anywhere near enough and Peterson sensed he was being squeezed out when Porsche approached March with an offer of £30,000 to include Jo Siffert in the works line-up alongside Amon. A highly valued member of the German company's endurance racing team, Siffert was being romanced by Ferrari with offers of both F1 and sports car programmes. If Porsche wanted to keep him, they had to find him an F1 berth. March accepted the moustached Swiss – and his bag of Porsche money – with open arms.

In addition, Firestone produced £27,000 to assist the effort and Mosley, ever the optimist,

An enormous amount of media attention attached to the new March, due partly to the fact that Ford bought two of the cars for Ken Tyrrell's team. This 'family group' shows Jackie Stewart in the cockpit, Ken on the car's left-front wheel and Ford's Walter Hayes on the right-front wheel. Cosworth's Keith Duckworth is to Stewart's right, alongside Dunlop's Dick Jeffrey, Herd and Alex Meskell. Number two driver Johnny Servoz-Gavin is sitting on the left-rear wheel.

calculated that a three-car works team (including Peterson's entry) would earn about £30,000 in prize money, bonuses and so forth. That meant the total projected income was around £112,000, excluding driver fees. With the cost of operating the team projected at around £140,000, and with Amon still to be paid a £40,000 retainer, it was clearly going to need more than a little creative accounting for the situation to make any sort of financial sense. I suggested to Max in 1989 that this really meant they couldn't afford to pay Amon. He thought for a moment, then replied: 'I think you've summed it up quite accurately!'

Meanwhile the March manufacturing facility was taking shape amidst a frenzied hubbub of activity at the Launton Road factory. Production versions of the F3 car were to be priced at £1870 for a rolling chassis with gearbox, and it was also anticipated that a handful of March 702 Formula 2 machines would be made available to private customers, these at £2600 for a rolling chassis. But the European F2 challenge was to be spearheaded by a semi-works team, Malcolm Guthrie Racing, run by the son of former BOAC Chairman Sir Giles Guthrie. Ronnie Peterson would drive the number one car, with Malcolm (now Sir Malcolm), who had previously campaigned a private Brabham BT30, in the second entry.

The next customer for a 701 was STP, now assuming the role of entrant. Mario Andretti, who had won the 1969 Indy 500 for STP, had also been intermittently involved in F1 with Lotus over the previous couple of seasons. Now he wanted to dovetail his Indy car commitments with a limited programme of F1, so a requisition for another March 701 was duly fed into the manufacturing system, such as it was, for Andretti's use under the management of Vince Granatelli, Andy's younger brother.

Enquiries came crowding in and Amon, who had originally been sold the idea of driving for the new team on the basis of a degree of exclusivity – just a couple of works cars for him and, perhaps, Peterson – was already beginning to wonder whether the March directors had not perhaps bitten off more than they could chew. Moreover there was still a major obligation to Ronnie. Eventually that was fulfilled by gaining sponsorship from Colin Crabbe's Antique Automobiles outfit, and another works-assisted March F1 entry was added to the seemingly never-ending list of potential runners.

At this point Ken Tyrrell entered the equation. After a great deal of soul-searching and not inconsiderable anxiety he and Jackie Stewart had decided that they would have to split with Matra, for whom they had won the World Championship in 1969. The French aerospace company was hell-bent on running its own V12 engine for 1970, but both entrant and driver knew that it wasn't really a match for the Ford-financed Cosworth DFV. In short the World Champion was casting around for a new chassis in which to install Duckworth's engine.

'I tried to get a Brabham or McLaren chassis but, not surprisingly, nobody wanted to sell me one!' says Ken Tyrrell with an infectious grin. While Max and Robin were talking to respected private entrant Rob Walker about the possibility of selling him yet another 701 for Graham Hill's use, a phone call came through from Tyrrell. He wanted to speak with the March directors. They remember him being somewhat aloof about the whole business, but Rees quickly sized up the situation and realised that, at the end of the day, Ken had no choice but to have the March. He was absolutely correct.

A March 701 rolling chassis cost in the region of £2500 to build. Mosley offered Tyrrell three chassis at £6000 apiece but, after Ken had paid the deposits, the March directors were called to a meeting with Ford's Walter Hayes in London.

'I told them that they would soon be out of business if they didn't price the cars higher than that,' Walter recalls. So March increased their price – and Ford ended up paying £9000 each for the two Tyrrell race cars. It was cheap money to keep Jackie Stewart on the books, although Max recollects that he made Ken squeal like hell by billing him direct for another £9000 for the team's spare chassis! 'But, since Ken couldn't really tell me that Ford had in fact already agreed to buy the cars, but only two of them, he couldn't do much more than grizzle,' laughs Max. 'But Walter's advice made the difference between staying in business and going under. At the end of the year we finished up with a nominal profit of £2000. If we'd sold the seven customer 701s we produced for £6000 each, we'd have lost over £20,000 and that would have been that.'

Section 1: The Grand Prix Cars

Chapter 2

The bright days of youth, 1970-72

By the start of January 1970 Chris Amon found himself facing something of a dilemma. He was both tantalised and frustrated at the prospect of Tyrrell also fielding March 701s during the coming season. He had yet to set eyes on the first of Robin Herd's new creations, but expressed grave reservations about the way in which the new team's efforts threatened to be spread too thinly over an excessive number of cars.

'It would have been all right if they'd stuck to their original intention,' he reflected. 'When I signed to drive, it was in a single-car team with a spare car. Within weeks, Siffert came along, and Peterson, and Andretti. And they were selling the damn' things to Tyrrell as well. I don't reckon I got the best deal out of that little operation.'

However, the prospect of having a crack at the reigning World Champion in equal machinery acted as a spur to his confidence. He liked and respected Stewart, but reckoned he could match him in terms of natural talent, although by no stretch of the imagination in organisation and business savvy.

Back at Bicester Max had set 5 February as the day on which the March 701 would be unveiled at Silverstone. There was a certain amount of symbolism about this. There was really no need for the cars to be ready by then, for the season was not scheduled to open until 7 March with the South African Grand Prix at Kyalami. Admittedly, there was a crucially important tyre-testing session preceding the race, but by the standards of the late 1980s, when some teams are virtually putting the finishing touches to their new cars in the pit lane on the morning of first qualifying at the opening Grand Prix of the season, March Engineering was being remarkably cautious. But people were watching for them to make the first slip. If they didn't make that unveiling date, the project's entire credibility would be called into question.

The March directors photographed with Vince Granatelli** (left, hiding Mosley). **Mario Andretti's STP 701, hurriedly wheeled out of the build shop minus its cockpit top, is on the left.

Alan Rees summed up succinctly the prevailing mood during those heady days prior to the launch. 'In some ways, the whole project only really survived on the enormous amount of publicity it received,' he grins. 'In fact, looking back at it all, I sometimes think perhaps it shouldn't really have worked. It all seems enormously ambitious.'

Finally the great day dawned. Mosley couldn't have stage-managed things better. Silverstone in February could just as easily have been under several feet of snow, but on this particular Friday in 1970 the Gods chose to smile on the audacious new boys. The weather was cold and bright. Two March 701s were on hand, stubby and not terribly attractive to the eye.

Tyrrell's blue car arrived in his distinctive transporter, which had itself been the subject of a fair amount of publicity a couple of years earlier. Its Leyland chassis had started life as a bus bound for Cuba, but the ship on which it was being carried sank in the Thames after a collision. When the salvaged remains of the cargo were sold off, Tyrrell enterprisingly acquired the chassis, which formed the basis of the transporter built to accommodate the F1 Matras he fielded in 1969. By the standards of the time it was very grand. By contrast, the lone works STP March arrived on a tiny trailer behind a rather grubby-looking Ford Transit van!

So there they were: two March 701s, all ready to go on the requisite date. In fact the STP car had been finished a day or so before, Amon taking the opportunity for a pre-launch warm-up at Silverstone, but Tyrrell's car was brand new. The paddock was brim-full of international motor racing personalities. Aside from the four March directors, there were Tyrrell, Jackie Stewart and his team-mate Johnny Servoz-Gavin, Chris Amon, Jo Siffert, Mario Andretti, Ronnie Peterson and Andy Granatelli; and just about every journalist and television interviewer in the game.

On closer examination the March 701 revealed itself to be a very straightforward and uncomplicated Grand Prix machine. It employed a simple 'bathtub' style monocoque manufactured from 18 swg aluminium, double wishbone suspension and outboard coil-spring/dampers. At 93 inches, it had the shortest wheelbase of any 1970 Formula 1 car (the yet-to-be-announced Lotus 72 would be the longest at 100 inches). With an all-up weight of 1280 lb, the March was also the heaviest. Predictably, at 1165 lb, the new Lotus would be the lightest.

The great moment arrives. Herd looks quizzically at the 701's nose section, while team driver Jo Siffert** (fourth from left, in sheepskin coat) **wonders what the future holds in store as he prepares to try the car for the first time at the Silverstone launch.

MARCH
ENGINEERING LIMITED
STP
STP

STP
Autolite
CHRONOSPORT
BP

STP

Jackie Stewart in the Tyrrell 701 at the Silverstone launch wearing the distinctive helicopter pilot's helmet he used briefly at the start of the season.

As Herd told the author: 'The car was desperately conventional. Everything was done in such a rush; all its weight was in the wrong places and too much was sacrificed in the way of lightness.'

A Serck water radiator was fitted under the bullet-shaped nose and the car was distinguished by additional cellular fuel tanks of aerofoil section to supplement the five interconnected bag tanks in the main chassis structure, thereby ensuring that the 701 would have ample capacity for the longest races on the calendar. This side pod concept had been suggested to Herd by aerodynamicist Peter Wright, who worked for Specialised Mouldings, the Huntingdon-based plastics company which had one of the first wind tunnels to be applied specifically to racing car development. Wright, who had originally experimented with a similar concept when he worked with BRM in 1968/69, later went on to Lotus, where, several years later, his experiments produced the ground-effect Lotus 78 and 79. He can be regarded as the father of this aerodynamic philosophy – and the March 701 was the first car to utilise its potential, albeit in relatively unsophisticated form.

The Tyrrell lads had done their own detail finishing work on the blue 701, which demonstrated subtly different oil piping and unions as well as additional bracing for the rear aerofoil, but there was no hint of the long-term plans going through Ken's mind as Jackie Stewart took to the circuit, on this occasion wearing an unusual helicopter pilot's helmet for experimental purposes.

Amon was well wound up, expressing himself quite content with the 701's performance on the relatively smooth expanses of the British circuit, but JYS adjudged the car too new to come to any conclusions. Servoz-Gavin had a run, then Siffert tried the works car before, finally, Ronnie Peterson was given a few laps in the STP machine for the benefit of Swedish television cameras. Ronnie's wrists still bore unpleasant red burns, the long-term legacy of his Montlhéry shunt the previous autumn, but he willingly shed his shaggy fur coat and donned his overalls to sample Cosworth DFV power for the first time. Later he confided, 'Christ...I'll never get used to anything that bloody fast!'

By the time the teams arrived at Kyalami for tyre testing, no fewer than five 701s were ready to go. Amon and Siffert had 701/1 and 701/5, Stewart and Servoz-Gavin 701/2 and 701/4, while Andretti's mount was 701/3, painted a vivid dayglo pink to distinguish it from the STP-backed factory cars. Mario shunted during testing, pushing the engine forward into the back of the monocoque, but some suitable fabricators were located at a nearby airport and the car was repaired in time for the start of practice. Another problem, common to all five Marches, was excessively high cockpit temperatures. But Peter Jackson of Specialised Mouldings just happened to be on hand 'on holiday' and was able to instigate suitable modifications to the nose cowlings.

Into action for the first time. Stewart's Tyrrell 701 leads Chris Amon in the works STP car round Copse Corner during the press launch at Silverstone.

DUNLOP
elf
elf
elf
elf
7

Jackie Stewart quickly concluded that the March 701 really wasn't a terribly nice car to drive, although it was undeniably quick enough against the stop-watch. The previous year at Kyalami he'd qualified his Matra MS80 fourth with a best lap of 1m 20.4s. Now, aided by Dunlop's new MP31-350 compound, he produced a 1m 19.3s in his Tyrrell-run 701 to take pole position, admittedly using the only 1970-specification Cosworth DFV in the field. But he reported the March to be uncomfortable and vague to handle on the limit. It didn't seem to him that it was a car with a great deal of potential. It didn't react positively to sudden changes of direction. The weekend was not without its lighthearted moments, however. At one point Jackie asked if he could try Amon's seat. It was a request met by blank stares from the March mechanics. Chris was just sitting on the floor of the cockpit. 'Seat? We can't afford a seat.'

Yet it was difficult to argue against the March 701's superficial effectiveness. Amon matched Stewart's time with the Firestone-shod STP works car, lining up in second place, while Jack Brabham's new Brabham BT33 (on Goodyear rubber) completed the front row on 1m 19.6s. The other March 701s were further back, in the order Siffert (9th, 1m 20.2s), Andretti (11th, 1m 20.5s) and Servoz-Gavin (17th, 1m 21.4s).

At the start Stewart, racing on Dunlop's CR84 Mk 1-350 compound tyres after the MP31s had proved to have excessively sudden breakaway characteristics, catapulted away to build up an early lead. Amon tangled with Brabham and Jochen Rindt's Lotus 49C going into Crowthorne Corner on the opening lap, found himself pitched into a spin and then retired after 14 laps with overheating. JYS led for 19 laps, but was passed firstly by Brabham and then, on lap 38, by Denny Hulme's McLaren, the Scot finishing third on his maiden outing in the new car. Siffert survived to take tenth after a spin, but Mario also went out with overheating after 26 laps, while Servoz-Gavin's engine expired on lap 57.

A fortnight later the Brands Hatch Race of Champions produced a welcome fillip for both Tyrrell and March when Stewart emerged victorious in the non-title contest at the undulating Kent circuit. He had to work overtime, however, hurling the 701 round in untypical opposite-lock slides to keep Brabham's mellow-handling BT33 in sight, only winning when his rival's engine turned rough in the closing stages. Jackie started from pole, 1.2s ahead of Amon, the works car failing to last the distance, this time succumbing to engine failure.

The second round of the championship took place over 90 exhausting laps of Járama, the tortuous 2.11-mile Spanish circuit just north of Madrid. The factory team and Tyrrell both had new chassis available, numbers 6 and 7 respectively, the former featuring a monocoque made from 20 swg aluminium, a saving of about 20 lb over the original-specification 701. The works car was a spare for Amon, but Servoz-Gavin used Tyrrell's latest chassis in the race. Inboard rear brakes were also seen for the first time, fitted in conjunction with redesigned side plates for the Hewland DG300 gearboxes.

Official practice was punctuated by a controversy over the number of cars permitted to start, a dispute which was badly mismanaged by the officials of the meeting. Among four cars virtually dragged off the grid shortly before the start was Siffert's STP works entry, a 'non-seeded' runner for the purposes of this dispute, which was at the same time both complex and trivial.

Brabham's BT33 took pole on 1m 23.9s from Hulme (1m 24.1s) and Stewart (1m 24.2s), but the Scot took the lead from the start and held it throughout, despite being shadowed by Jack for many laps. On the opening lap disaster intervened as Jack Oliver's BRM P153 broke a stub axle under braking on the downhill approach to a tight infield hairpin, the car spearing out of control and collecting Jacky Ickx's Ferrari 312B as the Belgian swung into the apex.

The two cars erupted in flame, both men scrambling out intact, although Ickx received some unpleasant, if superficial, burns to his legs. The track was then doused with extinguishant, most of which finished up clinging to the five lonely finishers at the end of the afternoon. Amon had again failed to survive to the chequered flag, his 701 eliminated by clutch and engine failure, but Stewart scored March's first Grand Prix victory, finishing a full lap ahead of Bruce McLaren's second-place McLaren. Andretti and Servoz-Gavin brought their 701s home third and fifth, sandwiching Graham Hill in Rob Walker's Lotus 49C.

Andretti's 701 would not now appear again until the British Grand Prix, as his USAC commitments, notably the Indy 500 with the STP McNamara, would monopolise his attention for the next couple of months. The two men hired to tend his car were Bob Dance, later chief mechanic at Brabham and Lotus, and Bob Sparshott, a future partner in the Luton-based BS Fabrications organisation.

First Grand Prix win for the marque. Jackie Stewart, well in command of the 1970 Spanish GP at Járama at the wheel of Ken's 701.

SEAT

Servoz-Gavin speeds to fourth place at Járama, his Tyrrell 701 streaked with extinguishant from the Ickx/Oliver conflagration on the opening lap. The young Frenchman would abruptly retire from the sport after failing to qualify at Monaco.

Dance: 'As I recall, it originally started out that Mario's was going to be a works car, then Vince Granatelli suddenly decided that he wanted to operate it separately. I'd originally joined March as one of the early boys, thinking I was working for them, and within six weeks I had to leave the company and become an employee of STP.

'We kept Mario's 701 at Bicester for six weeks or so, but after the Spanish Grand Prix it was flown to Chicago. Before coming back to Europe, Mario did some testing at Watkins Glen in June, after which we were located at McNamara's base at Lenngries, between Munich and Salzburg, where the McNamara Indy cars were being built. We all rather got caught up with the Indy programme and the F1 season rather fell by the wayside.'

Meanwhile Chris Amon's acute sense of frustration found some relief on 26 May in the Silverstone International Trophy race, the second of Britain's non-title events. Chris led the first heat commandingly throughout, and while JYS pulled away at the start of the second, his Dunlops working well on a still-damp track surface, Amon hauled back onto his tail as the circuit dried out. To ensure aggregate victory, he had to finish within 12 seconds of Stewart, a task he achieved with ease, crossing the line a couple of seconds adrift of the World Champion.

On 10 May Ronnie Peterson joined the Grand Prix set at Monaco at the wheel of his distinctive yellow Antique Automobiles 701, this still to the original specification with outboard rear brakes. During practice Amon gave his mechanics some unwanted extra work when he wiped a wheel off as he tried to lap the obstructive Pedro Rodriguez's BRM and shake his fist at the Mexican at the same time. He continued practice in the spare while his race chassis was fixed.

Stewart took pole on 1m 24.0s, Amon lining up next to him on 1m 24.6s. Siffert was 11th, one place ahead of Ronnie, while Andretti's commitments at Indianapolis meant the 'STP Oil Treatment Special' stayed back home in Bicester. After early morning rain on the Sunday, Monaco dried out in time for the race and the 701s produced an initially impressive display, Stewart and Amon circulating at the head of the field from the start.

By lap 22, however, Chris found himself displaced from second place by the tenacious Brabham and, just when it looked as though Stewart had his second Monaco triumph convincingly in the bag, the Tyrrell March suddenly began to misfire. A faulty spark box was the culprit and Stewart lost three laps in the pits having it replaced, resuming only to retire with engine failure. A suspension breakage eliminated Amon, leaving the dynamic Rindt to fluster Brabham into a last-corner error, the Austrian nipping by to win at the wheel of his trusty old Lotus 49C. Peterson finished a steady seventh, two laps down, while Siffert was classified eighth, despite stopping near the end with fuel-feed problems.

Servoz-Gavin had failed to qualify at Monaco, knocking a rear wheel off his Tyrrell 701 after a hair-raising moment when he clipped the chicane. The effervescent Frenchman, who had made his name by leading briefly at Monaco in the Tyrrell Matra a couple of years earlier, had been nursing a worrying secret. While out in an off-road vehicle the previous winter, the branch of a tree had hit him in the face, causing a loss of acuity in one eye. This was a potentially disastrous problem for a young Grand Prix driver and 'Servoz' subsequently told close friends that he had indeed experienced troubled vision during those early races of the year. After Monaco he opted for the prudent route and quit for good.

The next item on the agenda was the Belgian Grand Prix at Spa, an event surrounded by complex arguments about safety. Stewart, who had upended a BRM there in the rain four years earlier, had always been concerned about the quirky weather conditions in that area, which produce bright sunshine at one end of the circuit while rain is deluging down at the other. He talked it over with Tyrrell and recalls that Ken accepted the fact that, if it rained, he wasn't going to compete.

The March 701s were still looking moderately promising at this stage of the season, neither the Lotus 72 nor the Ferrari 312B having been sorted out to a competitive pitch, and Jackie planted the Tyrrell car on pole position with a time of 3m 28.0s. Alongside him on the front row were Rindt's Lotus 49C (3m 30.1s) and Amon's works 701 (3m 30.3s). Peterson lined up ninth and Siffert tenth, Ronnie having been fished out of gaol just for the race after an earlier altercation with a traffic cop.

If ever a race encapsulated Chris Amon's bad luck, it was the 1970 Belgian Grand Prix. He initially swapped the lead with Stewart, only for Pedro Rodriguez to sweep by in the notoriously unreliable BRM P153. Chris tailed him doggedly but – you've guessed it – this was the one day that the English V12 chose to hold together.

Chris Amon's Firestone-shod works 701 heads out of Silverstone's Woodcote Corner ahead of Denny Hulme's McLaren during the two-heat 1970 International Trophy. Chris beat Jackie Stewart's Tyrrell 701 on aggregate to score the first of the two wins in non-title races which were the only F1 victories he would achieve in a long career.

Overleaf: ***Amon in command. Chris leads the opening stages of the Belgian Grand Prix from Stewart, eventual winner Pedro Rodriguez's BRM and Jochen Rindt's Lotus 49C.***

Amon: 'Stewart went into the lead midway round the first lap, while I fought my way past Jochen's Lotus and caught Jackie halfway round lap two. I slipstreamed by into the lead and, although he reckoned at the time there was something not quite right with his car, I don't believe that.

'We were all strung out down towards Malmedy when I looked in my mirrors and saw a white car tucked in behind Rindt in fourth place. It suddenly whipped out past the Lotus and tucked in behind Stewart and I remember thinking, "Who the hell is that?" Then the white car nipped past Stewart, tucked in behind me and, as we went down the Masta Straight, it drew level and I saw it was Pedro Rodriguez in the BRM. He was running really quickly and driving extremely well.'

Chris admits that for the next few laps he consoled himself with the thought that it was

extremely unlikely that the BRM would manage to last the distance. 'But it soon became clear that I'd got a big problem,' he recalled. 'My March would pull 9800 rpm on its own down the Masta, but it was being towed up to 10,200 rpm behind that BRM. I did get past him just once, slipping through on the inside of La Source, but the damned thing was back past me by the time we got to the bridge at Eau Rouge.

'From then on I managed to get my front wheels level with his rears a couple of times on the Masta, but he beat me in the end by a couple of seconds. I suppose the only consolation is that he'd had to battle his way past Rindt and Stewart before he could have a crack at me.' Stewart's 701 succumbed to a major engine failure, Siffert had fuel-feed trouble and Peterson was eight laps down at the finish, unclassified after a lengthy stop to change a broken exhaust pipe.

Ronnie Peterson in the Antique Automobiles March 701 brakes hard for the Malmedy chicane during the 1970 Belgian GP. In order to take part in this race, the Swedish newcomer had to be released from a local gaol, having been incarcerated for a motoring offence!

The Dutch Grand Prix at Zandvoort on 21 June saw Tyrrell's 701/4 appear rebuilt round a lighter-gauge monocoque, while young F2 Tecno driver François Cevert was signed on to replace Servoz-Gavin. More importantly, Rindt had the sensational new Lotus 72 really working on this occasion, taking pole on 1m 18.50s ahead of Stewart (1m 18.73s) and Ickx (1m 18.93s) in the ever more promising Ferrari flat-12.

The Belgian driver got the jump on his front-row rivals off the grid, but Rindt was soon through and away. The Austrian drove smoothly away to a commanding victory, Stewart bringing his Tyrrell 701 home second, the only other runner to go the full distance. But neither man derived any satisfaction from his afternoon's work, for their close friend Piers Courage had been killed when his Frank Williams-entered de Tomaso plunged off the circuit and caught fire during the race. Among the other March runners, Peterson was ninth, Amon's car packed up on only the second lap and both Cevert and Siffert suffered engine breakages.

The die for the season seemed to have been cast. A fortnight later at Clermont-Ferrand Rindt won again in the French Grand Prix, although this time Ickx and the heroic Jean-Pierre Beltoise's Matra MS120 were early pacemakers. In fact it was something of a lucky win for the Austrian, with both the 12-cylinder cars encountering trouble and Stewart losing time changing a spark box, which dropped his Tyrrell March to ninth. Amon ended the race in a strong second behind the new Lotus, inwardly simmering about the 701's handling. Siffert hit a guard rail, wrecking his 701's monocoque, Cevert was 11th and Peterson rolled to a silent halt with crown wheel and pinion failure.

Andretti's car should have been back for Zandvoort, but a shortage of Cosworth DFVs prevented his reappearance there. When the STP machine arrived back on the scene for the British Grand Prix at Brands Hatch on 19 July, McNamara designer Jo Karasek had incorporated alterations to the cooling system, new uprights and rear suspension revisions.

There was a real furore during practice when Amon, exhausted and frustrated after battling over the undulations of the Kent circuit, told Mosley and Herd that he thought the March 701 was 'a heap of shit'. Moreover he expressed broadly the same sentiments, albeit in slightly moderated language, when interviewed over the public address system. Stewart, with characteristically less in the way of outward emotion, had also concluded that the 701 didn't have much future. Not that he was unduly worried. Several months earlier Tyrrell had decided to build his own chassis, under conditions of great secrecy. The new car was only weeks away now, so Jackie's escape route from the great dilemma was assured.

Rindt took the Brands pole on 1m 24.8s, a time matched by Jack Brabham, while Ickx completed the front row on 1m 25.1s. The fastest March driver was JYS, eighth on 1m 26.0s, while Mario was ninth on 1m 24.8s and Peterson 11th on 1m 26.8s. Chris couldn't break 1m 28s in his Firestone-shod works car and was so far back it hardly mattered. Come the race, all the Marches were out of contention, Amon ironically ending the day as the leading 701 driver, a lapped fifth. Cevert was seventh, Peterson ninth. Siffert, Andretti and Stewart all retired as Rindt collected another victory, but this time only after Brabham's BT33 had run low on fuel.

Yet another March 701 appeared on the entry list for the German Grand Prix at Hockenheim on 2 August, but its owner, former BMW saloon racer Hubert Hahne, was well out of his depth in such exalted company. The best he could manage was a 2m 07.1s lap, over seven seconds away from Siffert's fourth-quickest two minutes dead with the best-placed March on the grid. The 50-lap race produced a hectic four-way scrap at the front, Rindt and the Ferraris of Ickx and Clay Regazzoni all taking turns at leading, with Amon hanging on breathlessly in the works 701 before its engine expired 15 laps from the finish. There was to be no 701 in the points at the end of this gruelling event.

The March directors hadn't heard the last of Mr Hahne, however. Clearly, reasoned the German driver, I have paid £9000 for a car which is in some way sub-standard. As the works transporter made its way back to the Belgian border, mechanics Jon Redgrave, John Woodington and Ray Wardell were unaware that their progress was being shadowed by a police helicopter. Hahne had taken out a writ against March and the transporter was halted at the frontier, being allowed to continue on its way only after March had provided the necessary sureties.

The matter was sorted out at a private Silverstone test session where Peterson set a bogey time with his own car, the intention being to prove that he could match it at the wheel of the Hahne 701. Ronnie did his employers proud, wheeling the German's silver car round almost

Mario Andretti's STP March 701 swings into Druids Corner during the 1970 British GP, his car now featuring parallel link rear suspension and a revised oil tank which distinguished it from the factory machines.

François Cevert's March 701 heads for seventh place in the 1970 British Grand Prix. Ken Tyrrell's decision to sign the promising young Frenchman was to prove shrewd and perceptive.

STP
26

DUNLOP
2

two seconds faster than necessary. March was vindicated – and Hahne immediately decided to retire from racing.

The atmosphere within the works March team was by now a little tense, for not only was Amon expressing dissatisfaction with the machinery, but Mosley had also decided that the New Zealander wasn't worth the money he was being paid.

'Don't get me wrong, I liked Chris and there was no question that he was an extremely good driver,' recalled Max some 19 years later. 'But he was costing us a lot, bringing in no money. In my view the whole purpose of the Grand Prix racing programme was firstly to enhance the reputation of the company and secondly to make money.' Stewart and the Tyrrell connection were looking after the former priority while, in Max's view, Siffert and Peterson would have been a far more cost-effective partnership for the factory team to field.

Mosley felt so strongly about this matter that he went to the trouble of producing a complex and detailed internal company document which set out the financial rationale behind his thinking. He itemised areas in which not having Amon would lead to significant budgetary reductions. 'I figured that if we could have got the Firestone contract on the strength of Siffert's inclusion in the team, we would have ended up £34,000 better off over the year as a whole,' he concluded.

Chris was eventually paid something in the region of £30,000 'plus a couple of Can-Am cars', although the deal had opened at £40,000 and been up as high as £60,000 before the cunning Mosley had managed to get it 'restructured'.

By the middle of the summer Amon opened negotiations with Matra on the matter of a possible contract for 1971, his mood in no way brightened by another disappointing outing in the inaugural Austrian Grand Prix at the Österreichring. While Ickx and Regazzoni strode away to a convincing 1-2 finish, Chris was left floundering in eighth place behind Giunti. Stommelen's Brabham wound up third, but with the BRMs of Rodriguez and Jack Oliver fourth and fifth ahead of Beltoise's Matra, there were five 12-cylinder cars in the top six.

Andretti stands by his STP 701 in the Hockenheim pit lane. On the left, Bob Dance – later with Brabham and Lotus – discusses strategy with Vince Granatelli. Behind Mario, Bob Sparshott fiddles thoughtfully...

Stewart was an early retirement with a split fuel-line, while Andretti's 701 was wrecked in a big shunt after its throttle stuck open, bringing the American driver's all-too-fleeting F1 season to an end. 'It was then taken back to the STP base at Santa Monica, California, where we rebuilt it round a new chassis during the autumn before sending it out to the Tasman series to be driven by Amon and David Oxton,' recalls Bob Dance.

On 22 August Jackie Stewart gave the new Tyrrell its maiden outing in the non-title Oulton Park Gold Cup. The brand new machine was very quick, but troublesome, and although it was taken to Monza for the Italian Grand Prix on 6 September Stewart opted to run the March 701 in the race.

That Monza blast was one of Jackie's truly heroic races. Shrugging the emotional trauma of Jochen Rindt's fatal practice accident from his mind, the Scot ran consistently with the leading bunch, finishing second to Regazzoni's Ferrari at the end of the day. His 701 ran shorn of wings and spoilers in an effort to squeeze out every ounce of straightline speed, but it wasn't quite enough to match the lusty flat-12 Ferrari. Afterwards Stewart said that he hadn't been impressed by the way in which Regazzoni weaved on the straight in an effort to break the 'tow', but such complaints were swept away on the wind as the Swiss-Italian driver was cheered to the echo.

Jackie's had been the quickest March in qualifying, fourth overall on 1m 25.39s behind Ickx's pole-position Ferrari (1m 24.14s), Rodriguez's BRM (1m 24.36s) and Regazzoni (1m 24.39s). Behind the Tyrrell March were Giunti's Ferrari, Oliver's BRM and Siffert's works 701 (1m 25.09s), separated by a whole host of other cars from Amon, who was way down in 18th on 1m 26.67s after an endless catalogue of problems. He finished seventh, one place behind Cevert in the other Tyrrell 701.

Crossing the Atlantic for the Canadian Grand Prix was the next priority, the race taking place over 90 laps of the St Jovite circuit, set in the Laurentian mountains some way north of Montreal. Stewart confidently planted the new Tyrrell on pole with a time of 1m 31.5s, a scant tenth of a second quicker than Ickx, while Regazzoni's Ferrari was third on 1m 31.9s. Cevert, demonstrating his considerable flair, placed the Tyrrell March fourth on 1m 32.4s, then came John Surtees's TS7 and Amon, tying on 1m 32.6s.

The pit lane at the Österreichring during practice for the 1970 Austrian Grand Prix. Max Mosley (centre left) *clasps a timing board, while Amon* (beneath '4' sign) *regards his 701 with some anxiety. In the foreground Dance and Sparshott tend Mario's 701, while Andretti sits on the pit wall just to the right of team manager Andrew Ferguson* (seated).

Prior to the race Jackie had the last word on the 701. He played golf with Robin Herd shortly before practice in Canada and the March designer suggested that, if Jackie won the game, he should race the Tyrrell. If he lost, he should race the 701. Stewart replied: 'Robin, never has anyone had such an incentive not to lose a golf match before!' They played it out.

STP
ANDRETTI
Firestone
FORD

5
4
3
2
1

JYS finished one up...

At the start Stewart stormed away into the distance, only to be foiled by a broken front stub axle on lap 33, so Ickx and Regazzoni waltzed home to another Maranello 1-2, with Chris Amon joining them on the rostrum. Only a broken shock absorber mounting robbed the dynamic Cevert of fourth place, the Frenchman having chased Amon hard before a lengthy pit stop dropped him back to ninth at the flag.

JYS displayed the same form with the Tyrrell at Watkins Glen, only losing the United States Grand Prix after an oil-line fractured, starving his DFV of lubricant. With this event being held over 108 laps, the cars were clearly going to need every drop of their fuel capacity and, when Rodriguez brought his BRM in for a top-up a few laps from home, Emerson Fittipaldi slipped by to score a lucky win for Lotus. It was only the Brazilian's fourth Grand Prix outing.

More importantly for Chapman, it was a success which clinched the Constructors' Championship for Lotus and ensured that Jochen Rindt's points total could not be beaten in the battle for the Drivers' Championship. Although Amon finished a distant fifth, behind Rodriguez, Reine Wisell's Lotus 72 and Ickx's Ferrari, Herd and Mosley at least received a compliment from Chapman. The Lotus boss walked over to them after the race and said: 'I only brought my team to North America to prevent you lot from winning the Constructors' Championship in your first season!'

With Ferrari rounding off the year by scoring another Ickx-Regazzoni 1-2 in a chaotic Mexican Grand Prix where suicidally enthusiastic spectators spilled over onto the track edge, Amon's fourth place behind Hulme's McLaren could not prevent March from dropping to third in the final championship table. The score was Lotus 59 points, Ferrari 52 and March 48. The 'Bullshit Racers' had by no means been disgraced.

Yet somehow it didn't seem terribly satisfying at the time. The initial lustre surrounding March had by now dulled somewhat, the sense of impending achievement and initial excitement evaporating with the realisation that they had just been a vulnerable group of newcomers with a Grand Prix car that wasn't really quite up to scratch. The last three races had been something of a chore, to be survived before the season was over and fresh plans could be laid for 1971. Siffert was off to BRM and Amon to Matra, but Ronnie Peterson would be staying, of course, and there was an exciting new F1 challenger just around the corner.

For 1971 March would regroup and consolidate its position with a totally new car, concentrating on Ronnie Peterson's willing and uncomplicated efforts. That would amount to their prestige, number one challenge. But, in line with Max's philosophy that the company should make money, he concocted a deal for the supply of Alfa Romeo V8 engines for the second car for much of the season, an arrangement which was financially beneficial to the tune of £20,000 – and March did not have to pay for the engines. The disadvantage of this deal was that Alfa would nominate the drivers for this second car, Andrea de Adamich and Giovanni 'Nanni' Galli being the incumbents involved. Nice guys, but journeymen both...

But first there was Robin Herd's new car, the striking 711, which was as sleek, rounded and elegant to the eye as the 701 had been stubby and box-like. Its concept reflected the fact that Herd had rather more time at his disposal to produce the second-generation F1 March, much of the credit for which he gives to Geoff Ferris, whom he took on as a young designer to carry out the detail work.

Herd's top priority was to produce a very aerodynamic car with a low drag factor and he engaged the distinguished Frank Costin as a consultant to maximise the car's potential in this area. Later Max would fall out with Costin's business agent over the terms of their arrangement. Mosley: 'Frank and Robin did the most amazing engineer's deal in which the remuneration was a function of the aerodynamic efficiency of the completed car. It caused endless trouble.'

The 711 had a distinctive, bullet-shaped nose on which was mounted what came to be known as the 'coffee table' front wing, in reality an aerofoil of NACA laminar-flow section which – viewed from above – had the appearance of a pair of Spitfire wings joined together, minus the fuselage. It was mounted on an adjustable single strut and was to prove extremely effective.

The car was built round a full monocoque manufactured from 16- and 18-gauge NS4 aluminium alloy and, in its original guise, sported inboard-mounted 10½-in. ventilated disc brakes driven by shafts with constant-velocity joints on either end. The front coil-spring/dampers were mounted inboard too on a dural front bulkhead, which also held the pivot

The press conference at London's Dorchester Hotel prior to the 1971 season at which the new March 711 was unveiled. At table** (left to right) **are STP's Tony Gumbrill, Andrea de Adamich, Alan Rees, Max Mosley, Ronnie Peterson and the 'question master', Nick Brittan. Note the inboard front brake disc just behind the 711's left-front wheel and the all-enveloping rear bodywork. Neither was raced for long...

A frontal view of the new 711 at the Dorchester reception, showing off its distinctive 'coffee table' nose wing, shafts for inboard brakes and heavily cowled hip radiators.

WELCOME
RACE
FANS
STP
STP OIL TREATMENT
Firestone

STP

STP

STP

Minus its front wing, the first Alfa V8-engined March 711 lines up outside the factory, still fitted with inboard front brakes.

point for the forward rocker arm extension that activated the springs, and the steering rack. A second bulkhead, slightly further back, carried the anti-roll bar and the rearward suspension pick-up points. There was a wide-based lower front wishbone, which was duplicated at the rear, plus a transverse link and single radius arm. Rear coil-spring/dampers were mounted outboard in the airstream.

Water radiators at hip level were a Ferris suggestion (as were the inboard front brakes) based on knowledge assimilated during his time at Lotus working with Maurice Phillippe on the Type 72. The Cosworth DFV engine and Hewland FG400 gearbox were shrouded in an all-enveloping rear end, which would quickly be discarded when the cars showed signs of dire overheating during practice for the South African Grand Prix at Kyalami.

Above: ***Soler-Roig sits thoughtfully in the 711's cockpit at Kyalami, an open-faced helmet keeping him cool. The engine cover and radiator cowling have been shed to keep the DFV's temperatures similarly under control.***

Meanwhile an array of outmoded 701s had passed into fresh ownership. Frank Williams had ordered a new 711 for Henri Pescarolo to drive, but this was not ready for the non-title Argentinian Grand Prix at Buenos Aires on 24 January, so he fielded the Frenchman in 701/6, the 'lightweight' former works spare which he had also taken the precaution of acquiring. 'Pesca' finished second to Chris Amon in the Matra, while Derek Bell retired Tom Wheatcroft's 701, as did Siffert his own ex-works car.

Pescarolo still had to rely on Frank's 701 for the first round of the World Championship in South Africa on 6 March, the team's new 711 not yet ready. Peterson and Alex Soler-Roig, the well-heeled motor racing son of a top Barcelona orthopaedic surgeon who had thrown a further £15,000 into the pot for the privilege, fielded a couple of Cosworth-engined 711s, with de Adamich in a lone Alfa V8 car. Stewart's Tyrrell took pole position on 1m 17.8s, Ronnie only managing a best time 2.1s slower to line up 13th in 711/2. Pescarolo's old 701 was 18th on 1m 20.2s, with Rhodesian ace John Love's Team Gunston 701/9 21st (1m 21.9s) ahead of de Adamich (1m 22.2s), while Soler-Roig, out of his depth in F1, was last on 1m 25.8s. 'We really did need Soler-Roig's contribution very badly indeed,' recalls Max, 'although we tried to be quite casual and non-committal about it at the time.'

After Amon's non-title win in Buenos Aires, Kyalami provided the opportunity for another member of the March 701 'old boys' association' to shine, Mario Andretti emerging the winner at the wheel of his Ferrari 312B, Peterson's being the best-placed March in tenth position after a pit stop to change a punctured tyre. By finishing 13th and last, four laps behind Andretti, de Adamich at least gave the Alfa V8 its first F1 finish. Pescarolo was 11th, but neither Love nor 'Solenoid' finished.

A rear shot of the 711-Alfa, with the Italian V8 tucked snugly under the curvaceous engine cover.

All smiles from Ronnie Peterson, even though the organisers at Kyalami don't know how to spell his name on the labels gracing the 711's flanks. Note the dramatically low-profile Firestone rubber. To Ronnie's left are Dave James and Berni Ferry, to his right Alan Rees, Jon Redgrave and Pete Kerr.

Bottom: ***Delivered new to the South African F1 Champion John Love, the Team Gunston March 701 is seen contesting the 1971 South African Grand Prix at Kyalami. Love found the car difficult to drive – who didn't? – and later switched to a Surtees TS9.***

Left: ***Andrea de Adamich with the March 711-Alfa at Kyalami, about to be overtaken by François Cevert's Tyrrell.***

Below: ***Bob Dance unintentionally summing up the March management's philosophy after the 1971 South African GP. However, leasing a seat to Alex Soler-Roig definitely wasn't 'the thing'. He proved extremely slow and was replaced mid-season.***

Lucky escape. Peterson slams into the bank at Becketts Corner after the 711-Alfa's throttle jammed open during the 1971 Silverstone International Trophy race. He was concussed, but otherwise unhurt.

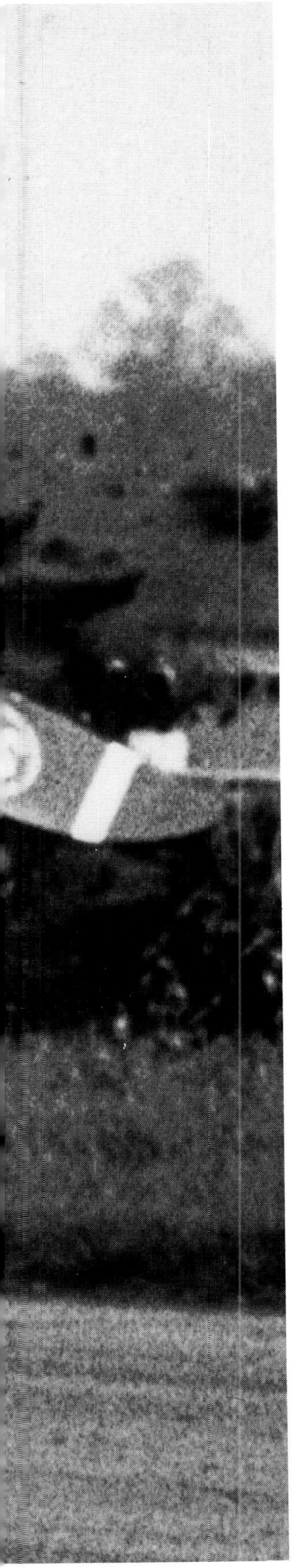

A fortnight later the Williams team's 711 made its race debut in the hands of Ronnie Peterson in the non-title Brands Hatch Race of Champions. It was a potentially disastrous outing, the Swede surviving a huge moment under braking for Clearways when a front brakeshaft failed and the car almost went into the bank.

There were also a couple of 701s in this race. Frank's entry for Formula 5000 exponent Ray Allen, who splashed home sixth, was financed by Motor Circuit Developments boss John Webb, who put up £1000 a time for the March to be handled by a 'local ace' in the domestic British F1 events, while a totally new 701/11 for F3 graduate Mike Beuttler was sponsored by a consortium of stockbrokers: Ralph Clarke, David Mordaunt and Alastair Guthrie, the brother of the 1970 March F2 entrant Malcolm.

Peterson had used the Williams 711 because his works car was in California in preparation for the following weekend's Questor Grand Prix at the Ontario Motor Speedway. Using a combination of the infield road circuit and the super-speedway, this non-title event marked another victory for Andretti in the Ferrari.

A detailed examination of the fractured brakeshaft from the Williams 711 led Robin Herd to conclude that the Brands Hatch breakage had been an isolated occurrence. But, despite plans to build a static test rig for such systems with a view to possible readoption on the 1972 car, the brakes were moved outboard on both 711s which appeared for the Californian event, the Williams entry being flown out after the Brands Hatch race. Also on hand was the Williams 701/6 for Bell and the ex-Andretti/Amon/Oxton 701/3 for American Formula A Champion John Cannon, the latter on the verge of a European F2 programme with a March 712.

Before the European leg of the World Championship got under way, Easter Monday saw the non-title Rothmans International Trophy take place at Oulton Park. Former F3 man Cyd Williams comprehensively demolished Williams's 701/6, actually managing to hit the Bailey bridge in a huge practice accident from which he was fortunate to escape unscathed. That left Alan Rollinson to take a steady fifth place with the ex-works, Siffert-owned car in the race, which was won by Rodriguez's BRM, and Beuttler to retire when the radiator support bracket fractured.

Stewart's March days were long behind him by the time he took the new Tyrrell out onto the starting grid at Barcelona's spectacular Montjuich Park circuit on 18 April. Although Ickx, Regazzoni and Amon made it an all-12-cylinder front row, the canny Scot wasn't to be denied in the 75-lap race. He quickly shouldered his way to the front of the pack and ran just fast enough to keep Ickx's Ferrari back in second place at the finish. By contrast, it was a dismal day for March, all four 711s failing to go the distance. Peterson was out first with electrical trouble, de Adamich suffered transmission failure, Soler-Roig a split fuel pipe and Pescarolo a broken aerofoil mounting.

The next month was to produce both joy and sadness among those close to the March organisation. Earlier in the year Graham Coaker had left the company he had helped found: the relationship hadn't worked and his fellow directors bought out his shareholding. The split was amicable enough and, as part of his settlement, Graham took a March 712 F2 car in which he planned to resume club racing.

Practising for an Easter Formula Libre event at Silverstone, Graham crashed and sustained a broken leg. Sadly, in hospital he was found to be suffering from cancer and died on the eve of the Monaco Grand Prix. His loss would temper the celebrations of the great result that March was to produce on the streets of the Principality.

Before Monaco, however, Ronnie found himself landed with driving the March-Alfa in the International Trophy meeting at Silverstone. It had originally been entered for Galli, but March had been prevailed upon to substitute their star driver at the last minute. Ronnie sulked about it, but Max told him not to worry.

Unexpectedly, Peterson reported that the engine wasn't too bad at all, finding it would run willingly to 10,000 rpm on sections of the circuit where the DFV-engined car would only manage 9,600 rpm. 'Take it to 10,600!' grinned Max. 'I can't,' replied Ronnie. 'It makes a funny noise at around 10,400.'

After qualifying on the second row for the first 26-lap heat, the Swede was delayed by a quick pit stop to secure an electrical lead. Then, approaching Becketts, the Alfa's throttles jammed open and Ronnie hurtled into the bank. The left-front wheel whipped back to catch him a glancing blow on the side of his helmet, but he regained consciousness in the ambulance taking him to Northampton Hospital and asked what had happened. Bruised and sore, he had sustained no serious harm.

Peterson heads his 711 towards a brilliant second place at Monaco. Did the well-protected photographer in the foreground get a good picture, do you suppose?

The 1971 Monaco Grand Prix was one of Jackie Stewart's greatest races. A broken brake-balance bar was discovered as his Tyrrell lined up in pole position, yet he still managed to win convincingly with most of the car's retardation confined to the front wheels. Yet Ronnie made his name by finishing a magnificent second.

Peterson's was the only works March to make the field, qualifying eighth on 1m 25.8s, 2.6s slower than Stewart's pole winner. Unsurprisingly, Galli's 711-Alfa (rebuilt round a new monocoque after the Silverstone excursion), Soler-Roig and visiting American Formula A exponent Skip Barber's private 711/5 failed to make the cut. Barber, a 34-year-old from Carlisle, Pennsylvania, was sponsored by a group of Philadelphia businessmen under the Gene Mason Racing banner. His single-seater experience up to that point amounted to little more than Formula Ford and he had originally only come to Europe to take delivery of his 711. As he was over, he thought he'd have a go at F1 while he was about it.

At the end of the opening lap Stewart was already easing away from Siffert's BRM P160, Ickx's Ferrari, Rodriguez and Peterson. By lap 13 Ronnie was up to fourth, climbing to third by lap 30 and occupying second place from lap 31 to the chequered flag. He was in no way daunted by the three 'heavy hitters' in front of him, pulling some dauntless overtaking manoeuvres to dislodge a trio of drivers who had a reputation for being extremely difficult to get by if they weren't in the mood. It was the day Ronnie Peterson came of age as an F1 driver, proving he now had the discipline and restraint to complement his lightning reflexes.

The 1971 season seemed to be studded with non-title events, the next being the Rindt Memorial thrash at Hockenheim, scene of Jochen's last Grand Prix win less than a year earlier. No fewer than seven Marches went out to the starting grid, Ronnie duplicating his Monaco performance with a fine second behind Ickx's Ferrari. Galli's 711-Alfa was fifth, Barber a creditable sixth and Soler-Roig eighth. Xavier Perrot, who had given March its first F2 victory in 1970, was unclassified in compatriot Siffert's 701 and Beuttler's gearbox failed. Finally, Ray Allen had fuel system problems on his second outing in the Williams 701, now reincarnated round an ex-Tyrrell monocoque following Cyd Williams's bridge-bashing exploits at Oulton Park.

The Dutch Grand Prix took place over 70 laps of a saturated Zandvoort on 30 June, the diabolical conditions favouring Firestone rubber and 12-cylinder engines – or, at least, those of Ickx, Rodriguez and Regazzoni, who filled the top three places at the end of a lurid afternoon. Peterson briefly dallied with one of the Alfa cars during practice, using it to earn 13th place on the grid with a time of 1m 19.73s. He switched to a 711-Cosworth for the race, however, finishing fourth. Galli shunted the Alfa car; Pescarolo's Williams 711, now red-liveried with Motul oil sponsorship, was unclassified, as was Barber; and Soler-Roig suffered engine failure.

Behind the scenes at March, however, all was not well. Mosley and Rees were increasingly at odds with each other about the way in which the company should evolve. Alan continued to feel that Grand Prix success was the number one priority, that commercial prosperity would flow from good results in the sport's most senior category. Nurturing Peterson as a potential World Champion was also his priority.

Max, on the other hand, remained determined that March should survive by means of financial stability. To this end, he courted Alfa Romeo intently and, despite the obvious deficiencies of its V8 engine, decreed that Ronnie should use it in the first French Grand Prix to be held at Paul Ricard, on 4 July.

Ronnie was absolutely furious and told Mosley what he thought of the idea. He didn't see why his championship aspirations should be compromised by Max and his business deals. But there was to be no argument. Mosley stuck to his guns and that was the end of the matter, but it was absolutely typical of Ronnie that he should hurl the 711-Alfa round Paul Ricard just as fast as he could manage.

He qualified quite well, all things considered, the quickest March on the grid with a 12th-fastest 1m 53.36s lap. But the Italian V8 was so gutless that Ronnie found himself being passed by at least one car every lap as he accelerated away from the tight right-hander before the pits.

Eventually the 711-Alfa was running a solid last, but Ronnie was released from his indignity when the engine expired, showering lubricant all over the circuit at the start of the back straight. Race winner Stewart successfully negotiated the oil slick, but Regazzoni's Ferrari and Graham Hill's Brabham BT34 both pirouetted off into the guard rail. All in all, it wasn't a good day for March: Soler-Roig, de Adamich and Pescarolo also failed to finish. But there

Trying yet again. Soler-Roig struggling at Paul Ricard. But time was running out for the Spaniard as far as March was concerned.

were a couple of old 701s still trailing around at the end, François Mazet five laps down in Siffert's and Jean Max nine laps behind the winner in the much-used Williams machine.

Soler-Roig was dropped from the team for good prior to the British Grand Prix, Galli taking over the Cosworth-engined 711/4 alongside Ronnie, while de Adamich was left in the Alfa car. Chassis 711/6, the car Peterson used at Paul Ricard, was rebuilt with a Cosworth engine for the Swede and 711/2 was on hand for Beuttler to run under the 'CMAG' stockbrokers' banner.

In practice Pescarolo crashed Frank's 711 after a rear upright broke, but damage was quite mild and the rear end was duly repaired for the race. The good Henri then brought a smile to his entrant's face with a steady and profitable run to fourth, while Peterson displaced Fittipaldi's Lotus 72 to take a strong second behind Stewart's victorious Tyrrell.

By the time the March team arrived at the Nürburgring for the German Grand Prix, Colin Chapman was sniffing round, making enquiries as to whether Peterson might be released from his contract for 1972. Chapman fully appreciated Ronnie's long-term potential and, by the same token, knew that Fittipaldi's number two, Reine Wisell, wasn't really displaying the same sort of flair. Put simply, he wanted a change of Swedes.

Of course, with Max Mosley having written Ronnie's contract, the document was bullet-proof. But that didn't prevent Chapman from winding up the March director in public. At

Above: ***Pre-race testing at the Circuit Paul Ricard with cranes still at work in the background completing the lavish pit buildings complex. Pictured are*** (left to right) ***Nanni Galli, Frank Williams, Dave James, Bob Dance, Ronnie Peterson*** (in car) ***and Firestone's Bruce Harre.***

Top: ***Outboard brakes now. Ronnie's 711 photographed at Ricard minus nose cone, showing off the inboard front spring/dampers activated by rocker arms, steering rack ahead of the driver's feet and anti-roll bar.***

Looking concerned at Ricard are (left to right) ***Herd, Henri Pescarolo and Peterson. The Frenchman drove a 711 for Frank Williams throughout the '71 season and would finish fourth in the British GP at Silverstone.***

POLITOYS
MOTUL
GOOD
SMOG

the Nürburgring Colin approached Ronnie and said, 'You'll have to drive for me or Ken [Tyrrell] next year if you're going to get your hands on the special new Ford engines.'

That message was relayed to Mosley and Herd by an understandably concerned Peterson, so Max engineered a paddock confrontation with Chapman. In front of Ford's Walter Hayes, Max asked his rival to elaborate on the subject of the new engines. Chapman, wily as ever, laughed it off.

Encouraged by Mosley's obvious sensitivity on the matter, Chapman came back with another suggestion. 'Tell you what, Max,' he said, 'I'll give you £60,000 for the balance of Ronnie's contract. If I take him, you'll save the £30,000 you'd have had to pay him and I'll give you Wilson Fittipaldi's contract which brings along another £30,000 in sponsorship.' Predictably, Mosley told him there wasn't a chance!

In the end Hayes promised an engine to the latest spec for Ronnie for 1972, Max appreciatively recalling Hayes as one of the few people he'd met in motor racing whose word could utterly be relied upon. The same went for Ronnie. 'We paid him £2000 in 1970, £5000 in 1971 and £10,000 in 1972,' says Max. 'He was the only driver I ever met who appreciated the risk we were taking in offering him a three-year contract as an inexperienced, unproven driver. He would never have thought of breaking that commitment.'

For the Nürburgring Bilstein gas-filled shock absorbers were tried for the first time on Peterson's car, while Galli's ex-Soler-Roig 711/4 was fitted with an Alfa V8 for this event. Stewart took pole on 7m 19.02s, a scant 0.2s faster than Ickx's Ferrari and almost seven seconds faster than Ronnie over the breathtaking 14-mile lap. The Scot won easily from teammate Cevert after Ickx spun off on the opening lap, while Peterson survived to take a distant fifth, plagued by tyre vibrations and badly worn shock absorbers. Galli made it to the finish in 12th place, while Beuttler was disqualified after taking a short-cut to the pits round the North Curve loop when he felt a tyre beginning to deflate.

The Austrian Grand Prix at the Österreichring, held on 15 August, marked an historic occasion, the F1 debut of a man who was to win no fewer than three World Championships in the years to come. Andreas-Nikolaus Lauda, at 22 years old one of several who had purchased a season in a 'works' March F2 car for the bargain-basement price of £8500, had now scraped together sufficient sponsorship to hire the works 711/1 for his home Grand Prix.

Lauda recalls the car as 'absolutely lousy' on that occasion, although that would not prevent him from concluding a deal with March for a full season in 1972 'as I reckoned they were the only team who could reasonably accommodate a novice'. Niki qualified last and retired early with handling problems.

The race proved a tremendous success for the BRM team, Siffert's P160 hanging on ahead to beat Fittipaldi's Lotus 72, despite the fact that the Swiss was grappling with a deflating rear tyre. Ronnie qualified a disappointing 11th and struggled home a lapped eighth, beset by serious understeer on the Styrian circuit's many fast corners. The Williams team had a tense time when Pescarolo's 711 failed to arrive until Saturday, the transporter having broken down *en route*, much to the frustration of the mechanics, who had toiled night and day at Morris Gomm's Woking premises to rebuild the car round a new monocoque. Thankfully, the car made it in time to qualify and the bearded Frenchman rewarded their efforts with a creditable sixth place.

The following weekend Oulton Park hosted its second non-title race of the year, the Gold Cup attracting a pair of 701s in addition to Pescarolo's Williams machine and Beuttler's semi-works 711. Henri crashed at Knicker Brook while in the lead after an earlier tangle with Peter Gethin's BRM, and Beuttler succumbed to engine trouble. Tony Trimmer crashed the Williams 701, leaving new-boy Jean-Pierre Jarier to creep home a cautious eighth in the car he had rented from Hubert Hahne.

Jarier recalls his F1 debut as a nerve-racking experience. He had been obliged to sign a waiver guaranteeing Hahne up to £10,000 in the event of an accident and the 701 was prepared by an F3 mechanic with little experience of Cosworth DFVs. 'It was fitted with four old Firestones and I kept it down to 9500 rpm all the way, trailing home six laps behind the winner,' Jarier reminisces. 'Of my £500 starting money, £450 went in mechanics' fees, as I recall.'

For the Italian Grand Prix at Monza on 5 September Peterson's works 711 was fitted with a brand new 11-series DFV and, after careful experiments during practice, it was decided to remove the nose wing in the interests of out-and-out straightline speed. This was the last year of the 'pre-chicane' Monza, the last time that the Milanese circuit would provide an unin-

Low-drag trim. Ronnie in the Monza pit lane, his 711 running minus its nose wing and fitted with a smaller rear aerofoil for this classic flat-out blind.

25
STP

Gulf
Shell
TOTAL
STP

Great stuff! Ronnie leads past the Monza pits with Mike Hailwood's Surtees TS9 right in his slipstream, then a small gap to Peter Gethin's BRM P160, François Cevert's Tyrrell and Howden Ganley's BRM.

hibited blast with which to round off the European season.

Chris Amon's Matra MS120B stole pole position from Ickx's Ferrari with a 1m 22.40s lap, although the Italian timekeepers didn't 'find' the former March driver's best time until the paying public had drifted home after final practice, content in the knowledge that a red car was in pole position. Siffert and Howden Ganley were next in their BRMs, followed by Cevert's Tyrrell and Peterson with a time of 1m 23.46s. Pescarolo was tenth on 1m 23.77s, Beuttler 16th (1m 25.01s), de Adamich's 711-Alfa 20th (1m 25.78s) and Jarier, now tackling his first Grand Prix meeting, right at the very back in the Hahne 701.

The race turned out to be a bitter disappointment for those local fans who'd invested their lire in the confident expectation of a Ferrari victory. Before even the 20-lap mark Ickx and Regazzoni were out with broken engines. Stewart's Tyrrell retired with a similarly shattered motor on lap 16, Ganley's brakes were fading and the main issue seemed to lie between Amon, Peterson, Cevert and Mike Hailwood's Surtees, the leading bunch swapping places several times a lap, all jousting in an attempt to be in the right place at the right time on that crucial final lap.

Mosley and Herd could hardly bear to watch. As the race moved into its final phase, Amon began to flex his muscles, confident that he was at last on the verge of winning his first Grand

Prix. His Matra V12 was quite capable of out-gunning the others among the leading bunch, but he fully appreciated that he would have to position himself perfectly.

Reaching for the grimy, oil-stained 'tear-off' visor on the front of his helmet, Chris peeled it off and hurled it overboard. It was his intention to leave a clear visor beneath, but he inadvertently managed to pull them both off, ruining his chances in the face of a 200 mph slipstream.

Now it was down to a three-way battle at the front, with Ronnie's 711 doing the lion's share of the leading. But none of the leaders noticed Gethin's BRM gaining steadily. 'I was trying to beat Cevert,' explained Ronnie afterwards, 'because he seemed the fastest. I knew I must lead into Parabolica, because I figured his Tyrrell hadn't the speed to pass me between there and the line.' Parabolica, of course, is the tricky right-hander which swings the cars through 180 degrees and leads them out onto the start/finish apron.

Into the last lap Peterson led Cevert by a wheel. Despite his engine being slightly down on power due to a cracked exhaust, Ronnie positioned the March perfectly as they came rocketing down to Parabolica for the last time, cheered on by the madly enthusiastic crowds.

As he swung the red 711 towards the apex of the corner, Ronnie suddenly noticed Gethin coming up the inside at a million miles an hour, front tyres chirping under the strain. For a moment Ronnie thought his plot had been foiled. The March drifted wide, but he stayed level with the Yardley-liveried BRM as they hurtled out of the corner.

Ronnie was in the wrong place, for he suddenly realised that his rival's V12 engine was capable of out-accelerating his Cosworth DFV to the finishing line, a quarter of a mile hence. So he swung the March back across into Gethin's slipstream. The rev-counter needle jerked up as the slipstream effect took over and, at the end of the pit barrier, he swerved out from behind the BRM, pulling alongside as they took the chequered flag. But he was fractionally too late; Gethin had won the Italian Grand Prix by the minuscule margin of one-hundredth of a second!

Gethin does it. As the leading bunch lap Jo Bonnier's painfully slow McLaren** (far left), **Gethin pops his hand out of the BRM's cockpit to acknowledge a split-second victory over Peterson's 711. Cevert was third, ahead of Hailwood and Ganley.

Jean-Pierre Jarier makes his GP debut at Monza, 1971, at the wheel of Hubert Hahne's March 701. This was the car over which a legal action had arisen during the summer of 1970 after Hahne proved unable to qualify it for the German GP at Hockenheim.

In many ways Monza 1971 represented the high spot of the March/Peterson relationship, a race which ranked alongside Monaco as Ronnie's best performance at the wheel of a 711. It would be unfair to suggest that his rapport with the March directors deteriorated from that point onwards, but he never really achieved that sort of conspicuous success again, although his run to second place behind Stewart's Tyrrell in the Canadian Grand Prix a fortnight after Monza was not to be sniffed at.

That year the Canadian race was transferred to Mosport Park, near Toronto. Peterson was partnered on this occasion by Galli and Beuttler in the works team, the Englishman using de Adamich's usual car with his own DFV plugged into the back. Stewart bagged pole position with a lap in 1m 15.3s, ahead of Siffert's BRM P160, Cevert, Fittipaldi, Amon and Peterson (1m 16.2s). Pescarolo had a miserable time in practice, his Williams 711 consuming two engines before he skidded off through some catch-fencing, straining his neck too badly to take part. In the race Ronnie battled bravely for the lead, eventually settling for the runner-up position after damaging the nose wing lapping George Eaton's BRM. Galli and Beuttler were but footnotes to the main event, while the optimistic Skip Barber popped up again, only to retire with engine trouble. The same day, under sunny skies in far-distant Bulawayo, John Love's March 701 was busy beating Dave Charlton's Lotus 72 into second place in the non-title Rhodesian Grand Prix!

Right: *Peterson demonstrated his considerable wet-weather prowess, a crucial index of ability, in the 1971 Canadian GP. Here he keeps his March 711 ahead of Jackie Stewart's Tyrrell at a streaming wet Mosport Park, although JYS would turn the tables by the end of the race.*

elf
11

By the time Peterson sped to third place in the United States Grand Prix at Watkins Glen a fortnight later, March had effectively swept 1971 under the carpet and was firmly focusing its efforts on 1972. Robin Herd, reasoning that he would have to pull something special out of the bag if Ronnie was to be persuaded to stay beyond his three-year contract (which expired at the end of 1972), set to work on a brand new concept. Mosley, meanwhile, concluded the contract for Niki Lauda to join the team as number two. At the time it looked as if he was taking candy from a baby.

By the end of September 1971 Lauda had raised the necessary sponsorship to guarantee himself the second works F1 March seat alongside Ronnie the following year, also undertaking whatever F2 events could be combined with this programme. The recollections of Mosley and Lauda are at variance where the cost of this project is concerned. Max insists that the figure for Niki's 1972 programme of F1 and F2 amounted to 2½ million Austrian schillings (about £42,000 at the prevailing exchange rate). Niki, however, has stated in his memoirs that the 'buy-in' price was £100,000 – which would have been right at 1988 rates of exchange. Moreover he states that he had paid just over £20,000 for a season of F2 the previous year (1971), although at the time March said it was charging its 'rent-a-drivers' £8500.

Lauda's 1971 backing had come from an Austrian bank, the Erste Oesterreichische Sparkasse, and he duly negotiated an extension of this sponsorship to cover his second season of racing with March. Until, that is, his grandfather intervened with the bank's directors and they called off the deal. It was an episode which caused a breach between Niki and his elderly relative that would never be healed. Lauda confessed that he never spoke to his grandfather again.

However, on the strength of that sponsorship, he had signed his March contract and Mosley was now pressing for payment, hinting that he'd got a queue of candidates for the drive stretching all the way down into Bicester town centre. He hadn't, of course, but wasn't above a little gamesmanship.

Mosley: 'I told him that I could only keep the deal open if he got a written guarantee from his father, which he did.' Niki, meanwhile, went out and negotiated an interest-free loan with another Austrian bank, the Raiffeisenkasse, which was secured with an insurance policy on his life. It was a loan, though, not sponsorship...

'There was no way I could let March down by failing to deliver my part of the contract, so I had to rush round all over the place getting the money I'd committed to them,' Niki told the author. 'It was an interest-free loan in return for wearing their decals on my overalls and helmet. But I just had to earn some money to repay the loan, which was over a five-year period.'

On the subject of finance, March Engineering itself had suffered badly from a commercial standpoint throughout 1971 as a result of the relative lack of management experience of its three surviving founders. 'To a large extent, we'd made the classic error of confusing turnover with profit,' Mosley recalls. 'The company had sold a lot of cars but, for all practical purposes, we were bust. We'd managed to lose £71,000, which was a simply massive sum in those days, far beyond our personal means.'

Events now polarised between Rees and Mosley. 'He still believed the company could race itself out of trouble,' Max recalls, 'but I had made it clear that either I had control of the financial side of the business or I couldn't see much point in staying on.' Mosley duly got his way and, through his step-brother Jonathan Guinness (who briefly became a March director), negotiated a line of credit with a merchant bank as well as extra finance secured against a new issue of convertible loan stock. This eased the monetary crisis, if not the personal pressures, and, after toying with the idea of running some semi-works March entries in new premises away from the main factory, Rees eventually left the company early in 1972.

Meanwhile Herd was beavering away finalising the design of a 'stopgap' F1 chassis which would be used by Peterson and Lauda until his imaginative new design was complete. Sure enough, on 1 December 1971 the STP March 721 was unveiled at a press conference in a London hotel. The interim car retained the 'torpedo-shaped' full monocoque of the 711, but had been subjected to a general strengthening all round, with more rigid suspension pick-up points, improved fuel and lubrication systems and revised suspension geometry. The car also featured a reprofiled 'bullet' nose and perhaps came closer to Costin's original concept with an all-enveloping rear body section.

The unproductive Alfa engine deal had come to an end and the team announced its impending switch from Firestone to Goodyear rubber for 'political reasons'. It was also

The team assemble behind the first 721X, its bluff full-width nose section well illustrated in this high frontal shot. Pictured are (left to right) ***Mosley, Peterson, Redgrave, Herd, Kerr, Dave Buller, Dave 'Beaky' Sims, Mike Turner and Wayne Eckersley.***

GOODYEAR
STP
OIL TREATMENT
TREATMENT
STP
GOODYEAR
GOODYEAR
Ford
Ford

revealed that Beuttler would continue to have a March and that another would be sold to German caravan magnate Heinz Henericci for Rolf Stommelen to drive under his Eifelland banner.

Immediately after the press conference the first 721 was shipped to California for Goodyear tyre testing at the Ontario Motor Speedway, where it was completely destroyed in a massive accident on 9 December. Ronnie had earlier turned a 165 mph lap on the USAC oval using Goodyear's G26 F1 mix, before switching to a different compound cover to tackle a mixture of the banking and the road circuit. Approaching Turn One at around 170 mph, a probable component failure caused the car to turn right into the wall. Miraculously, Ronnie emerged with little more than a shaking, but he attracted misplaced sympathy when he came hobbling through Customs at Heathrow a few days later, having managed to bruise himself rather more seriously after the shunt while messing about on a pedal-bike!

The 1972 season kicked off with the Argentinian Grand Prix at Buenos Aires on 23 January, where Ronnie's 721 was the only Cosworth runner to have a 12-series DFV installed. He wasn't able to make best use of this during practice, a nasty stomach bug causing him to miss the first day. In fact doctors had advised him to stay in bed until Monday, so Wilson Fittipaldi was asked to stand by as a possible replacement. But Ronnie forced himself round to grab tenth place on the grid, with Lauda, slowest of all, sharing the last row with Soler-Roig's BRM.

In the race Ronnie found himself troubled by his gearbox intermittently jumping out of fourth, was balked by Helmut Marko's BRM and then spun, recovering to finish sixth behind the Surtees of his Maidenhead neighbour Tim Schenken. Lauda slogged home 11th and last, while Pescarolo finished eighth in his brand new 721/3, purchased by Williams notwithstanding his assurance to *Motoring News* at one point that 'I'll never buy another effing March.'

Rees had formally departed from Bicester by the time the South African Grand Prix took place at Kyalami on 4 March, Peterson qualifying ninth on 1m 17.8s, less than a second away from Jackie Stewart's pole-position time with the Tyrrell. The Swede pulled through to third place by lap 46, aided by retirements, but then faded to fifth after a fractured rear wing-stay caused the 721 to start vibrating ominously. Lauda performed respectably to take seventh, 0.3s behind an obstructive Graham Hill's brake-troubled Brabham BT33. Pescarolo was 11th, Stommelen 13th in the debutant Eifelland 721, which sported striking bodywork devised by designer Lutz 'Luigi' Colani, and Carlos Pace 17th on his F1 debut in the Williams 711.

Driving a 721, Niki Lauda finished a promising seventh in the South African Grand Prix, the second round of the 1972 World Championship. For his next race, however, he would have a 721X...

Meanwhile, back at Bicester, the factory mechanics under Dave 'Beaky' Sims were working an endless series of all-nighters to complete Robin's radical new brainchild in time for a debut in the Brands Hatch Race of Champions on 19 March. When the wraps came off the new March, dubbed the 721X, it stopped most people in their tracks.

The fundamental principle behind the new car's design was the concentration of as much weight as possible within the wheelbase in an attempt to reduce the 'polar moment of inertia' – an expression which would hang round Herd's neck like a dead albatross for years after the 721X's ignominious failure.

Gone was the 'unicorn' front wing, replaced by a bluff, full-width nose cone. Side radiators at hip level were retained, but the most significant alteration was the incorporation of a gear cluster ahead of the rear axle-line. In adopting this concept, Robin admittedly relied on positive input from dear old Ronnie, always a hopeless test driver. The previous summer he had shared the winning Alfa T33/3 sports car with de Adamich in the Watkins Glen 6-hour race and returned enthusing about the gearbox on this car.

It was this gear cluster, installed within a new casing manufactured to March's own specification, that Herd employed on the 721X, together with a system of quick-disconnect hydraulic lines, intended to ease the problems of changing ratios. A Weismann differential was fitted. The rear suspension was another novel aspect of the design of the 721X, using angled coil-spring/dampers mounted on top of the gearbox and operated by a system of cranks and levers. The first car was scheduled for Lauda's use, but Ronnie drove it on its race debut at Brands.

It is an indication of how far the 721X was from the prevailing pace that Peterson could only manage a time of 1m 25.6s, good enough for eighth place on the Race of Champions grid and 2.7s slower than Fittipaldi's pole-position JPS Lotus 72. Ronnie trailed round near the back, pitting briefly with a suspected loose rear wheel. Lacking suitable springs, the 721X proved an enormous handful, understeering madly on its bump rubbers under brak-

Vital stumble: the March 721X, semi-naked, outside the Bicester factory doors. Note the triangulated roll-over cage, unusually strong and elaborate by the standards of the time, and the spring/damper units at the rear mounted atop the inboard Alfa Romeo-derived gearbox.

STP
GOODYEAR
STP

STP
FINA
FORD
FORD

Even worse. Peterson found the 721X absolutely at sea during the rain-soaked Monaco Grand Prix and languished down with the tail-enders. By now, Herd could see this car was not the answer.

CINZANO
LOP
OIL TREAT
VICK
cough drop
FINA
GIRLING
STP
FINA

ing, then oversteering madly out of the corners. Ronnie also complained that the gearchange was balking slightly on his way to a distant 12th place at the finish.

A fortnight later Peterson enjoyed a brief remission from the impending problems, speeding to second place in the non-title Brazilian Grand Prix at Interlagos at the wheel of a 721, the second works car being hired to local hero Luis Bueno, who finished sixth. Carlos Pace made his second appearance in the old Williams 711 but, like Pescarolo in Frank's 721, he was sidelined as a result of jammed throttle slides on the opening lap.

The 721X made its World Championship debut in the Spanish Grand Prix at Járama on 1 May, Peterson's 721X/2 weighing in some 40 lb lighter than the prototype thanks to the use of a magnesium gearbox casing and titanium elsewhere in the chassis. Peterson qualified an heroic ninth on 1m 19.86s, Lauda a bewildered last more than five seconds slower.

Lauda might not have been the most obviously talented driver at this early stage of his career but, as he later proved, he was a supremely logical and lucid individual. His comments about the 721X, made to the author during an interview at the end of 1973, put the problems surrounding this F1 March into sharp perspective.

'At the start of the season it had been extremely hard for me to judge the original 721 because I simply did not have the necessary experience,' Niki recalled. 'I just said, "Oh, very nice", and drove off in it. But when the 721X came along, I just couldn't believe what was happening.

'I remember being allowed five laps at the end of the first session at Járama. I think I did three or four laps before I spun it. I must say that I wasn't somebody who spun a lot – I tried to get used to a car, feeling my way before I pushed hard.

'I thought, "Oh dear, how did I spin?" Then I realised that this bloody Alfa gearbox was just impossible to drive with. If you pushed it from fifth into fourth, sometimes you would get second or first. All the time it was just pure luck if you got the right gear. The handling wasn't any good either – the thing just snapped from acute understeer to quick oversteer. As soon as the car began to slide, you just had to say "forget it" and wait for it to spin. There was no margin between driving and sliding.'

He didn't get much change from the March directors when he returned to the pits with his complaints. Robin said soothingly, 'When you've had as much experience as Ronnie, you too will be able to drive this car.' In the race Niki managed seven slow laps before retiring with a sticking throttle and a faulty limited-slip differential. Peterson, having been debarred from using the spare 721, was eliminated by a fuel leak.

Lauda: 'I was quite sad about all this. I thought I must be a complete idiot and went off on holiday for a week after the race. I was really worried. I kept thinking about what Robin had told me and there was no way I could work it out. The way I saw it, experience is important, but you should be able to drive a car, even slowly, without it spinning all the time.'

In the fortnight prior to the rain-soaked Monaco Grand Prix both 721Xs were rebuilt with different roll bars, revised brakes and fuel pick-up systems, also being equipped with Salisbury differentials for this race. Ronnie could only qualify 15th, Lauda was right down at the back and both of them simply floundered in midfield throughout. Peterson finished 11th after a late stop to secure a loose steering wheel, despite running into Ickx's second-place Ferrari, which slowed suddenly on the last lap. Niki came home 16th, drenched in fuel from a broken pressure gauge.

It was clear that the 721X concept was severely lacking and a hastily revised machine, equipped with a 'standard' Hewland FG400 gearbox, was readied for Peterson to drive in the Oulton Park Gold Cup on 29 May. A spacer was inserted where the Alfa gearbox had previously been and the revised car sported 721 suspension. But it was an inconclusive outing as he collided with Wisell's BRM accelerating away from the grid and got no further than the first corner.

The 721X finally met its Waterloo in the first Belgian Grand Prix to be held at Nivelles-Baulers on 4 June. Ronnie had the revised car once again, practising badly to line up 14th on 1m 13.0s, compared with Fittipaldi's pole-winning time of 1m 11.43s. Peterson finished ninth and Lauda 12th after another fiasco.

Niki again: 'In the quick corners you could drive it through without sliding, but in the slow ones there was no way in which you could get the car round. With Ronnie's revised transmission, at least he could change gear. On my car they just had to blank off fifth gear and run with the four remaining ratios. Robin reckoned it would be better to start with four gears we knew we could get.

Niki Lauda's first full season in Grand Prix racing brought endless frustration, although he would put the lessons learned during his time with March to good use.

STP
FERLAM

Perhaps so, Robin – but did the customers always agree?

Ronnie Peterson snuggles deep into the 721X cockpit, while Robin Herd keeps a smile on his face.

'I kept arriving at the hairpin and understeering straight on, so, to get the car round, I had to wait until I'd got onto the grass and, as soon as the outer rear wheel began to spin, I heaved the car back onto the circuit. It was hardly the best way to go about putting in a fast lap.'

By this stage Lauda felt he was reaching something of an impasse with Herd. 'There was really no way with this car. I could see Robin was getting more and more upset – and *I* was extremely upset – because there was nothing we could do with it. Then – and I don't know whether he was joking or not – he asked "Beaky" Sims to put some STP into the differential "because it might help the understeer".

'Now, I don't know whether my appreciation of English humour was lacking at this stage in my career, but I really thought he was being serious. I rushed out of the pits, did two or three laps, and then came back and told him his bloody car was still no good. And he was very upset indeed.'

Later that same year Robin complimented Niki glowingly on his whole attitude. 'He was an exceptionally good test driver with a really analytical temperament. Everything he told us to follow up has been absolutely right. I just wish we'd taken more notice of him when he told us that there was "no way" with the 721X. He's in a class of his own as a test driver and I can't think of anyone with a better mental make-up to be a World Champion than Niki.' Robin then spoiled this piece of crystal-ball gazing by adding, 'The only thing I question is whether he's simply got sufficient speed to get to the top.' Ouch!

The escape route from the disastrous 'X' project had been charted as early as the Spanish Grand Prix, where Beuttler had arrived to drive the March 721G 'stockbroker special' prepared by Space Racing, an alliance of former March mechanics Bob Sparshott and John 'Ace' Woodington. The car, based round a 722 F2 tub, was a logical development of the F5000 Rover V8-engined 72A which had been showing promise in the hands of John Cannon. The new car was conceived and constructed in the phenomenal period of nine days, its designation 'G' standing for Guinness (as in *The Guinness Book of Records*!).

The basic March 722 tub had been reworked with pannier tanks on either side, increasing the fuel capacity to 40 gallons, and the rear bulkhead and radius arm pick-up points were dramatically strengthened. Larger 721X radiators were fitted and the Cosworth DFV was

Harvey Postlethwaite, photographed in 1972, when he was working on the March design staff. He would first make his name in F1 working on James Hunt's Hesketh March 731 the following year.

installed as a stressed member. At the rear the more conventional 721 suspension layout was employed. In Beuttler's hands it wasn't quick, but it certainly seemed promising.

After the Belgian race Niki was despatched to Vallelunga with a regular 721 for the non-title Gran Premio Republica Italiana, but he shunted the car badly in practice and failed to start. But he did have the chance to try Beuttler's 721G and reported back favourably.

Niki: 'That comparative test was really the main purpose of my trip. I reckoned it was a better car to concentrate on for the future and, after both Ronnie and I spent a day at Silverstone with both the "G" and the "X", everybody agreed that this was the route to take. The team then had one hell of a struggle building new cars in the middle of the season and, in the end, we were not as competitive as we should have been due to the lack of time to sort everything out.'

Spurred on by the challenge, March constructed two completely new 721Gs for the French Grand Prix at Clermont-Ferrand on 2 July, incorporating over 30 revisions to the specification of the original Beuttler car. Peterson had an eventful practice, blowing an engine and glancing a guard rail on his way to ninth place on the grid with a time of 2m 58.2s – just under five seconds away from Amon's pole-winning lap with the Matra. He looked set for third in the race, but a broken front roll bar dropped him to fifth in an event that rightly deserved to be Amon's, but eventually fell to a lucky J.Y. Stewart. Lauda was out early with a broken driveshaft, Beuttler ran out of fuel and Pescarolo had the first of many shunts that summer at the wheel of Frank's 721. Williams was by now running his older 711 on a regular basis for the promising Carlos Pace, who had first driven at Kyalami earlier in the year.

Peterson and Lauda found the 721G an awful handful over the 'vertical corners' at Brands Hatch, Ronnie's car sporting stronger front wishbone mountings in addition to a fully adjustable rear wing. He ran fourth in the closing stages and was just pondering whether to come in for a fuel top-up when his DFV cut out abruptly at Paddock Bend. He slammed off the road, clipping Cevert's abandoned Tyrrell before smashing into Hill's parked Brabham BT37. He was classified seventh none the less, two places in front of Lauda, the Austrian some three laps behind Fittipaldi's victorious Lotus. Pescarolo switched unsuccessfully to Williams's new Len Bailey-designed 'Politoys' for this event, but Pace looked good in the 711 before retiring with differential failure.

Ronnie was at least finding the 721G a more responsive proposition than its predecessor and he managed to qualify fourth at the Nürburgring, despite a troubled practice, the result of a stone blocking an oil pressure relief valve. Having initially run in second place behind Ickx's Ferrari 312B2, he spun back to fifth but was promoted to third after Fittipaldi and Stewart dropped out in the closing stages. Lauda, plagued by fuel pressure problems, retired early in the race with a split oil tank. Stommelen's Eifelland succumbed to electrical gremlins, Pescarolo shunted again and Pace was unclassified, but Beuttler claimed a promising eighth place.

By now the March directors could see their hopes of retaining Peterson's services slipping away. At the Austrian Grand Prix on 13 August the 721G oversteered badly and even the conversion of the spare car to front-radiator specification, with a full-width, bluff nose section, did nothing to improve matters. Ronnie was a distant 11th on the grid on 1m 37.58s, almost two seconds away from Fittipaldi's pole time, but once the race got under way he came storming through to fourth, climbing to third as Stewart's Tyrrell dropped away. Revson's McLaren then breezed past, but the Swede looked set to take fourth place until fuel starvation intervened. After a late stop he stuttered home 12th. Lauda's metering unit had to be changed on the grid and he finished 10th. Pescarolo had yet another practice shunt in the Williams 721 and failed to start.

During the month following the Österreichring March carried out extensive tests at Goodwood, but there was just insufficient time left to convince Ronnie that he should stay. He said later, 'I might have stayed if the 721G had proved more competitive earlier on. I think it would have been nice to stay with March but, if I'd turned down Lotus, I might have regretted it for the rest of my career.'

Overleaf: ***Better by far was the compact March 721G, seen here heading for third place in the German Grand Prix at the Nürburgring in Peterson's capable hands. It formed the basis of all March F1 cars over the next five years.***

Ronnie finally signed a two-year contract with Team Lotus on 28 August 1972. Mosley responded by giving him a really hard time at Monza where, distracted, he made several errors in practice, culminating in his hitting the Vialone chicane on Saturday. He started from the back of the grid in a hastily prepared car, clipped another chicane, stopped for a replacement wheel and finished ninth. Niki was five laps down at the end in 13th place, the Austrian staring unemployment for 1973 in the face.

10
STP
march
Ford
GOODYEAR
GOODYEAR

GOODYEAR
STP
VICK
Ronnie Peterson
OIL TREATMENT

A pensive Robin Herd, late 1972. Musing about low polar moments, perhaps?

Niki's 721G was kitted out in front-radiator specification for the Canadian Grand Prix, but he damaged the front of the car in a practice shunt, so it was rebuilt for the race in side-rad trim like Peterson's. Ronnie's tail-out style got him onto the front row, his time of 1m 14.0s being beaten only by the McLaren M19Cs of Peter Revson and Denny Hulme. He led the first three laps, then held second behind Stewart's Tyrrell until a brush with Hill's Brabham damaged his steering. Having stopped beyond the pit exit, he pushed the March back into the pit lane for repairs, but was later black-flagged after resuming the chase.

Niki also fell foul of officialdom. His throttle slides jammed shut on the opening lap, so two of the mechanics came out and 'talked him through' the repair procedure. But they also helped him fasten his seat harness; this was deemed to be illegal 'outside assistance' and although he continued to the finish, 15 laps down, he wasn't included in the official results. Beuttler survived a first-lap shunt caused by a broken suspension link, continuing to the finish after attention in the pits, while Skip Barber snapped his 711's throttle cable in his attempts to free the mechanism when it apparently jammed shut, but, after repairs, was still running at the flag, many laps behind.

At Watkins Glen on 8 October Peterson's 721G became the first F1 car to be fitted with Herd's latest secret weapon – a cockpit-adjustable anti-roll bar. But, typically, Ronnie wasn't sure whether or not it represented an improvement. In what everybody thought would be his last race for March the Swede stormed through from 26th on the grid to finish fourth, his practice having been punctuated by two broken engines and a crash on a wet track surface. Lauda was 19th, bringing to an end a season which had promised a great deal and delivered very little.

It hadn't been all gloom, though, as Lauda summed up: 'I had a very bad time from the results viewpoint, but I learned a tremendous amount, even from that wretched 721X. I did a lot of testing and got to know a great deal about how a Grand Prix car behaves. If I'd driven a more competitive car, I don't think I would have learned so much. Unfortunately, it was my money that I had to spend to learn all these things.'

Twelve years later, as he announced his retirement for the second and final time, triple World Champion Niki Lauda conceded that the investment had been worth it. He had earned enough to pay back the £8000 a year for five years outstanding on the loan that had taken him into F1 for the first time with March Engineering.

Star quality. Between them, Ronnie Peterson and Niki Lauda would win 35 World Championship Grands Prix during their careers. When this shot was taken, after they had finished 1-2 in an F2 race at Oulton Park in September 1972, that glittering record of achievement had yet to begin.

Where it all began. The first two STP March 701s outside the Murdock Road, Bicester factory at the start of the 1970 season.

15

elf
elf

Left: *The heady taste of victory came early for March in F1, although it was not destined to be sustained. Here Chris Amon heads for victory in the 1970 Silverstone International Trophy.*

Below left: *The wee Scot heads his Tyrrell 701 towards victory in the 1970 Spanish Grand Prix at Járama. Even at this early stage, Jackie Stewart realised that something better than the March would be needed.*

Ronnie Peterson (above) *in the Antique Automobiles-backed March 701 at Hockenheim during the 1970 German Grand Prix. The Swede had originally been destined to partner Amon in the works team, but this semi-works deal kept him on the 'back burner' until he took over the team leadership the following year.*

STP
OIL

Peterson at Kyalami, 1971, in the aerodynamic March 711, showing off its 'coffee table' nose wing, compact hip radiators and low-mounted rear aerofoil. Peterson used it to good effect, taking four Grand Prix second places to finish runner-up in the championship behind Stewart.

GOODYEAR
STP
STP
OIL TREATMENT
STP
4
STP

Left: ***Bright new talent. Niki Lauda heading for seventh place in the 1972 South African GP at Kyalami, his March 721 fitted with a 'shovel' nose rather than the full-width front wing set-up pioneered on the 711.***

Peterson in the F2-based March 721G on his way to third place in the 1972 German Grand Prix at the Nürburgring, chasing the Tyrrells of Stewart and Cevert for all he is worth.

27
JAMES
HUNT

Far left: *James Hunt made his name with Lord Alexander Hesketh's privately fielded March 731 during 1973. Engineered by Harvey Postlethwaite, it easily eclipsed the works car's performance, and is seen here at Watkins Glen, where the extrovert Englishman finished second in the United States Grand Prix, a few lengths behind Ronnie Peterson's Lotus 72.*

Robin Herd discusses the set-up of the Beta Tools-sponsored 751 with Vittorio Brambilla at Anderstorp, scene of the 1975 Swedish Grand Prix (left). *The car worked particularly well on this circuit, which is characterised by a series of slightly banked, constant-radius corners, and Vittorio qualified in pole position. In the race, however,* (overleaf) *his early lead proved short-lived.*

AGB
AGB
TRICO TRICO TRICO
AWAB
22
Atlas
Atlas

Beta
9
GOODYEAR
GOODYEAR

TEXACO
TEXA
DUCKHAMS
DUCKHAMS
GOODYEAR

Left: ***Ronnie Peterson's March 761 on the climb from Ste Devote towards Massenet during the early stages of the 1976 Monaco Grand Prix. He is running ahead of Clay Regazzoni's Ferrari 312T2 and the Tyrrell P34s of Patrick Depailler and Jody Scheckter.***

Max and Ronnie. There were times when Mosley got rather schoolmasterly with the Swede, although second time around the relationship between March and Peterson was less romantic, more pragmatic.

Above: ***Peterson again in action with the 761, this time sporting First National City sponsorship for the weekend as he battles his way to victory in the 1976 Italian Grand Prix at Monza.***

Marlboro
TEXACO
BELLE-VUE
27
BELLE • VUE
TEXACO
saudia
27

ROTHMANS
10
ROTH MANS
VALVOLINE
VALVOLINE
GOODYEAR

Ian Scheckter (below left) ***in the Rothmans-backed March 761B at the 1977 Belgian Grand Prix. Jody's elder brother tried hard, but there was no sense of overwhelming commitment about the March factory's programme that season. It was pure commerce, nothing more.***

Left: ***Ironically, while the works March F1 effort dwindled during 1977, Frank Williams was laying the foundations of his future success with one of the company's cars. Frank's 761, handled by Belgian Patrick Neve, set the scene for Patrick Head's splendid Williams FW06 the following year.***

Above: ***Scheckter's partner in the March F1 line-up was genial Brazilian Alex Ribeiro, seen here hard against the wall at Long Beach. Passing is the Surtees TS19 of Hans Binder.***

Epsilon
MODULAR WHEELS
PIVEC
PACIFIC COAST
HARDWARE
G&E
READY MIXED
CONCRETE
DAETWEILER CO.
JOKER
GUINNESS
17
RIZLA
RIZLA

ROTHMANS
Newsweek
ROTHMANS
17
ICI
RECORD
Valvoline
AVON

Section 1: The Grand Prix Cars

Chapter 3

Ronnie's intermission

Towards the end of the 1973 season Robin Herd was heard to joke privately, 'We'll have to make next year's car really good if we're to attract Ronnie back to the team.' Yet, despite the sentimentality and affection with which Peterson was regarded by the March directors, neither of them can seriously have believed that the Swede could possibly be lured away from his newly established niche at Team Lotus. By the end of 1973 he had not only won his first Grand Prix at the wheel of Chapman's Lotus 72, but three others as well. However, as things were to turn out, Ronnie would eventually return to what, at the time, was regarded as his spiritual home. 'I don't care whatever anybody says,' Mosley once remarked, 'Ronnie would really have liked to stay with us.'

Unquestionably that was true, but the Swede knew he owed it to himself to try Lotus. Although he always came across as a man who was most comfortable in surroundings he was familiar with, he was no soft touch. Beneath that unflustered outward countenance was a man who had a shrewd appreciation of his own talent. And he knew he had the ability to win races.

Derek Daly (left) ***vainly trying to qualify the RAM March 811 at Long Beach in 1981. This alleged Williams FW07-clone was badly overweight and unreliable.***

Adrian Reynard had some input into the March 821 design, but it was essentially a development of the 811. This is Rupert Keegan (below left) ***in action during the Swiss Grand Prix at Dijon-Prenois where he spun off early on.***

Once Mosley knew that Peterson was lost to the team, he began casting around for a replacement and the focus of his attention quickly fell on former March man Chris Amon. Chris had spent a typically unproductive couple of years with the French Matra-Simca F1 team, getting tantalisingly close to victory in a World Championship Grand Prix on a couple of occasions (at Monza in 1971 and at Clermont-Ferrand in '72) only for success to trickle through his fingers like gold dust. At the end of 1972 Matra decided to quit, so he was on the market again.

A deal was struck and Chris spent a day behind the wheel of a 721G at Goodwood before returning to his native New Zealand for a well-earned winter break. In half an hour he had managed to lap quicker than Lauda had done in a couple of days. That might not have seemed a major achievement at the time, but it certainly wasn't too dusty. There were plans for him to test again at Silverstone before Christmas, but the session was rained off. Amon went off to New Zealand convinced he'd got a deal with Max.

The next development in the saga came immediately after Christmas when March announced that 'due to a snag with financial arrangements' the agreement had been terminated. This was followed by Andy Granatelli's decision to suspend STP sponsorship of the March F1 team 'until Amon, or a driver of similar calibre, has been signed'. It seemed unlikely that the boss of STP was going to be satisfied with the nomination of a driver such as Jean-Pierre Jarier, the Frenchman already signed to spearhead the team's BMW-propelled F2 challenge.

With the Argentinian Grand Prix less than a month away, it appeared that Amon had received a cable from Max stating that the agreement was cancelled. Unhappily, the telegram didn't reach Chris's home in rural Bulls until shortly after the news had broken on the local radio. Amon claimed that there was no final agreement and he wanted more money, while, according to Max, the whole deal had been finalised until he received a letter from Chris asking for a larger retainer.

Max told *Motoring News* at the time, 'I don't want to rubbish Chris while he's away, but the deal was completely done before Christmas – right down to who was to pay for the engine oil in the plane we were going to share next season. But, before he left, he put a letter in the post to us saying that he might not be able to race with us after South Africa unless we came up with more money. We haven't got any more money and, even if we had, we wouldn't give it to him under these circumstances.

'Chris told us on the phone that he hasn't got any other offers for F1 and I believe him. As for who we'll replace him with, that's the great unanswered question. There's a great list of unemployed F1 drivers who, for one reason or another, haven't been offered number one seats.

Another family shot: Pete Briggs** (far left) **returned from Surtees to manage the F1 programme, but was to be sadly disappointed. Kerr, Herd and Mosley complete the group.

The great question is whether we have one of those, or gamble on a novice.'

This was somewhat at odds with Amon's recollection of events and, the following week, he put out this statement via his journalist friend Nigel Roebuck:

> Last August negotiations started between March Engineering and myself with a view to my driving for them in 1973. At the time, I was told that I would be paid a retaining fee, and that it would be comparable with those paid by other teams to an experienced Grand Prix driver. The exact amount was not specified, as this was dependent on sponsorship. There was no doubt that the necessary sponsorship would be found.
>
> At that time I was under contract to Matra. Rumours were circulating to the effect that the French team would quit F1 at the end of the year. I was unwilling to commit myself to March until Matra had made clear their plans for 1973. At Watkins Glen I was informed that Matra had decided to abandon Grand Prix racing, and there then followed more negotiations with Max Mosley of March.
>
> I was now told that the figure originally envisaged could not be met, but it was hoped that about half of it could be found. At this time, I was approached by another team (with which I should certainly have signed had I been aware that March did not intend giving me a retainer). After I had turned this down, I was informed by Mosley that there was no longer any question of any retainer whatsoever. My earnings would be 45 per cent of the car's earnings and I would be expected to pay my own expenses for travel etc. Mosley said he would try to obtain more sponsorship, and this would be used to pay my retainer should he succeed. No figures were quoted and no guarantees given. Having now no other option, I reluctantly agreed. No contract of any kind was signed. After reviewing my financial situation, I came to the conclusion that I had to have a retainer of some kind.
>
> Having tried, unsuccessfully, to telephone Mosley, I wrote a letter to him immediately prior to my leaving for New Zealand, on December 17. In it I stated that if, after the South African Grand Prix, no retainer was forthcoming, I would have to review the situation. By this time the word 'retainer' was referred to as the sort of figure a second year Grand Prix driver might expect, and considerably less than one would be paid for a sports car drive. I certainly do not consider that anyone could accuse me of being greedy. By saying 'after the South African GP' my intention was to give Mosley three more months to find some sponsorship. A good deal more reasonable than most of my colleagues would have been, I suspect.
>
> The conclusion of the affair came on December 30 when I heard on a New Zealand radio broadcast that March Engineering had cancelled their agreement with me due to the fact I had asked for more money (i.e. SOME money). In fairness to March Engineering, I must point out that they were courteous enough to inform me personally of their decision a few hours after I had heard it on the radio. I received a telegram stating that they had informed the press that they had terminated the agreement due to difficulties with the driver.
>
> I consider any further statement to be superfluous.

The following week March announced that Jean-Pierre Jarier would, in fact, be driving the sole F1 works entry after all and that STP had reviewed the situation and would be continuing its sponsorship, at least for the Argentinian, Brazilian and South African races. Jarier's inclusion in the line-up was sweetened by the promise of some £60,000 in sponsorship from the French Meubles Arnold furniture company, whose boss Marcel Arnold had previously supported his youthful protégé for an intermittent programme of F2 races in a 'renta' March co-sponsored by Shell during 1971 and '72.

Mosley later admitted that he had explored several avenues which he had hoped might produce some measure of personal sponsorship for Chris, in order to avoid the potential problem of a retainer having to come from March Engineering's own financial resources. Interestingly, Max recalls that he originally spoke with Chris as early as the week following the 1972 French Grand Prix at Clermont-Ferrand, when he was alerted to the possibility of Ronnie switching to Lotus.

'I heard from other sources that Ronnie had signed an option with Lotus,' he recalls, 'so I realised we would need a replacement, although Ronnie denied that he'd signed anything binding.' At this point he began talking to Amon and claimed, in an interview published early the following year, that Chris had even discussed taking over the role of test and development driver, just contesting a few Grands Prix in a second car. The idea of Ronnie staying on as number one driver, driving cars set up by Amon, who would also be on hand in an advisory capacity, had a certain appeal because Peterson was a truly hopeless test driver.

'But then Ronnie said, "Oh, there's this piece of paper – but I don't think it means anything,"' Max relates with a shrug. 'Well, of course there was no way in which I could see Colin Chapman asking him to sign a totally meaningless document and, when I examined it, sure enough it was an option that could be exercised by Lotus before August 30th. That was the moment I realised, whatever else happened, we'd lost Ronnie.'

STP
march
Ford
TREATMEN
JARIER

Jean-Pierre Jarier's ex-Lauda 721G battling round Buenos Aires at the start of the 1973 season. The Frenchman failed to finish this race and had an unhappy year in the works F1 team, although he won the European Championship in the BMW-engined F2 March 732.

Amon summed up the whole unfortunate saga by saying, 'What upset me most was the implication that I'd been sacked. At the time Mosley made a big deal out of the fact that March was paying my insurance policy, but every team I'd ever driven for up to that point had done that and there was no way I would ever have driven for anybody who didn't. But it really was a great shame. On paper, money apart, everything looked absolutely right.'

Many people have concluded, given Max's ambivalence towards an F1 programme that was anything less than self-financing, that the March director had been looking for a way out of the Amon deal so that he could accept Jarier's sponsorship package. Even if that wasn't the case, the whole episode degenerated into an unholy muddle and Max should have known from previous experience that dear old Chris was an organisational disaster area. Bearing in mind what James Hunt would later manage at the wheel of the Hesketh March 731, the failure of the partnership between Amon and the works team to get off the ground can be seen in retrospect as a tragically missed opportunity.

Jarier was a self-confident youngster with a high opinion of his own talent. Undeniably quick in both F3 and F2, he was hard on his machinery and remarkably little in the way of hard success was destined to come his way throughout an F1 career that continued, intermittently, through to the end of 1983. When he lined up in Buenos Aires to do battle for the March works team in the 96-lap Argentinian Grand Prix, his mount was the ex-Lauda 721G, modestly updated with a repositioned oil tank at the rear which, together with the rest of the ancillaries, was on a hinged 'lift-up' frame to permit the gear ratios to be changed. This was a tweak originally developed for the BMW-engined March 732 which Jarier would use to barnstorm his way to victory in the European Championship.

In the sweltering heat Jarier qualified 17th on 1m 14.27s, 3.7s away from Clay Regazzoni's pole-position time in the Marlboro BRM P160. Beuttler was one place behind, albeit 0.9s slower, with his CMAG entry and neither of them was classified at the finish. Beuttler's mount retired with six laps remaining when a radius rod mounting sheared through, while Jarier, although still running 12 laps down, had been delayed by gear linkage problems and a wayward side pod.

Things were no better in the inaugural World Championship Brazilian Grand Prix, staged at Sao Paulo's spectacular Interlagos circuit a fortnight later. Jarier's works car, now fitted with Lockheed brakes, succumbed to a broken crown wheel and pinion, while Beuttler's engine expired. And in the South African race on 3 March both cars were unclassified.

On 11 April a reception at London's Hyde Park Hotel saw the wraps officially come off the uprated 1973 car, still the ex-Lauda 721G which had been rebuilt with the deformable structures down its flanks which were to become mandatory from the first race of the European season. The car featured a narrower front and rear track than its predecessor and sported forward-facing bracing stays to supplement the roll-over bar's effectiveness. The modified machines were generally referred to as 731s.

Losing Amon had considerably dimmed the spark of March Engineering's F1 ambition. In preparation for Chris's recruitment Mosley had set up an excellent support team, with the highly respected Kiwi Pete Kerr as chief mechanic and Pete Briggs as team manager. Briggs, a contemporary of Kerr and Alan Rees at Winkelmann Racing, where he had been the 'lad', had joined March at the start but was turfed out by Max in a post-Rees 'clear-out' at the beginning of 1972 after plans for Alan to run the semi-works programme, in which Briggs was to have been involved, fell through.

An infectiously cheerful optimist who today runs the successful Edenbridge Honda dealerships in rural Kent, Briggs recalls those days with affection and not a little amusement: 'After I left March, I joined John Surtees and ran his Formula 2 team in 1972. And, of course, with Mike Hailwood driving, we beat the works Marches to the European Championship. Towards the end of the year Max approached me and asked me if I'd come back to run Amon in a one-car works F1 team. It was really ambitious stuff. "We're going to win races," he told me. So I had a meeting with him and agreed to join.

'But, within about three weeks, the Amon deal had fallen through and we were lumbered with Jarier. What could you do? From that moment on the F1 team was completely ignored by Max and Robin, who were concentrating their efforts on the BMW-supported F2 programme. It was a shame, because Kerr did a superb job on the preparation side, although it was a complete shambles trying to assemble the car at the start of the year. We would suddenly find that we wanted a top link for the rear suspension and, because there wasn't one to be found, then we'd just have to make one on the spot.'

Winning the European F2 Championship with the 732-BMW was such an important priority that Jarier had to miss those Grands Prix which clashed, so Henri Pescarolo was shoehorned into the works entry for the Spanish Grand Prix at Barcelona's Montjuich Park circuit on 29 April. He qualified in 18th place, immediately followed by Beuttler, the pair reversing positions in the race to finish 7-8, the stockbrokers' car in front. Meanwhile, at the front of the field, Ronnie Peterson was paralysing the opposition with a sensational drive in Chapman's Lotus 72, only to be forced into retirement. From the pits, Pete Kerr was the first to smell the vanishing lubricant. 'Ronnie's got a gearbox oil leak,' he predicted accurately several laps before the Swede succumbed. Nobody could really blame him for being more interested in monitoring Ronnie's progress than Pesca's...

March continued to go through the motions at the Belgian Grand Prix on 20 May, Jarier qualifying in 16th place, 2.4s away from Peterson's pole-winning time. This was the famous race in which the Zolder track surface crumbled like a meringue, but Jarier kept it on the island until, with ten laps to go, he pirouetted off the tarmac, slamming into Peter Revson's abandoned McLaren M23 which had departed the circuit earlier. Beuttler later crashed at the same corner.

Meanwhile, behind the scenes, the March contingent in F1 was set to double at a stroke in time for the Monaco Grand Prix on 3 June with the arrival of cars for James Hunt (Hesketh Racing) and David Purley (a Lec Refrigeration-sponsored 'semi-works' entry). Of the two, Hunt's machine represented by far the more serious challenge. Having moved into F2 fleetingly the previous year with a March 712M, Lord Hesketh had originally planned a full European F2 Championship programme with a private Surtees TS15. However, he hired an F1 Surtees TS9B for Hunt to drive in the non-title Brands Hatch Race of Champions and was so encouraged by the young Englishman's third-place finish that the decision was taken to jump straight into Grand Prix racing. The original scheme was to have a Surtees TS14 which had initially been intended for Andrea de Adamich, but a late change of plan saw the team take on a March 731, running on Firestone rubber. More importantly, together with the car, his Lordship acquired the services of Dr Harvey Postlethwaite.

Postlethwaite, a Morgan fan and former amateur Clubmans sports car racer with a U2, had qualified from Birmingham University with a B.Sc. in Mechanical Engineering and a Ph.D. in Automobile Crash Research. After initially working at ICI's research and development department at Runcorn in Cheshire, he craved something a little more exciting than such a 'think tank' environment. Seeing an advertisement in *The Daily Telegraph* for a vacancy in the March design team, he applied and won the position in the face of competition from 250 other applicants. Not for the first time would March provide design department training for those destined to go on and build significant reputations elsewhere.

Among other projects, Harvey had a lot to do with the aerodynamic development of the F2 title-winning 732-BMW and tells some wonderful tales of testing at Goodwood with Graham Hill and a taciturn Scot whose single-seater exploits did not, shall we say, immediately reveal the talent he would subsequently display as a car developer and businessman. That individual was Tom Walkinshaw, later to gain fame as the mastermind behind the Jaguar racing renaissance of the late 1980s.

Harvey remembers that 'Not much aerodynamic work was done on the F1 car at the time,' but he personally stepped up the pace of such a programme on the Hesketh 731 which was operated out of a base at Easton Neston, the Hesketh family seat on the fringes of Towcester. Managed by the enterprising Anthony 'Bubbles' Horsley, steered by a highly motivated driver and with the team all pulling in the same direction with enormous enthusiasm, the performances of the Hesketh 731 would quickly put those of the Goodyear-tyred works effort firmly in the shade.

Returning to the Monaco race, Purley's machine was run by works-based mechanic Bob Evans and was the only one of the four to retain the previous year's wider-track front suspension. Evans was quoted as saying, 'It's built from 90 per cent new parts,' adding in the same breath, 'although the monocoque has been adapted from an existing tub.'

Writing in *Motor Sport*, Denis Jenkinson made the point that Jarier was in 721G/4, which could also be called 731/4 'depending on whether you view it as last year's car, rebuilt and rebodied, or an entirely new car'. He continued: 'There were two more Marches, both virtually new, but constructed from 1972 parts, either used or unused, depending on whether they originated from the workshop floor, under the bench or from the stores.' That put the haphazard, profit-orientated mood of the 1973 March F1 operation nicely into perspective.

STP
STP
STP
STP
STP
STP
OIL TREATMENT
Marlboro

Jean-Pierre Jarier three-wheeling at Monaco. March had laid ambitious plans for the 1973 season, but in the event commercial considerations took priority over the search for success on the track.

Jackie Stewart placed the Tyrrell on pole for what was to be his last Monaco Grand Prix (although we didn't know it at the time) with a 1m 27.5s best. Jarier was 13th (1m 29.4s), Hunt an impressive 17th (1m 29.9s), Beuttler 19th (1m 31.0s) and Purley 23rd (1m 31.9s).

Purley was an abnormally brave, enormously charismatic former parachute officer from Sussex. The son of self-made millionaire Charlie Purley, the founder and boss of the Bognor Regis-based Lec Refrigeration empire, he had previously hired a 721G to drive in the Rothmans 50,000 'super-libre' all-comers meeting at Brands Hatch the previous August, but this was his first attempt at a proper World Championship race. In no way inhibited by DFV power, on this occasion David's 731 would retire when a fuel collector tank split and the engine just ran out of fuel. By the end of the season his reaction to somebody else's tragedy would make him a national hero.

Jarier succumbed to another gearbox failure on lap 68, but Hunt survived to within five laps of the chequered flag before the engine in the Hesketh 731 expired, so he was officially classified ninth on his maiden Grand Prix outing.

Two weeks later Anderstorp's Scandinavian Raceway hosted the first World Championship Swedish Grand Prix, the locals only being denied a glorious victory by their darling Peterson when his Lotus 72 picked up a puncture towards the finish and Denny Hulme nipped by with his Yardley McLaren M23 on the very last lap. Beuttler's 731 sported a new oil radiator layout at the rear end for this race, while the car Purley rented at Monaco had been given a quick blow-over with yellow paint so it could be hired to Swedish driver Reine Wisell's sponsors. The former Lotus and BRM works driver did a good job to qualify it 14th, 2.5s slower than Peterson's pole-position time, but Reine's race was literally over before it began, for when he applied the brakes on the warm-up lap, the lower left-front wishbone mounting broke, so all he could do was limp back to the pits with the wheel lolling in at a drunken angle. Beuttler finished eighth, just out of the points, while Jarier retired with a broken throttle cable.

Mike Beuttler was a regular March F1 contender in 1972/73, his programme sponsored by a group of stockbroking friends. Here his 731 is seen in the early stages of the 1973 British GP at Silverstone.

Wisell got a second outing for March at the Circuit Paul Ricard on 1 July, this time at the wheel of the 'CMAG' 731, Beuttler missing the race due to the after-effects of an F2 accident the previous week. Jarier demonstrated Cosworth DFV durability by running throughout practice and into the race on the same engine, only to succumb to a driveshaft c/v joint failure early in the contest. The Frenchman did extremely well in qualifying, bagging a place in the middle of row three, so his race retirement was a big disappointment. Wisell went out with engine trouble, but Hunt, whose Hesketh 731 had lined up on the outside of row six, came home a joyous sixth to take a point in only his second Grand Prix, an event which marked Ronnie Peterson's long-overdue first F1 triumph.

By now tensions were building up between Mosley and Jarier's sponsors, who were dragging their heels on the subject of payment. The French driver didn't believe Max's threats that he would be replaced unless some of the agreed finance was forthcoming, so he was stunned when the March works entry in the British Grand Prix turned out to be for Roger Williamson.

A product of the British club racing scene, Williamson was born on 2 February 1948, the son of a garage owner and former speedway rider based in Leicester. He made his name in karting and later enhanced his reputation with winning performances in an 850 cc Mini and a one-litre Ford Anglia.

Max recalls the Williamsons, father and son, arriving on the March stand at the London Racing Car Show at the start of 1971 to buy a March 713M on hire purchase. It was a risky step to take, but Roger soon impressed everybody on his modest budget and the down-to-earth youngster, who in this writer's view sprang from the same sort of no-nonsense mould as Derek Warwick, soon attracted the shrewd and sympathetic sponsorship of Leicester builder Tom Wheatcroft, the man who would later restore Donington Park to its former glory as an active race circuit.

Roger continued in F3 throughout 1972, first with a March and later a GRD, but he switched back to the Bicester marque with the Donington boss's continued sponsorship in 1973, winning the Monza Lottery that June after a superb drive in his 732-BMW. Now he was going to tackle his home Grand Prix in the works STP March, benefiting again from additional backing from Tom Wheatcroft.

Purley and Beuttler were back on the scene in 'their' 731s, but it was Hunt's Hesketh machine that did best in qualifying, James planting it in 11th place on the grid. Purley qualified 16th but then slid off at Becketts, damaging the monocoque beyond immediate repair,

James Hunt ruffled a few feathers with the Hesketh 731 during the 1973 season. Here he presses Ronnie Peterson's Lotus 72 during the British GP at Silverstone, where they finished second and fourth respectively.

STP

EXPRESS
"ALWAYS IN THE LEAD

so he was forced to miss his home Grand Prix. Four years later to the weekend he was to crash his own Mike Pilbeam-designed Lec CRP1 at the same corner, sustaining dreadful leg injuries which would bring to an end his serious motor racing career.

Williamson was 22nd, two places ahead of Beuttler, but young Roger became an innocent victim of the massive multiple pile-up triggered by Jody Scheckter's wayward McLaren M23 at the end of the opening lap, the works 731 being so badly damaged that he could not take the restart. By the end of the afternoon Hunt had won his F1 spurs superbly, hanging on to the leading bunch and slamming across the line fourth, a few yards behind Revson's victorious McLaren, Peterson's Lotus 72 and Hulme's McLaren. Beuttler was eleventh, two laps down.

What followed at Zandvoort on 29 July would go down in contemporary motor racing history as a scandalous example of ineptitude and a lack of co-ordination on the part of the safety services at the Dutch circuit. Early in the Dutch Grand Prix Williamson and Purley had settled into their own private scrap over 13th place, the two novices gaining experience with every lap, but on lap eight neither of them came round. For those who had been present in 1970, when Piers Courage crashed to his death, the sight of an ominous pall of smoke rising from the distant sand-dunes at the back of the circuit offered a sickening sense of *déjà-vu*.

Williamson had lost control going through the first of the two fast fifth-gear right-handers leading towards a slower, recently reprofiled section of the circuit, almost certainly due to the failure of the March's left-front tyre. The left-front wheel had impacted with the barrier which, unbelievable as it may sound, was mounted on steel posts which were just sunk into the soft sand without any discernible packing.

The guard rail simply sprang back, allowing the March partially to mount it, then recoiled, flipping Williamson's 731 over onto its roll-over bar. The March then skated to a halt on the right-hand side of the circuit, still upside down, and on fire. Purley had a grandstand view of the whole accident and immediately stopped, leaping from his own car and sprinting to the scene of the disaster.

Jarier was replaced in the works team by the promising British driver Roger Williamson, but the new partnership ended in tragedy. He is seen practising for the Dutch Grand Prix at Zandvoort, the race in which he crashed and, as a result of scandalously inadequate marshalling, was burned to death.

With a mounting sense of desperation, Purley single-handedly attempted to right the burning March, but all in vain. The fire erupted more widely and, as the shambolic safety services did nothing to help, the race continued with cars hurtling through a curtain of smoke at the accident scene. Williamson died in the wreckage and Mike Hailwood, one of the race's other participants, later told the author that he felt 'desperately guilty that none of the rest of us had realised what was happening and we didn't stop to help'. Hailwood was demonstrably far from a coward himself, having plunged into an inferno at Kyalami earlier that same year to rescue Clay Regazzoni from his blazing BRM.

Mosley: 'The whole thing was absolutely outrageous. He could certainly have been got out; Purley was the only person who did what ought to have been done. If the accident had occurred opposite the pits, everybody would have been across the barrier to help and, in fact, a number of spectators, with no protective clothing, attempted to intervene, but were prevented from doing so by the marshals.' But, of course, it was clear that the Sussex driver had done what the officials on the scene were only too reluctant to do when faced with such a crisis, the measure of his heroism being acknowledged when he was awarded the George Medal in the following New Year's Honours List. Appropriately, the same award went to Hailwood for his heroism in South Africa.

Williamson's accident inevitably overshadowed yet another fine run by James Hunt, this time to third place behind the Tyrrell twins Jackie Stewart and François Cevert. Beuttler went out, unnoticed, on the second lap with electrical trouble.

Two things happened in the wake of the Williamson disaster. Firstly, STP withdrew its sponsorship after what had admittedly been a lukewarm involvement up to that point in the 1973 season, and Pete Briggs was so upset by the aftermath of the tragedy, being left to clear up all the driver's personal effects, that he took the decision to quit the sport and stayed away for almost three years. 'It was one of the worst moments I've ever experienced in motor racing,' added Max. 'Tom Wheatcroft, of course, behaved impeccably and we appreciated his sympathetic touch.'

David Purley in his privately sponsored March 731 at Zandvoort. Confronted with Williamson's accident, this brave former paratroop officer abandoned his car and struggled, unaided, to rescue his compatriot from the upturned works March.

The works team missed the German Grand Prix, as did Hesketh, so only Purley and Beuttler represented the marque at the Nürburgring, finishing in 15th and 16th positions, one 14.18-mile lap behind Stewart's triumphant Tyrrell. Jarier was back in the fold for the Austrian Grand Prix, now at the wheel of the works-operated machine previously driven by Purley. The Frenchman, furious at being dropped prior to the British Grand Prix, had taken

GOODYEAR GOODYEAR
STP
WHEATCROFT
STP STP
STP
STP
GOODYEAR
GOODYEAR

18
DAVID PURLEY
CHAMPION
DAVID
PURLEY

James Hunt drove brilliantly in the Hesketh March 731 to take third place in the 1973 Dutch GP behind the Tyrrells of Jackie Stewart and François Cevert. Here he sweeps past Carlos Pace's slowing Surtees TS14.

27
JAMES
HUNT
27

The Hesketh March 731, benefiting from the attentions of Harvey Postlethwaite, ended the season in impressive form at Watkins Glen, where James Hunt finished a couple of lengths behind Ronnie Peterson's victorious Lotus.

legal advice and accepted an offer from Ferrari for 1974, even though March had an option on his services for two further years. Max immediately intervened, telexing Maranello to inform them of Jarier's continuing obligations. As a result, Niki Lauda found his way to Ferrari, although Jarier left March anyway, as things turned out, to pursue his Grand Prix career with Shadow from the start of the following year.

Postlethwaite's aerodynamic development ideas, most of which had been tried in the MIRA wind tunnel, manifested themselves on the Hesketh 731 at the Österreichring, the white March sporting a new nose cowling which incorporated a wide, shallow aerofoil with a long, wide lip, while the rear aerofoil was moved forward. Rear suspension geometry changes had been made to complement these alterations and cutaway sides to the cockpit enhanced the water radiators' efficiency. An extra day's testing prior to the race produced a nasty moment when a rear tyre deflated due to a rear wheel rim being produced with too small a diameter, but James got away with only a slightly rumpled rear wing.

Emerson Fittipaldi's Lotus 72 took pole on 1m 34.98s, James being the best March with a ninth-fastest 1m 36.63s, only two places ahead of an on-form Beuttler who eased out Jarier by one-tenth of a second. Hunt succumbed to a broken fuel injection control on the third lap, Jarier's engine failed, and Beuttler's oil-coolers were ripped apart when he was hit up the rear by Hailwood's Surtees on the opening lap.

The season now petered out as far as the works March team was concerned, although Hunt and the Hesketh lads kept hope alive right to the end of the year. At Monza, though, James hit one of the tight chicanes, damaging the monocoque badly and obliging the team to withdraw from the race. Purley drove the works car as Jarier was away competing in Formula 2; he finished ninth, one lap down on Peterson's winning Lotus, after a trip up a chicane escape road when attempting to outbrake Graham Hill's Embassy Shadow.

Two North American races followed, Hunt finishing seventh in the chaotic wet/dry/wet Canadian Grand Prix at Mosport Park before rounding off the season with a stunning second place in the United States GP at Watkins Glen, by which time the Hesketh 731 had been developed to the point where it qualified fourth overall. Hunt was only 0.4s behind Peterson's winning Lotus 72 at the end of the race, a performance which raised the Hesketh team's hopes for 1974 when Postlethwaite would design the team its own chassis.

Beuttler and Jarier wound up in tenth and eleventh positions, Jean-Pierre having been on course for seventh place when he crashed heavily on the last lap, making a real mess of his 731. It was the last-ever race for Beuttler, the English driver failing to pick up a drive the following year. A confirmed bachelor, he drifted away from motor racing, and indeed England, settling eventually in San Francisco where he died in 1988 at the early age of 45. David Purley too would never drive an F1 March again; after finally quitting motor racing in 1980, he switched to aerobatics to keep the adrenalin flowing. Sadly, this larger-than-life personality was killed in the summer of 1985 when his Pitts Special biplane crashed into the sea a few hundred yards off the beach at Bognor Regis, in full view of his friends John Watson and Mike Earle, who were playing tennis at the time.

Although his F1 relationship with the team had been neither productive nor harmonious, Jarier had managed to keep the works 732-BMW out of trouble for long enough to clinch the European Championship in the first year of the March-BMW partnership. But that was only the start. BMW Competitions Manager Jochen Neerpasch hit it off well with both Mosley and Herd and, during 1972, they collaborated to tempt one of the most exciting young German drivers away from the Mike Kranefuss-run Ford saloon racing team.

The driver concerned was Hans-Joachim Stuck, the 20-year-old son of the famous prewar Auto Union ace who was an acknowledged star at the Nürburgring and won a pair of German Grands Prix over the demanding *Nordschleife* in the 1930s. As a member of the Ford factory Capri team Stuck Junior had quickly carved out a reputation as something of an ace. By the end of 1972 Neerpasch had persuaded him to join BMW and virtually made it a condition of the March-BMW alliance that 'Hanschen' should have some outings in the F2 team from time to time.

Mosley says that Stuck Senior was a willing accomplice in all this and remembers with relish 'visiting the old boy at his home near Garmisch-Partenkirchen. We walked down long, dark corridors lined with, shall we say, ominously familiar pictures. At one point we got to a section with photographs of Stuck in company with...some well-known pre-war German personalities. I had the feeling that it was a little better illuminated than it might have been for some other visitors.'

Stuck duly drove a handful of F2 races in 1973, out-qualifying Jarier sensationally to take pole for the Eifelrennen. A gregarious, lanky, golden retriever of a lad with a hearty sense of humour and enormous zest, 'Hanschen' Stuck was a natural for promotion into F1 the following year. OK, so he drove single-seaters in the same way he threw about BMW CSL coupés, but he had a lot of obvious natural flair.

There wasn't any obvious major sponsor on the horizon, but with a small amount of German support, probably arranged by BMW, Mosley secured Stuck's services, partnering him with the unflappable Kiwi Howden Ganley for the first race of the 1974 season at Buenos Aires on 13 January.

Robin Herd penned a brand new car, the 741, although its basic monocoque was a logical derivative of its immediate predecessor. In fact all F1 Marches from the 721G through to the 771 five years later were basically derived from the original 712M F2 monocoque with which Ronnie Peterson had blitzed the F2 opposition to win the 1971 European Championship. The new 741s were finished in almost-unmarked green livery, and, quoting out of my own notebook from that race, had 'a wide chassis tapering forward, conventional wishbone suspension all round...lower parallel links, radius arms and single top links at the rear'. In other words, nothing out of the ordinary.

Most strikingly, the 741s sported simply massive rear wings, their side plates shrouding engine oil-coolers on each side. In fact the wings were a gnat's whisker too wide and Mosley

GOODYEAR
10
GOODYEAR
GOODYEAR
GOODYEAR

GOODYEAR
Beta
10
10
Beta
GOODYEAR

was left with the task of getting the approval of every other team manager in the pit lane before the cars were permitted to run. Needless to say, that was no problem.

Good old Ronnie planted the now-ageing Lotus 72 on pole with a time of 1m 50.78s, while Ganley was tenth (1m 54.21s) and the debutant Stuck 23rd (1m 54.67s). In the race, won by Denny Hulme's Marlboro McLaren M23, Stuck retired with clutch problems after 33 laps, while Ganley suffered the frustration of losing sixth place on the last lap when his 741 ran out of fuel, eventually being classified eighth.

Those teams attempting to bring components out to Sao Paulo for the Brazilian Grand Prix a fortnight later found their efforts thwarted by the absurdly pronounced *mañana* attitude adopted by Customs officials at the city's Viracopos international airport. For example, a replacement monocoque for Jarier's Shadow, damaged in a first-lap collision at Buenos Aires, took three days to emerge thanks to nothing but bloody-minded inefficiency. Herd managed to get through carrying some new brackets for the 741 side water radiators, to increase the minuscule clearance between them and the rear wheels, and Stuck really began to show some form on the magnificent five-mile circuit, qualifying 13th, less than three seconds away from Fittipaldi's pole-winning best with the McLaren M23.

The race was flagged to a halt eight laps early owing to a thunder shower, Fittipaldi still ahead, but by then both Marches had retired, Stuck with a broken driveshaft and Ganley due to an engine problem.

By the time the South African GP took place at Kyalami over two months later, on 30 March, Ganley had been announced as the contracted driver of the Japanese Maki F1 car (an undistinguished no-hoper of a project as things turned out), so he was no longer available to March. In his place, with sponsorship from the Italian Beta Utensili tool-manufacturing concern, Vittorio Brambilla was drafted in to partner Stuck.

Popular Kiwi Howden Ganley drove a couple of races in the works March 741 at the start of the 1974 season. Here he is seen at Buenos Aires where he ran out of fuel on the final lap.

More than ten years Stuck's senior, Vittorio Brambilla was a member of a Monza-based motor racing dynasty. Both he and elder brother Ernestino had raced motor cycles, and 'Tino' got as far as becoming a member of the works Ferrari F2 team, even practising an F1 Ferrari for the 1969 Italian Grand Prix at Monza. But he proved well out of his depth and was replaced by Pedro Rodriguez for the race.

In F2 circles the Brambillas gained a reputation for being wild and unpredictable. But there was no doubt about it: Vittorio was quick when he kept on the track. In 1973, driving a March 732-BMW sponsored by Beta, he had shown signs of trying to put his accident-prone days behind him. Prior to climbing into the works March 741 at Kyalami, his experience of a Grand Prix car was limited to a few laps round Misano-Adriatico in the painfully slow Tecno PA123, the Alan McCall-designed car which Chris Amon had abandoned as being totally useless midway through the previous season.

The 741s sported extended 'F2-style' nose sections for the South African race, Stuck qualifying splendidly in seventh place a mere 0.4s away from Niki Lauda's pole time in the Ferrari 312B3. The German scored his first-ever championship points with a fifth-place finish, Brambilla keeping his nose clean to take a steady tenth, one lap down on Carlos Reutemann's winning Brabham BT44.

Having missed the Silverstone International Trophy, for which his 741 was hired to Japanese driver Noritake Takahara, who finished 11th, Vittorio reverted to form in practice for the Spanish Grand Prix at Járama, crashing heavily at the end of the start/finish straight. At first it seemed that he'd gone off on oil dropped by Rikky von Opel's Brabham, but some detective work by the respected Peter Jowitt, on hand as a consultant to the F1 Constructors' Association, identified the precise cause.

The Farnborough aviation crash inspector, one of Britain's leading technical scrutineers at the time, pin-pointed a rear aerofoil collapse as being the start of the problem. That in turn pressed a rear brake pipe onto a hot disc, the fluid leaked out and Brambilla experienced a complete loss of retardation on the rear wheels. With the braking load now solely on the front end, the car locked up and slid straight on. Not much is ever as it seems in F1.

Vittorio Brambilla on his debut outing for March in the 1974 South African GP. Despite his 'wild man' image as a driver, the rugged Italian proved a very competent car-sorter and was held in high regard by both Herd and Mosley.

A brand new car was built up for Brambilla in time for the Belgian Grand Prix at Nivelles-Baulers, strengthened wing side plate mountings being incorporated on both 741s. Stuck, who had earned fourth place in Spain, took up where Vittorio had finished at the previous GP, the German crashing heavily on Friday, but this time the car was repaired for the race. Brambilla started right at the back following two days of serious engine trouble, trailing home ninth, while Stuck was out early with clutch problems.

At Monaco Brambilla managed to get embroiled in a multi-car shunt going up the hill

Hans-Joachim Stuck, son of the pre-war Auto Union ace, was a staunch March performer for three seasons. He is pictured heading for fifth place in the 1974 South African GP at Kyalami, his first helping of championship points.

GOODYEAR
GOODYEAR

from Ste Devote towards Casino Square on the opening lap of the race. When Hulme's McLaren tangled with the BRM P201 of Jean-Pierre Beltoise, Arturo Merzario braked hard in his Williams – and Vittorio ran into the back of him. The March driver managed to limp round as far as the pits before calling it a day. Hardly had the dust settled when Stuck ran over the back of Hunt's Hesketh 308 on the descent to Mirabeau, eliminating the other March midway round lap four. Hans had been trying to get by for several laps and James closed the door quite blatantly. Max personally believes that this shunt rather took the wind out of Stuck's sails and that, after it, he never performed quite as well in F1 as he otherwise might have done.

It was turning into a long, hard and unproductive season for the March team. With Stuck away driving in F2, Reine Wisell was again invited to have a guest outing in the Swedish Grand Prix and qualified 16th, one place ahead of Vittorio. Wisell retired when a pivot bolt broke in the 741's rear suspension, and Brambilla stopped just short of the finishing line on the last lap when the engine began to seize, dropping from sixth to tenth as Jody Scheckter and Patrick Depailler came home to score a splendid 1-2 for Tyrrell.

Stuck returned to the cockpit at Zandvoort, crashing on the opening lap, and was so detuned by his accidents in Monaco and Holland that he failed to qualify for the French Grand Prix at Dijon-Prenois. He bounced back well to earn ninth on the grid at Brands Hatch, but crashed out of the British Grand Prix after 36 laps, almost certainly earning the distinction of having scattered the circuit with the debris on which Lauda's Ferrari punctured a rear tyre. That, in turn, led to chaotic scenes when Niki found the pit lane exit blocked following the inevitable pit stop. Among the non-qualifiers at Brands Hatch was British F3 graduate Mike Wilds in his Dempster-backed ex-Purley March 731/3.

Brambilla finished tenth at Zandvoort and eleventh at Dijon but retired with a broken gearbox and a loss of fuel pressure at Brands Hatch. Returning to his spiritual family home, the Nürburgring, even the irrepressible 'Hanschen' couldn't work miracles with the 741. Although he qualified sixth, he was a full 16 seconds slower than Lauda's pole-position Ferrari. But at least he survived to take seventh place at the end of the race, in front of his many cheering fans. Finally, on 18 August, Brambilla scored his first championship point, taking sixth place – the last unlapped runner – in the Austrian Grand Prix at the Österreichring, which was won by Reutemann's Brabham BT44.

Unfortunately, at the Italian Grand Prix at Monza the excitement rather got to Vittorio; barnstorming through to fifth in the early stages, he got carried away, clipped the chicane just beyond the pit exit, and bounced into the guard rail – hard. It was a bad day for Bicester. On lap 12 Stuck trailed in to complain that the handling felt distinctly spooky. Cursory examination revealed that two engine mounting bolts had fractured and the 741 was in severe danger of becoming articulated!

The season finished on a low note: Brambilla and Stuck failed to qualify at Mosport Park and Watkins Glen respectively; Hans and Vittorio failed to finish at Mosport Park and Watkins Glen respectively. Mosley and Herd couldn't really see any point in continuing the March F1 programme on this sort of also-ran basis, so the initial decision was taken to drop out of Grand Prix racing for 1975. Of course it was a lot easier to come and go from F1 in those days, there being no obligation to take part in all the races. But the programme was suddenly reactivated at short notice when Beta announced that they wanted Brambilla to continue in F1.

Consequently, a singleton 741 was hastily prepared for the Argentinian Grand Prix, Vittorio qualifying it 12th and finishing a lapped ninth. He was out on the second lap of the Brazilian Grand Prix when engine failure intervened, but had a 'new' 751 on hand for Kyalami. A tidied-up, lighter evolutionary version of the 741, the new car's narrow track paid off on the South African circuit's long straight and he qualified seventh, only 0.6s away from Carlos Pace's pole-position Brabham BT44B.

Mosley's willingness to do almost any sort of deal for money was thrown into sharp focus with the arrival of a second March entry onto the scene at Kyalami. An approach, via an intermediary, from Italian industrialist Count 'Googhie' Zanon led to Lella Lombardi's inclusion in the team with backing from the Lavazza coffee-producing concern, in which Zanon's wife's family had a stake. To be fair, this young lady wasn't a total disgrace in F1, at least qualifying for her first race before retiring after 23 laps with a loss of fuel pressure. Brambilla's oil-cooler fractured, so he stopped after 16 laps.

After Lella finished 12th in the non-title Silverstone International Trophy, the Grand Prix

Glorious moment. Vittorio qualified in pole position for the 1975 Swedish GP at Anderstorp and is seen here leading the pack into the first corner, easing out Patrick Depailler's Tyrrell, Jean-Pierre Jarier's Shadow DN5, the Brabham BT44Bs of Carlos Reutemann and Carlos Pace and Niki Lauda's Ferrari 312T.

action moved to Barcelona for the Spanish Grand Prix. Montjuich Park was beset with circuit security problems on this occasion, and the sloppy installation of guard rails produced a strike by members of the Grand Prix Drivers' Association which effectively wiped out official practice. But then Jacky Ickx broke ranks for Lotus, followed quickly by Brambilla, who may well have been galvanised into action by threats from Mosley to replace him with fellow Italian Giorgio Pianta if he didn't feel inclined to drive.

Vittorio did well to qualify fifth and finished the race in that position, with Lella Lombardi completing the top half-dozen – to this day the only woman ever to finish in the points in an F1 Grand Prix. Tragically, the race was marred by an accident to Rolf Stommelen's Hill GH2, which suffered a rear wing-support failure while in the lead, just as it crested the fast brow beyond the pits. The car flew over the guard rail, killing four onlookers and seriously injuring the German driver. The race was flagged to a halt prematurely, with Jochen Mass's McLaren leading, and the top six were awarded only half points. It was truly a day to forget.

Lombardi failed to qualify at Monaco, but Vittorio again bagged a fine fifth on the grid for the thrash through the streets of the Principality on 11 May, only to be bumped to the back of the queue in the opening-lap traffic jam. He retired later, but continued to prove that there wasn't much wrong with Herd's 751 when he popped up on the second row of the grid at Zolder in practice for the Belgian Grand Prix.

Third behind Pace and Lauda on the opening lap, he moved through to lead on laps four and five before slipping back down the field as the *bête noire* of the 751's performance, brake problems, manifested itself. By the time he retired on lap 54, the fluid had boiled and one pad was down to the bare metal. But before making his first pit stop at the end of lap 49, he had been sailing along confidently in fourth place. Lella retired with a seized engine, brought on by a leaking oil-cooler.

What came next made all the March team's rivals sit up and take notice. In practice for the Swedish Grand Prix Vittorio bagged pole position by 0.4s from Depailler's Tyrrell, the stiffly sprung 751 proving ideal for the constant-radius 180-degree corners which abound at Anderstorp. Looking superbly neutral and well balanced, the orange March was in a class of its own.

Herd immediately found himself at the centre of a milling crowd of curious journalists. How had he done it? Robin really didn't seem too certain. 'Our car is quite light,' he ven-

GOODYEAR
NORTON
Mark Donohue
FIRST NATIONAL CITY
28
TRAVELERS CHECKS

GOODYEAR

tured, 'it's quick on the straight and we've made it so that it's extremely good going into the corners.' Moreover Ferodo had provided March with a specially thick set of brake pads. They were available to other teams, of course, but only March tried them.

At the start of the race Brambilla went straight into the lead, but didn't get away. Within a few laps, the previously fine-handling 751 began showing the first signs of time-consuming understeer. After 15 glorious laps Vittorio relinquished first place to Reutemann's Brabham, and the 751 quickly fell away, pitting for fresh rubber only three laps later. He resumed quickly, but soon succumbed to a broken driveshaft universal joint. Still, it made you wonder what a top-line driver might manage in one of Robin Herd's machines.

Vittorio's hopes of repeating this performance at Zandvoort were thwarted when he qualified in midfield and found his 751 savaged by Depailler's Tyrrell as they accelerated away from the grid. He was out on the spot with damaged rear suspension. Lella trailed home 14th. Vittorio made the fourth row at Paul Ricard for the French Grand Prix, but a damper failure eliminated him after half a dozen laps. Then it was on to Silverstone, where the March ranks were swollen by none other than Mark Donohue after Max Mosley pulled a commercial coup by selling a 751 to Roger Penske!

Donohue had emerged from a brief spell of retirement the previous year when Penske, one of the most respected entrants on the US racing scene, had decided to expand into Formula 1. His company established a manufacturing base at Poole, in Dorset, where former March engineer Geoff Ferris produced the team's first car, the PC1.

Despite enjoying a near-legendary reputation at the time for his car-sorting abilities, 38-year-old Donohue hadn't been able to get a great deal out of the PC1 and an instant panacea for the team's ills appeared to be the purchase of a 751. This was Max's salesmanship at its very best and looked for all the world like a rerun of the Tyrrell deal five years earlier. Having a highly regarded outfit such as Penske running one of its cars could only enhance the prestige of March Engineering.

Mark Donohue switched from Roger Penske's own car to a March 751 in time for the British GP. Sadly, the charismatic American driver was to die as the result of injuries sustained during an accident at the Österreichring a few weeks later.

In the space of five days Penske took delivery and thoroughly race-prepared the 751 in readiness for the British Grand Prix and Donohue was warm in his praise of the new chassis. 'It's more sensitive to tuning than our car,' he enthused. 'When you do something, you can feel the difference. It's easy to drive, has the right aerodynamic properties, it's simple and it's light.'

Meanwhile Brambilla's works car had been extensively revamped for this race, featuring new suspension geometry all round, a larger engine airbox and large horizontal panels mounted low on the outside of the rear wing side plates. Wind tunnel experiments had shown that they eased aerodynamic turbulence behind the rear wheels, a fact confirmed by Vittorio's observation of something like an additional 200 rpm on the straight. Predictably, their legality was called into question by a rival team manager but, after much studying of the rule book, the scrutineers deemed them to be acceptable. 'It was a loophole in the regulations,' laughs Max. 'We only did it to infuriate the other teams!' Hans Stuck also rejoined the factory line-up, thanks to expanded backing from Lavazza, with Lombardi relegated to what had hitherto been the test car.

Stuck's return to the March fold was punctuated by a terrifying moment when a rear suspension upright clevis pin snapped at around 170 mph, going into Abbey Curve. 'I closed my eyes, waiting for the shunt,' he recounted. But the 751 shuddered to a halt without any disastrous contact. Tom Pryce qualified his Shadow DN5 on pole on 1m 19.36s, while Vittorio made the inside of the third row, fifth-fastest. The race was eventually brought to a premature halt when a torrential thunderstorm doused the circuit, no fewer than 12 drivers being involved in accidents before Emerson Fittipaldi's McLaren M23 was flagged in the winner.

Those classified second to fifth – Carlos Pace (Brabham BT44B), Jody Scheckter (Tyrrell 007), James Hunt (Hesketh 308) and Donohue's Penske March – all ended up entangled with the catch-fencing, leaving Brambilla to struggle home sixth. Stuck had crashed ten laps earlier and Lombardi suffered ignition problems.

Robin Herd produced this novel rear aerofoil set-up for Brambilla's 751 at the 1975 British GP where, although some rivals looked askance, the scrutineers deemed it within the regulations. Cleaning up the airflow behind the rear wheels produced a bonus of a couple of hundred revs on the straight, but it wasn't seen again.

Predictably, Stuck was the fastest 751 in qualifying at the Nürburgring, starting the German Grand Prix seventh, only four seconds away from Lauda's pole-winning time with the Ferrari 312T. Ironically, of the March brigade, only Lombardi survived the race, struggling home a lapped seventh. Donohue retired with a puncture after only a lap, grinding home on the rim having damaged the suspension pick-ups, while a similar problem put Brambilla out later on. Stuck's engine broke after only three laps.

Tragedy and triumph lay in store for March at the Österreichring, where Stuck and Brambilla proved fastest of all in one session, 'Hanschen' eventually nailing fourth place on the grid, only half a second slower than Lauda's pole-position Ferrari. Brambilla was eighth, Donohue a disappointed 18th after running on full tanks in the session where the two works cars set their quickest times.

Sunday morning's 45-minute warm-up session produced an awful catastrophe. Donohue's March speared over the guard rail on the left-hand side of the circuit as it started to negotiate the fast right-hander at the top of the hill immediately after the pits. From the scrape marks on the road, and other evidence, the finger of suspicion pointed to a left-front tyre failure. The March rammed straight on into the rows of catch-fences on the outside, buckling the nose of the car badly, then swapped ends, destroying the rear end in more fencing.

The wreck ploughed on, mowing down another 50 yards or more of fencing, the mesh of which, together with the broken posts, gathered into a snowballing mass underneath the car. When it finally arrived at the steel barrier, instead of stopping, the American's March was pitched over the top. The point of impact sadly coincided with a marshal's post where two helpers were badly hurt, one later dying from his injuries. As the car went over the barrier, it appears that Donohue hit his helmet hard against one of the tubular steel poles supporting an adjacent advertising hoarding.

Fittipaldi, Bob Evans and Stuck all stopped to help rescue the American driver who duly regained consciousness and seemed extremely lucid, although he had no recollection at all of the accident. Removed by helicopter to hospital in nearby Graz, he appeared to be making positive progress, only to die unexpectedly of internal haemorrhaging the following Tuesday.

Before the start, scheduled for 14.15, the circuit was doused by a torrential shower and mist hung ominously from the fir trees as the cars splashed round on their warm-up lap. Although the rain was no longer falling, the track was still soaking as the cars took their places on the final grid and Lauda's Ferrari 312T burst out of a wall of spray to lead up the hill on the opening lap.

By the end of three laps Niki was over three seconds ahead of Hunt's Hesketh, while Depailler's third-placed Tyrrell was busy fending off Stuck. Brambilla was already seventh...then sixth, fifth, fourth...It was as if a strange metamorphosis had overtaken the Italian. Even though the circuit was briefly drying, he looked as convincing as any of his rivals. Then, when the rain suddenly returned with renewed vigour, craggy old Vittorio was without equal. March had taken the decision to set up the car in ultra-high-downforce trim, realising that if it really poured Brambilla would have a huge advantage.

Meanwhile Lauda was in trouble. Although he'd been trading fastest laps in the early stages of the race, his Ferrari's 'semi-wet' chassis settings were proving far from ideal as the track became saturated. By lap 15 he was being crowded by Hunt, but Brambilla's orange March was catching them both. First Hunt slipped past the Ferrari, then Vittorio. Now the Beta March was challenging for the lead!

On lap 19, as Hunt came up to lap his new Hesketh team-mate Brett Lunger going into the Boschkurve, Brambilla zapped by into the lead on the inside, almost as if the circuit were bone dry. The rain was simply sheeting down now, visibility diminishing by the second. Stuck had already pirouetted into ignominious retirement; surely Vittorio was destined to follow suit very shortly?

No way. Brambilla barrelled enthusiastically ever onwards. In the pit lane drivers' spokesman Denny Hulme, now retired from the cockpit, beetled about urgently canvassing opinions from the entrants as to whether they would be happy for the race to be stopped. Mosley, realising that March's F1 travel benefits for 1976 were now in the bag, agreed enthusiastically that it would be a good move. The officials were hoping to hang on until 60 per cent of the scheduled distance (i.e. 33 laps) had been completed, so the race could be flagged to a halt and regarded as complete. But the conditions were so frightful that the surfing contest was brought to an end after 29 laps. And Brambilla was still ahead.

Then came a touch of vintage Vittorio. As he crossed the line to take the chequered flag, punching the air with delight, his March began to get away from him. By the time he passed the end of the pits, it was almost broadside, and veered into the guard rail halfway up the hill. Its nose cone badly rumpled, the March was still drivable and Brambilla – who'd driven on in plenty of cars more seriously disassembled than this in his time – splashed happily round to be greeted by his delighted mechanics.

Half points it might have been, but it was a wonderfully popular victory for this stocky

Victorious Vittorio! Nose askew, Brambilla's 751 completes its slowing-down lap at a saturated Österreichring after winning the rain-soaked Austrian GP.

journeyman driver, not one of the most obviously talented exponents of the F1 art, but a willing and enthusiastic performer none the less. Yet there were moves afoot to restart the race. Max Mosley, FIA rule book in hand, moved onto the defensive.

'I'm afraid we can't do that,' he chimed in sweetly. 'It says here in the regulations by which we are all bound to abide that we may restart the race only when it has initially been stopped by the chequered flag in conjunction with a black flag. Did anybody see a black flag?' Much shuffling of feet followed. Nobody had...

The Italian adds to the deluge (below) ***with the traditional outpouring of champagne as he shares the rostrum with James Hunt and Tom Pryce.***

There were only two more races to follow on the 1975 calendar, neither of which produced much in the way of hard results. Clutch failure eliminated Brambilla on the opening lap of the Italian Grand Prix, Lombardi crashed and Stuck retired after his March was vaulted by Harald Ertl's Hesketh. At Watkins Glen Brambilla and Stuck trailed home in seventh and eighth places, out of the points, Lombardi by now having been dropped from the works team.

Reflecting on 1975 in general and, in particular, on Brambilla's doughty efforts, Max remarked: 'Beta paid barely enough to run a sensible programme for Vittorio. We paid him a sensible retainer, but he wasn't getting anywhere near the astronomic money earned by the established top six at the time. Beta was a relatively small, albeit very efficient, concern with only about 300 employees. They had the sort of turnover and profits that you'd naturally associate with a company of that size and their sponsorship in '75 wasn't large, although it was bigger than it had been in 1974 because the exposure and publicity the programme generated for them was way beyond what they expected.'

Taken as a whole the last two races were a disappointing note on which to end the year after the Austrian success, but the 751's overall performance throughout the season set Mosley thinking seriously about some really ambitious plans to re-form a March 'dream team' for 1976. Mosley and Herd remained inwardly convinced that, if they could get Ronnie Peterson back, and strapped him into the cockpit of a strong, uncomplicated March chassis, then he would still do the rest. Moreover Max knew only too well that Ronnie was fast growing out of love with Team Lotus. The failure of the Ralph Bellamy-designed Type 76 had obliged Chapman to fall back on the ageing Type 72, now into its sixth season, and 1975 had turned out to be a barren year for Britain's most famous F1 team.

Coincidentally, the author recalls getting an insight into Chapman's feelings about his drivers at this time. Prior to Christmas 1975 I visited Hethel, where Colin, covering his backside for the lamentable failure of his racing cars, made an obliquely scathing reference to Ronnie as a 'ninety per center'. To this day I still believe that short-term expediency prompted that remark, for Chapman knew exactly what Mosley knew. Give Ronnie the car and he would do the job. But expecting him to sort out a chassis problem...not a chance. You might just as well have employed the cat!

What had become clear was the untenable nature of the Chapman/Peterson relationship. It plunged to rock bottom after the opening race of the 1976 season at Interlagos, when Ronnie and Mario Andretti, both wrestling with the spooky 'all-adjustable' Type 77, somehow managed to collide with each other during the Brazilian Grand Prix.

By this stage Max had done his homework, checking with Ronnie behind the scenes. Sure enough, the Swede indicated that he wanted to leave Lotus. The philanthropic Count Zanon agreed to underwrite Ronnie's proposed £110,000 March retainer – and Max prepared to pull probably the most enterprising legal stunt of his entire motor racing career!

In 1975 the British F3 title had fallen to the determined Swede Gunnar Nilsson at the wheel of a works March 753. Nilsson was a pal of Peterson's and Max knew that Chapman liked the look of the young charger. With a temerity that knew no bounds, Mosley proposed a deal whereby, if Lotus released Peterson to March, then March would release Nilsson to Lotus. In all the resultant negotiations Chapman failed to appreciate a very subtle, yet crucial, point. Namely, that while Nilsson was contracted to March Max could only release him – not tell him what to do once he was released!

'What the contract said, in effect, was that we'll release Gunnar to Lotus as long as he wants to go,' explained Max with relish more than a decade later. 'I remember the day I did the deal, coming back to meet Gunnar and Ronnie at their London health club, and saying, "I think, to be honest, I've rather broken the rules on this one." Ronnie shot me a glance, deadpan. "With Colin, there are no rules," he said seriously. Then we all went off to celebrate at the Hard Rock Café.'

Herd's 1976 challenger was another logical refinement of its immediate predecessor. 'In reality, I suppose you could call it a 751B,' he told the author in Brazil. The factory was again fielding Brambilla and Stuck for the opening race at Interlagos (where 'Hanschen' finished fourth) and then the operation was expanded to take in Ronnie's entry at Kyalami, the second race on the schedule.

Mosley: 'When he rejoined us he was pretty well the same old Ronnie as a person, but he was certainly a great deal more philosophical as a driver. That last year-and-a-bit with Lotus

Outwardly similar to the previous year's machine, the March 761 was a far more refined product, incorporating much aerodynamic improvement

Lella Lombardi scored a half-point for sixth place in the 1975 Spanish GP and the Italian girl retained a place in the March line-up for the following season thanks to sponsorship from the Lavazza coffee concern. Here she is seen at Sao Paulo's Interlagos circuit in the Brazilian GP. Left: *Lella tries Brambilla's 761 for size, watched by Robin Herd and Vittorio.*

Back in the fold again. Ronnie Peterson rejoined the March team in time for the South African GP at Kyalami. He went well in the agile 761, but was eliminated from the race when Depailler's Tyrrell collided with him.

GOODYEAR
GOODYEAR
LELLA
CHAMPION
10
10
LAVAZZA
LAVAZZA
GOODYEAR

GOODYEAR
Ronnie Peterson
10
Shell
GOODYEAR

STRIKE
FIRST NATIONAL CITY
TRAVELERS CHECKS
OUT FOR...
LUCKY
STRIKE
GOOD YEAR

had genuinely demoralised him. He had become much more used to the fact that things could go wrong, and was more prepared to wait for things to come right.

'He wasn't instantly quick in the 761, either, which was surprising. It took until Monaco before what we described as his "enormous go" characteristic began to reassert itself. You could always tell when Ronnie was trying hard, because he came into the pits breathing really deeply. Whatever he might have said to the contrary, he wasn't really trying unless you could see him breathing like that.'

According to one March source, Ronnie's return to the fold at Kyalami was 'a real case of going back to an old lover; it takes time to get settled in together.' But SuperSwede certainly looked smooth, confident and assured. Although Brambilla's 761 qualified sixth, only half a second away from James Hunt's pole-position McLaren M23, Ronnie closed onto the Italian's tail soon after the start. Sadly, on lap 15, Patrick Depailler's brake-troubled Tyrrell spun in front of Ronnie going into the Crowthorne right-hander at the end of the start/finish straight. Peterson tried to dodge round the outside, but smashed his 761's right-rear suspension on the near-stationary Tyrrell.

At Long Beach, for the inaugural United States Grand Prix West, Ronnie was the fastest March qualifier, lining up sixth with a time only 0.2s away from Clay Regazzoni's pole-winning lap with the Ferrari 312T. Clay led from the start, in head-down style, all the way to the chequered flag, but Ronnie briefly got up to fourth before the 761's brake fluid boiled and he had to make a pit stop. He was eventually classified tenth on a bad day for Bicester, which saw Brambilla out in a first-corner collision with Carlos Reutemann's Brabham BT45-Alfa and Stuck bouncing into Emerson Fittipaldi's Copersucar second time round.

March was very efficient when it came to race-to-race deals for sponsorship of the nose cones of its 761s. At Long Beach Ronnie's car carried the oriental hieroglyphics of Hong Kong enthusiast Teddy Yip; John Day Model Cars and First National City became regular benefactors, while the McConnell Mason art gallery, which was owned by another great enthusiast, David Mason, and had its headquarters in London's West End, was identified on Ronnie's 761 at Monaco and Brands Hatch. A sliding-scale tariff of £6,000–12,000 per race was applied for this arrangement, based loosely on an unusually equitable approach, namely the sponsors' ability to pay!

The 1976 Spanish Grand Prix will be recalled by most fans for the shambles of James Hunt's post-race disqualification, the result of a dimensional infringement at the rear of his McLaren. For March it was a truly hopeless affair: Peterson's car succumbed early on to a transmission breakage, followed in short order by Stuck (gearbox) and Brambilla (another shunt). The race also marked the arrival of Arturo Merzario in a rented 761, run, like Stuck's car, out of a 'B' team base at Reading.

Vittorio ran well once again at Zolder, qualifying on row three, only to break a driveshaft after six laps of the Belgian Grand Prix. Ronnie fumbled an overtaking manoeuvre against Reutemann, spinning off into the catch-fencing, and Stuck wobbled to a halt with dodgy suspension after a wheel had worked loose.

Monaco looked better. Robin was getting all the worthwhile technical feedback from Brambilla, then communicating it to Max who was in charge of Peterson's car. Thanks to a lot of cosmetic 'leaping about' in the pit lane on the part of the March mechanics, Ronnie was really pumped up and qualified third behind the two Ferrari 312T2s. In the race he elbowed Regazzoni aside and chased Niki for all he was worth in the opening stages. Then, on lap 27, Ronnie fell foul of an oil slick at Tabac, pirouetting into the barrier with sufficient force to take off the rear wing and a bit more besides. Still, 'Hanschen' finished fourth. Brambilla's 761 broke its suspension.

Seventh on Peterson's home ground wasn't much to talk about, but at least he was three places ahead of Brambilla, while third place seemed on the cards at Paul Ricard, only for the Swede's Cosworth DFV's fuel metering unit to play up a mere three laps from the flag. Ronnie's return to March had seemed like a good idea at the time, but it was somehow difficult to rekindle the magic. Both partners desperately wanted it to work, but it was as if they couldn't find the precise recipe. Or maybe time had just passed them by and they each went into the project with romantic notions of what it might be like to work together again. Make no mistake, everybody at March Engineering who ever worked with Ronnie thought he was terrific.

People would later talk of Lotus being Peterson's 'spiritual home'. Not so. March had

The 1976 South African Grand Prix saw the old firm of Mosley, Peterson and Herd back in business. However, it proved impossible to recapture the magic of the early days.

tutored him, indulged his excesses and helped hone his talent to the point that he was virtually an instant Grand Prix winner by the time he moved to Lotus in 1973. Far more sentiment attached to his relationship with the March guys. It's all fading into history now and Ronnie has been dead over ten years as I write these words, but Max still nods approvingly – 'He was something special,' he says – while Robin becomes misty-eyed with affectionate nostalgia at the mere mention of his name.

Of course there was to be one more glorious moment, the high spot of the entire March/Peterson alliance. And, ironically, it was to come a few weeks after Ronnie had decided to turn his back on Bicester and sign for Tyrrell for 1977, a move that might have looked sensible on paper, but in reality almost sank his career without trace. He won the 1976 Italian Grand Prix, at the time of writing the only full-length World Championship victory scored by the March factory team.

Monza 1976 was the scene of the great row over fuel octane ratings which saw James Hunt's McLaren and John Watson's First National Citibank-backed Penske PC4 demoted to the last two rows of the starting grid. With Niki Lauda making his comeback for Ferrari after suffering those grievous injuries at the Nürburgring, many people felt that McLaren and Penske, as two established front-runners, had been 'fitted up' to keep the pressure off the Austrian. Either way, it prompted Citibank's man on the spot, Fred Stecher, to do an overnight deal to get FNCB identification onto Ronnie's 761 for the race. It turned out to be a fortuitous move.

Jacques Laffite qualified the Ligier-Matra JS5 bravely in pole position on 1m 41.35s ahead of Jody Scheckter's Tyrrell P34 (1m 41.38s), Carlos Pace's Brabham BT45-Alfa (1m 41.53s), Depailler's P34 (1m 42.06s), Lauda (1m 42.09s), Stuck (1m 42.18s), Carlos Reutemann's Ferrari 312T2 (1m 42.38s) and Peterson (1m 42.64s). And they say F1 has become close in 1989 as if it were for the first time.

Jody set the pace from the start with Laffite hanging on in second place, but Ronnie stepped up the pressure from the word go. For the first ten laps he was embroiled in a ferocious scrap with the Tyrrell twins, but forced his way by into the lead on lap 11 and was never headed again. A mid-race shower threw officials into confusion and produced a half-hearted attempt to bring proceedings to a halt. But by the time most drivers noticed, the rain had stopped and the crisis passed. Ronnie broke the challenge of the hard-charging Regazzoni with the race's fastest lap on the penultimate tour and ran out the winner by just over two seconds from Clay, who was followed by Laffite and the truly heroic Lauda.

'But I didn't have any regrets about leaving March, not even after that Monza win,' he later confessed thoughtfully. 'I really couldn't see an end to the problems we were experiencing with the 761 or a sign that the team might finally get on and do things properly. When I signed for them, it was agreed that we would do a lot of testing and, in the end, we didn't. Trying to run three or four cars was just too much. We had a lot of reliability problems, mainly connected with front brakes and tyre-wear problems, so Monza was really rather lucky. That rain shower came at just the right time to cool down the front tyres. It was a cool afternoon, anyway, as was proved by the fact that I equalled the pole-position time on the last-but-one lap.'

Mosley was later to be proved correct in his assertion that Tyrrell was the wrong berth for Ronnie: 'I spent a great deal of time talking to him about that, you know. In my heart, I just couldn't see him getting the best out of the six-wheeler. It was far too complicated for Ronnie. I'd always believed that if he was going to have a chance of the championship, then he either had to be joint number one with the man who was going to set up the car, or would have to be given a machine which was relatively straightforward to adjust.

'Although, in fairness, he gave us quite a lot of feedback from the 761 during his time with us, he wasn't in the same street as a Fittipaldi, Lauda or Andretti in that respect. I tried to tell him that the Tyrrell wouldn't be his cup of tea and I think he believed me. Give Ronnie an uncomplicated car, easy to set up, and let him do the rest.'

Ronnie's parting shot was equally well aimed: 'Robin should spend more time on his Grand Prix cars. If he did that, then he would be able to design a winner, for sure. Max? Well, he's a great businessman – but he should concentrate on making money and not try to manage the team.'

The end of the 1976 season marked a significant turning-point for March Engineering as people had come to know it over the previous seven seasons. It was almost as if Peterson's Monza victory had been its last great push, the final effort. In 1977 the team adopted a more

Hans Stuck, another recent March returnee, tackles Monaco's hairpin in the 1976 race. The sponsorship from John Day Model Cars was one of several 'nose cone deals' charged at varying rates during the course of the year.

Ronnie held second place at Monaco in 1976 before parking his 761 against the guard rail at Tabac. Here he levers himself dejectedly from the cockpit.

JOHN DAY
MODEL CARS
GOODYEAR

MONACO
FINE ARTS
GALLERY
FINA
CHAMPION
DUCKHAMS
GOODYEAR
10

Ronnie Peterson scored a brilliant victory in the 1976 Italian GP at Monza, his March 761 sporting First National City sponsorship in a deal arranged over the weekend by the enterprising Mosley. Here Ronnie races wheel-to-wheel with Jody Scheckter's Tyrrell P34 in the early stages of the race, going on to take the chequered flag (right)***. The illuminated scoreboard in the background tells us that Regazzoni's Ferrari (no.2) and Jacques Laffite's Ligier-Matra (no.26) are in second and third places.***

FINA
FINA
FINA
FINA
FINA
FINA
10

Young Brazilian Alex Ribeiro did his best but was usually unable to qualify his Hollywood-backed works March 761B.

ruthlessly commercial attitude than ever before, fielding a couple of 761Bs for new boys Alex Ribeiro from Brazil and South Africa's Ian Scheckter. It proved to be nothing to get excited about.

The 761B was, predictably, another revamp of the existing machines, engineer Martin Walters doing the detail design alterations with Robin looking over his shoulder from time to time. Changes included the incorporation of revised front uprights to cater for twin-caliper brakes, while repositioned front and adjustable rear roll bars were fitted. But it all added up to a less-than-inspired effort, neither driver having the experience or technical back-up to do anything more than flounder around, scratching like hell even to qualify on most occasions.

Ribeiro, no champion in the making but a worthy performer who had jousted regularly with Nilsson in the 1975 March works F3 set-up, squeezed his 761B onto the grid for the first 'long-distance' races (Argentina, Brazil, Kyalami and Long Beach). But, once back in Europe, the fields expanded with an additional bunch of hopefuls, all trying to make a name for themselves on an intermittent basis. Alex had no chance. He failed to make the grid in Spain, Monaco, Belgium, Sweden, France and Britain. Having qualified at Hockenheim, he missed the boat in Austria before making the grade at Zandvoort, only to fail again at Monza. He then earned the right to race in the three remaining events held outside Europe (Canada, USA and Japan) where the fields thinned out again. In all he made the grid ten times in 18 races, but only three of his starts were gained in the maelstrom of European competition.

Ian Scheckter looked a more convincing performer from the outset, Jody's elder brother having F1 experience under his belt from his native South Africa's domestic series as well as a few outings for Williams and Hesketh over the previous couple of seasons. For this reason he was nominated to use the new March 771 when it was completed (in time for the Swedish GP), although he frequently reverted to the 'proven' 761B, feeling that the older car was a better-known quantity in many circumstances.

He was unable to qualify at Monaco, though, so for the first time since Stewart and Amon had lined up together on the front row in 1970 there was no March on the grid for this prestigious event. Hans Stuck stood in for him at Kyalami, and Brian Henton at Long Beach, after he injured his legs in a Formula Atlantic accident at Cape Town, but he was back in time for the start of the European season. Needless to say, neither he nor Ribeiro ever looked like collecting a championship point.

The March factory team's efforts were played out against a background of expectancy, however. For years Herd had been toying with the possibilities of four-wheel drive and, in early December 1976, he took the wraps off a revamped 761 with four tiny driving wheels at the rear. In railway locomotive terminology it was a 2-4-0!

The March 761 '2-4-0' six-wheeler was one of Robin Herd's more imaginative projects. As usual, the team lacked the financial resources to develop the idea much beyond the concept stage.

Robin had taken a long look at the then-current Tyrrell P34 six-wheeler and reckoned it was all very well, but it still had an enormous amount of aerodynamic drag from its huge, conventional rear tyres. So Robin adapted a standard Hewland transmission, removing the backplate and, with the use of a special pinion shaft, taking the drive into a second differential facing the rear of the existing gearbox.

Each pair of rear wheels had its own inboard-mounted pair of disc brakes and outboard coil-spring/dampers, while there were two sets of lower parallel links from each modified March Formula B upright. A familiar upper/lower radius arm arrangement was employed, these simply being extended by straight, parallel rods to the tops of the trailing uprights. It never raced, although Howden Ganley tested it on several occasions, and it certainly earned March (and Scheckter's sponsor Rothmans) a great deal of promotional ink over the following six months.

It had been intended that this system would, in due course, be grafted onto the rear of the brand new 771 which, at the time, was touted by Herd as being March's 'first proper F1 car' in the sense that it marked a break with the derivatives of the F2-based 751 which had been the mainstay of the Bicester team's efforts for more than two seasons.

Although similar to the 761 in appearance, the new car differed in many respects, notably the use of a front-mounted water radiator and a very much more rigid aluminium monocoque, wider than the 761's by some ten centimetres. The driving position was also

GOODYEAR
ARTURO
CHAMPION
speedline
37
FINA

ROTHMANS
ROTHMANS
Castrol
Castrol
GOODYEAR

Left: ***Arturo Merzario fielded the most effective March throughout the 1977 season. His private 761 was operated on a shoestring budget but comfortably outstripped the works machines.***

Back in business on his own after splitting with Walter Wolf, Frank Williams took the first step down the long road to fame and fortune by fielding this 761B for promising Belgian driver Patrick Neve. The team had little hard success, but the season provided a worthwhile apprenticeship for engineer Patrick Head.

moved forward by about two inches and the space created within the tub by these two alterations was used to relocate the fuel cells, the load now being split between a seat tank and two side tanks at the rear of the tub.

After several false starts Scheckter finally raced the 771 at Zandvoort in the Dutch Grand Prix at the end of August. He finished tenth, a lap and one place ahead of Ribeiro's 761B. Was it better than the earlier machine? 'Let's say it's a very nice rent-a-car, a bit like a Simca 1000,' replied the South African laconically. He rounded off his season by being refused permission to enter Japan owing to visa problems, so his 771 lay idle and unused throughout the Grand Prix weekend at Mount Fuji.

Private March 761s proliferated throughout 1977, but few were anything more than make-weights and none proved any more successful at scoring points than the works cars. Arturo Merzario performed energetically with his 761B, and was generally quicker than either Scheckter or Ribeiro, as indeed he ought to have been, while Brian Henton had a handful of decent outings with his private 761. Motor trader John MacDonald, himself a former saloon racer and previously the entrant of ex-works Brabham BT44Bs for a variety of also-rans, raised sponsorship from the Dutch F and S Properties organisation to run Boy Hayje and Mikko Kozarowitsky in Europe. British amateur Andy Sutcliffe tried his hand at Silverstone in one of Mac's cars, failing to pre-qualify for the British Grand Prix, while probably the most celebrated private machine of all was Frank Williams's car for Belgian Patrick Neve. This modest project marked the British entrant's first step down the road to re-establishing the highly successful Williams Grand Prix Engineering concern, one of the front-line F1 teams of the Eighties.

For March it was truly the end of an era. Mosley, now 37, 'figured I'd had enough of running an unsuccessful F1 team and trying to sell production racing cars. The business no longer really needed me and I'd run out of enthusiasm for it.' At the end of the year he sold his shareholding, moving off to seek pastures new. Ever since, Max has been a legal sounding board for Bernie Ecclestone and the Formula 1 Constructors' Association, and was right up at the sharp end, defending the constructors' corner, in the acrimonious FOCA/FISA wars which nearly tore F1 asunder in the early 1980s. He is now President of the Manufacturers' Commission, representing the world's motor manufacturers within FISA, and also acts as Ligier's representative within FOCA.

Ian Scheckter in the long-awaited March 771 in the Italian GP at Monza. Only one such machine was built, and it was entrusted to the South African, who found it no more competitive than his 761B.

It certainly did look as though March had sounded the last post as far as F1 was concerned, Robin's critics suggesting that he had never really been sufficiently motivated as far as building Grand Prix cars was concerned. But Mosley disputes this viewpoint: 'Robin wasn't in the position of somebody like, say, Gordon Murray, who was just employed to design racing cars. He had budgetary considerations to keep in mind, plus the company's future as a whole and the responsibility for designing cars in several other categories as well.'

Derek Daly and Eliseo Salazar struggled through the early races of 1981 with this overweight March 811, designed for the John MacDonald/Mick Ralph RAM team after Robin Herd had made a close study of the Williams FW07. Only when Adrian Reynard arrived on the scene and pared off a considerable amount of weight did Daly (below right) *begin to demonstrate the car's potential. This was the machine from which the March 81C Indy car evolved.*

Although March would design cars for the 1978 British national F1 series, the Bicester company was off the Grand Prix map completely for the next three years and it seemed that there would be no way back. Then, at the end of 1980, the resilient, always optimistic John MacDonald decided he would like to try Grand Prix racing again, but this time properly. His RAM team had run a pair of ex-works Williams FW07s in the 1980 Aurora British F1 series and a few GPs, operating from premises owned by Herd on the Telford Road Industrial Estate at Bicester, little more than a mile from the March Engineering headquarters.

MacDonald commissioned March to build him a series of ground-effect F1 racers, the design of which was to be the responsibility of Alan Mertens and Paul Brown (who later went to Zakspeed) under the close scrutiny of Herd himself. Usually Robin simply produced a two- or three-sheet document laying out the design parameters and let his juniors get on with it, but this time he personally oversaw every drawing. Undoubtedly Robin was anxious to make his first ground-effect F1 machine competitive, but it turned out to be a real lemon. The drivers were the cheery Irishman Derek Daly and Chilean newcomer Eliseo Salazar, but the season looked worryingly like a rerun of 1977, only rather worse.

MacDonald's problems were compounded by the fact that his was a small team operating at a time when the F1 regulations were in disarray, effectively being 'rewritten' or 'clarified' every other weekend. Yet none of that could justify the major chassis failure experienced on Daly's 811 in practice at Rio, where the lower left-front wishbone pulled bodily out of the monocoque, reflecting the stark truth that the car was neither strong nor stiff enough.

Herd flew straight back to England in order to instigate a programme of front-end strengthening, but the cars were effectively no-hopers for a long while before first Gordon Coppuck and then, more spectacularly, Adrian Reynard began to make some progress with them. Coppuck, who had left McLaren in 1979, joined March to work on their F2 programmes, but occupied some spare time on the calendar trying to make MacDonald's Marches perform. But they didn't really begin to shine until Silverstone, where a chassis reduced in length by 12 inches from which Reynard had slashed 58 lb took Daly speeding to an impressive seventh place on Avon rubber. He also scored a good 11th-place finish at the Österreichring, but Salazar was so depressed that he took his sponsorship away and joined Ensign before the season was half over. The RAM Marches scored no championship points.

For 1982 Reynard, who had already established a considerable reputation in his own right as a designer, driver and manufacturer of Formula Ford and FF2000 machines, produced a logical evolution of the final 1981 RAM March derivative for MacDonald's team. Through connections established by the German driver Jochen Mass, who was signed up along with Brazil's Raul Boesel, the team obtained sponsorship from Rothmans. But Mass was nearing the end of his single-seater career and finding it hard to become motivated. 'F1 sometimes leaves me with the taste of cardboard,' he told the author in a somewhat introspective moment at Rio.

Results were again hard to come by. The genial Jochen pulled an eighth out of the bag at Long Beach and a seventh at Detroit. But when he blundered into the path of Gilles Villeneuve's Ferrari during final qualifying for the Belgian Grand Prix at Zolder, Mass ensured that he would be remembered for his involvement in one of the great F1 tragedies of the decade. The French Canadian was killed in the ensuing accident, his Ferrari somersaulting to destruction over the March's left-rear wheel.

This accident further diluted Mass's enthusiasm for F1; when he crashed spectacularly in the early stages of the French Grand Prix at Paul Ricard after tangling with Mauro Baldi's Arrows, his March ended up against a spectator fence with four onlookers injured. Nursing cracked ribs, he returned to the cockpit briefly at Hockenheim, but chose to stand down for the rest of the year. His place alongside Raul Boesel was taken by the irrepressible Rupert Keegan, but whatever steam there had been was gone from the RAM March efforts and they petered out, almost unnoticed, during the remainder of the season.

TECFIN
din
JOKER
18
MICHELOB

JOKER
GUINNESS
17
Esso

DATSUN
NISSAN
MICHELIN
Newsweek
ROTHMANS
17
RECORD
Valvoline

Newsweek
ROTHMANS
RIZLA+
RECORD
17
CHAMPION
Valvoline

Below: ***The RAM March 821 was a development of the previous year's car, engineered by Adrian Reynard*** (right) ***and driven by Jochen Mass*** (centre) ***and Raul Boesel*** (left). ***Mass never seemed totally convinced that he'd done the right thing returning to F1. Later, after being tragically involved in Gilles Villeneuve's fatal accident and another shunt in the French GP, the genial Jochen withdrew from the team. The two RAM March 821s are seen in the Rio pit lane*** (bottom left) ***during practice for the Brazilian GP.***

Left: ***After Mass's retirement, Rupert Keegan was drafted into the March F1 team, but achieved little in the way of results. Here he is seen at Las Vegas, where his 821 was classified 12th after brushing one of the concrete barriers.***

Right: ***The RAM March 821s were smartly turned out, but John MacDonald*** (left) ***and Jochen Mass had no worthwhile results to show for their efforts.***

Section 1: The Grand Prix Cars

Chapter 4

Restoration

Throughout the early 1980s, with March making such a momentous impact on the Indy car establishment, the possibility of a return to Formula 1 never really seemed to be on the agenda. Yet, for Robin Herd, Grand Prix racing always represented unfinished business at the back of his mind. March Engineering had been founded in such a welter of F1 publicity over a decade earlier, yet had only fleetingly experienced Grand Prix success.

The catalyst for March's unexpected return to F1 came in the form of young Italian driver Ivan Capelli and his manager and mentor, a genial, roly-poly wheeler-dealer called Cesare Gariboldi. Capelli was a product of that rich vein of Italian kart racing talent from which the likes of Riccardo Patrese, Eddie Cheever and Elio de Angelis had sprung to racing prominence in the 1970s.

He won the Italian Junior Kart Championship at the age of 13 and first tackled the Italian Formula 3 series in 1982. The following year, now aged 20, he secured that title, building on that success in 1984 with victory in the European Championship as well as the prestigious F3 classic supporting the Monaco Grand Prix. Despite having less than perfect uncorrected vision, and consequently needing to wear spectacles or contact lenses, Ivan was clearly an exceptionally talented youngster. In fact he would display all the signs of being one of the few to confound the theory that racing drivers who have less than totally outstanding vision don't make it to the top.

For 1985 Gariboldi's Genoa Racing outfit obtained a March 85B F3000 car in which Ivan contested the first European Championship for this category which had replaced Formula 2 as the holding area for potential Grand Prix talent. Despite being run on a shoestring budget (the car and equipment were often carried round Europe in whatever space could be cadged in generous rivals' transporters), Ivan won at the Österreichring and turned more than a few heads. The following season Genoa Racing acquired a new March 86B. On a budget of barely £200,000 Ivan edged out compatriot Emanuele Pirro to win the championship at the final round after scoring race victories at Vallelunga and the Österreichring (again).

During that summer Ivan went to Suzuka to drive a March 86J in a round of the Japanese Formula 2 Championship, one of three such outings that year for the Italian. (Japan would not follow Europe's example in adopting F3000 until 1987.) The March to be driven by Ivan was entered by the Leyton House Racing Team, owned by long-time motor racing enthusiast Akira Akagi, the Chairman of the giant Tokyo-based Marusho property group, a company with an annual turnover approaching $200 million.

The evening prior to the race Capelli and Gariboldi were in a restaurant dining in company with the British freelance journalist Ian Phillips, their table adjacent to that of Mr Akagi's party. By chance, Nelson Piquet was also present at Suzuka, carrying out promotional work for Honda, and Capelli introduced him to the Leyton House boss. Later Stefan Johansson appeared on the scene and Capelli steered the recently signed McLaren recruit to the Akagi table. According to Phillips, both F1 stars were quite a hit with the Japanese businessman and his guests.

'We were joking with Ivan that those introductions could hardly do his chances of Leyton House sponsorship any harm,' reflects Phillips, 'but I don't think Ivan or Cesare gave it a second thought.' Ivan duly competed in the race and then, together with Gariboldi, dropped in on Akagi on the Monday morning, just to thank him for the drive. What happened next was as amazing as it was unexpected.

After some preliminary chat Akira Akagi asked Capelli what he wanted to do in 1987, whether he fancied moving up into F1. Ivan explained that, yes, that was what he really wanted to do, but raising the necessary sponsorship was a problem. At this stage he had already had a couple of guest drives for the Tyrrell team, finishing a splendid fourth in the 1985 Australian Grand Prix, but it hadn't led to anything for the following year apart from a couple of outings with AGS. Then Mr Akagi asked how much he would need...

The scope of the question was such that, initially, it completely missed its target. Cesare Gariboldi began babbling excitedly to the effect that, well, you could have a badge on Capelli's overalls for such-and-such an amount. Akagi said 'No, you miss my point' – or words to that effect! So Gariboldi went rambling on about how much it would cost for sponsorship of a rear wing on an F1 car before he realised that the Marusho Chairman was trying to get a figure for a complete sponsorship package.

Capelli remembers with glee that 'By this time Cesare had his hands together in front of

Forging a new partnership: (left to right) ***Robin Herd, Akira Akagi and Ivan Capelli at the start of the Leyton House/ March alliance. Two years later, the smiles had evaporated...***

him, dripping with perspiration.' Gariboldi named a figure of around $3 million. Without further hesitation, Akira Akagi told Capelli he'd got himself a deal and also gave him $60,000 with which to complete his F3000 season.

Gariboldi then flew directly from Tokyo to Miami in order to meet up with Robin Herd, who was visiting the USA for the final round of the CART series at Tamiami Park (ironically one of only three Indy car races out of 17.not won by a March 86C that season). At this point Robin had already received a proposal from former Ligier team manager Gérard Larrousse and his business associate Didier Calmels that March should consider building a car for the new F1 team they were launching in 1987.

Gariboldi's arrival with the new offer from Leyton House injected an element of confusion into the situation and, for a while, a Leyton House/Larrousse Calmels/Capelli/March collaboration was discussed. Ian Phillips, at this stage acting purely as a close pal of Robin's, was one of several who counselled strongly against an arrangement with Larrousse and Calmels because it would have been nothing more than an engineering partnership. It was easy to see that, in the event of any sort of racing accident, there would always be a temptation to point a finger of suspicion at the supplier. While it would not exactly be a no-win situation for March, the odds could certainly be heavily stacked against Bicester.

In the event, March decided to do it on their own and the LC team forged a deal with Eric

The March 871 was based on the marque's F3000 design, a straightforward and relatively uncomplicated machine. Here Capelli is seen in the 1987 San Marino GP at Imola, the 871 wearing an ungainly, and ineffective, airbox on this occasion.

Broadley's Lola company for the manufacture of its car. A new company, March Racing, financially separate from March Engineering (and not to be involved in the March PLC flotation on the Unlisted Securities Market in 1987), was established in the premises previously occupied by the RAM team on the Telford Road Industrial Estate at Bicester. Working against the clock, an intensive programme to get organised in time for the first race of the season was initiated.

Herd had to find a team manager for this new project and, after interviewing three highly respected and established managers from categories outside F1, rang up Ian Phillips and asked if he would consider the job. Phillips admits to being flabbergasted when Robin confronted him with the question 'Why haven't you ever tried it?'

Ian confessed that it was something he had always wanted to tackle, but had somehow never got round to. 'Why don't you try it now?' asked Herd. And thus the deal was done.

In fact Phillips was a fine choice for the job and had been a close 'family friend' of March for several years and, fleetingly, a customer! Back in 1978, admittedly in a drunken stupor, he had rashly pledged his house to buy Stefan Johansson an F3 March to replace the Swede's Chevron, which was proving uncompetitive. 'At the time Dave Reeves, March's production manager, wouldn't release the car, but he was eventually persuaded to when Robin said it was OK,' Ian shudders. 'I don't think I've enjoyed motor racing less, watching Stefan driving – and crashing – what was in effect my own house. In the end March were very good, buying it back from us at the original purchase price, less VAT.'

A former editor of the British weekly motor racing magazine *Autosport*, Ian had left journalism in 1976 to take up a post as General Manager of Donington Park and later organised the Gunnar Nilsson Cancer Treatment Campaign in memory of the Lotus F1 driver who fell victim to that terrible disease at the end of 1978.

In 1980 Phillips picked up as a journalist again and not much that went on in motor racing missed his attention. Unlike many team managers, who can't see the wood for the trees, his years as a journalist had given him a sensible perspective on the sport as a whole, and F1 in particular. Once Leyton House March got up and running, you always got the impression he was one of the lads. He, Capelli and the rest of the team would prove that F1 didn't have to be all long faces and narrow outlooks.

For the first race of the 1987 season in Brazil, there was simply no way in which the team's definitive race car could be ready in time. But, rather than follow the LC Lola team and choose to miss the race, paying a $50,000 fine to FISA in lieu of turning up, March made the trip using a beefed-up version of the 1987 F3000 chassis originally designed by Andy Brown, but now modified by Gordon Coppuck and newly recruited chief draughtsman Tim Holloway. With a fuel capacity of only 28.6 gallons/130 litres, there was no earthly way in which the car would ever last a race distance.

As things turned out, this wasn't a worry. The team blew up one Cosworth DFZ as Capelli was about to start second qualifying and, when its one remaining engine displayed signs of imminent failure in the race morning warm-up, Capelli was withdrawn in order to conserve the precious V8. The 1987 season marked the start of a transitional period in F1 and naturally aspirated 3.5-litre engines were admitted in preparation for the end of the turbo era at the start of 1989. With Tyrrell, March and Lola all contesting this 'second division', interest in which FISA had attempted to bolster by the introduction of the Jim Clark and Colin Chapman Cups for drivers and constructors respectively, engine supply would become a growing problem as the year wore on.

The 'definitive' March 871 made its first appearance at Imola for the San Marino Grand Prix, designer Gordon Coppuck having essentially developed the original F3000 concept, incorporating a bigger fuel tank and longer wheelbase. Capelli retired from the race after 18 laps with ignition trouble, having qualified an unobtrusive 22nd. During practice Ivan had had to spend some time behind the wheel of the old 87P hack while minor gremlins were sorted out on the new 871. It didn't help that the spare was fitted with a Cosworth DFL 3.3-litre sports car engine simply because the team couldn't get its hands on sufficient DFZs. In optimistic anticipation of Ivan's move into F1, Cesare Gariboldi had reserved six DFZs through Swiss engine specialist Heini Mader the day after Capelli clinched the 1986 F3000 title. March received the sixth in time for the Japanese Grand Prix, the penultimate race of the year. They were not impressed.

Throughout the summer of 1987 March stuck at it, regarded with lofty disdain by some members of the establishment as a group of lads having a good time, but nothing more than that. Rival team principals sidled up to Akira Akagi at regular periods during the year suggesting none too subtly that he might beneficially switch his sponsorship in 1988. He listened politely before telling them that he was perfectly content with the fledgling March organisation.

Interestingly, the distinctive Miami blue livery of the Leyton House Racing Team was created before any branded Leyton House products or services became available for public consumption. Having attained a certain profile in the motor racing world, mainly through F1, but also thanks to involvement at Le Mans and in European F3000, Leyton House used the sport as a springboard from which to organise successful international merchandising programmes. By the start of 1988 Tokyo would boast three Leyton House restaurants and two Hotels Leyton. In Italy a fashion house began producing designer clothing for export to Japan under this label. Akagi and his business associates were well satisfied with progress on this front too.

For the Belgian Grand Prix at Spa-Francorchamps March abandoned the 871's distinctively tall airbox; although it produced an extra 300 rpm on the straight, the uncomfortable buffeting round Capelli's helmet just wasn't worth the marginal benefit. In qualifying Ivan displayed tremendous verve, simply hurling the March over the Eau Rouge bridge with the confidence of somebody far more experienced.

As it turned out, he was lucky to make the start. An electrical failure stranded him on the warm-up lap, so he ran back to be strapped into the under-tanked, DFL-engined spare. But when the Tyrrells of Philippe Streiff and Jonathan Palmer tangled on the second lap of the race, out came the red flags and Capelli got a welcome second chance. The 40-minute interval prior to the restart allowed the March mechanics to retrieve, and repair, the original 871. Capelli

LEYTON HOUSE
16
Data General
COURTAULDS
Tyrrell
3

then ran away with the normally aspirated division before the engine failed after 15 laps.

Come Monaco time and the engine problems persisted. Ivan struggled gamely to take 19th place on the grid, the team still trying to sort out horrendous oil consumption problems as well as grappling with a misfire on one of the two freshly prepared Mader DFZs which had been delivered directly to the paddock from the premises of the Swiss engine builder. In the event Capelli had a splendid run to sixth place, not far behind Palmer's Tyrrell, to score the first championship point for Leyton House March. It was a performance made all the more creditable by the fact that Ivan drove the whole race distance without a rev-counter. Prior to the start it had been disconnected, on the off-chance that it might have had something to do with the practice misfire.

In Detroit poor handling and overheating in practice left Capelli in a lowly 22nd position. The battery broke after nine laps. By this stage tensions with the engine suppliers had built up to an almost impossible level. Phillips admits to having a 'blazing row' with Heini Mader as early as Spa and when he managed to acquire another DFZ from Williams he promptly sent it to Brian Hart, the highly regarded Harlow-based engine specialist, to be race-prepared.

Phillips: 'It was Brian who warned us about potential piston ring problems with our early DFZs which were simply drinking oil. Then he had a look at our wiring system and asked why we'd done it like we had. We told him that Cosworth had insisted that was the way.' The net result of that was £3000-worth of new wiring looms on both 871s fielded at Paul Ricard for the French Grand Prix, by which time March had concluded that there was little future in pursuing a Cosworth relationship for 1988.

'One of the first of half a dozen phone calls I had the day after joining the company had been from John Judd, who told me he was planning an F1 version of his F3000 engine for 1988,' Ian continues. 'It seemed like a good way to go, being lighter and more modern than what Cosworth was offering.' The engine was derived from a Honda design and this was where Akira Akagi's connections helped enormously. To Judd's disbelief, Phillips phoned him back on the Monday after Spa and said, 'OK, it's a goer, we've got Honda's agreement for you to supply them to us.' Judd initially didn't believe it, doubting that Honda would ever have made up its mind so quickly on such an important issue. But Akagi had spoken to Honda's F1 racing manager, Yoshitoshi Sakurai, and got the green light for a March-Judd partnership for 1988.

There was nearly a very nasty accident in the March pit garage at Paul Ricard when the spare 871 fell off its jack, quite badly damaging its monocoque. Mercifully, nobody was working beneath it at the time. Capelli was again running away with the non-turbo class, harrying Christian Danner's Zakspeed, when the engine expired on lap 53.

The team was learning all the time. During practice at Silverstone a faulty fuel collector pot obliged Ivan to run with a full fuel load for much of the time. Having qualified 24th, he retired with gearbox problems after three laps. At Hockenheim, where the Italian was rapped over the knuckles for over-revving a precious engine in qualifying, distributor failure put him out of the German Grand Prix. But things were better in Hungary where he finished tenth, the third naturally aspirated finisher.

In Austria Capelli won the non-turbo class, taking 11th place overall, and at Monza, despite being a worrying 10 km/h down on straightline speed during qualifying, he ran non-stop to 13th. But possibly Ivan's most satisfying performance of the year came during qualifying for the Spanish GP at Jerez, where less than one-tenth of a second separated him from Nakajima's Lotus 99T-Honda.

Portugal had produced a fine ninth overall – and another victory in the non-turbo category – but there were to be no finishes scored in the last three 'long distance' races in Mexico, Japan and Australia. Unreliability had dropped Capelli to fourth in the Jim Clark Trophy contest, behind the Tyrrell twins and Philippe Alliot's LC Lola. But close scrutiny of Ivan's performances pointed to March being the best long-term bet.

The season also had the ironic benefit of defusing a potential rival. On the basis of 1987, Ken Tyrrell misread the standards of future naturally aspirated competition so dramatically that his team found itself struggling hard throughout the following year, while March, accurately judging what would be required to keep up with prevailing technical trends, enjoyed considerable success.

Capelli scored the first championship point for Leyton House March with a strong sixth place at Monaco in 1987. Here he accelerates out of the Loews hairpin on the tail of Jonathan Palmer's Tyrrell DG/016, which finished ahead of him.

In addition to engineering a switch to Judd power, March needed a brand new, much more sophisticated chassis design for 1988. Leyton House, heartened by what it had seen in 1987, agreed to an appropriate increase in the budget which not only envisaged expansion to

The Judd V8 installation in the Newey-designed 881 (above) *incorporated a sharply waisted rear end, but the CG891* (right) *was even narrower at the back thanks to longitudinally mounted coil-spring/dampers and an inboard gear cluster.*

include a second entry, but also allowed Adrian Newey to be recruited as technical director, joining the team on 1 August 1987. A graduate from Southampton University with a degree in Aerodynamics and Astronautics, Newey's determination to work in motor racing led him into a post with Fittipaldi Automotive in 1980, working alongside Harvey Postlethwaite. From there he moved to March, where he engineered Johnny Cecotto's F2 car in 1982 and later designed the sports cars which won the GTP category of the American IMSA series in 1983 and '84.

However, it was to be Newey's experience in the aerodynamically challenging CART arena which would equip him for his role as the creator of the new March 881. Having gained his first taste of Indy car racing in 1984, engineering Bobby Rahal's TrueSports March, he was responsible for the design of the 85C, the car which represented March in the following season's championship, and his designs were to claim a hat-trick of Indianapolis victories between 1985 and '87. At the end of 1985 Adrian moved from Rahal's team to work with Michael Andretti and the Kraco organisation, which benefited from a certain degree of support from the March factory. He was then briefly involved with Carl Haas's FORCE F1 team, outlining its stillborn contender for the 1987 Grand Prix season, and stayed with the Chicago-based entrant to oversee the technical operation of Mario Andretti's CART Lola.

In finalising the concept of the 881, Newey drew extensively on his American oval racing experience. 'Indianapolis is all about aerodynamics,' he reflects. 'When cars are averaging 200 mph, aerodynamics become absolutely critical, as does the set-up of the cars. Indy car racing taught me a great deal about the subtleties of chassis set-up, both aerodynamically and through suspension tuning. The basic profile of the 881 was wholly evolved in the wind tunnel. It was my aim to produce a small, neat car, integrating our aerodynamic aims with the new 1988 technical regulations which demanded that the driver's feet be placed behind the front axle-line.

'Achieving that balance took up a lot of the initial design time. We had to move a lot of components around to get the weight distribution we were looking for now that the driver's feet had in effect to be moved back by 15 inches. There were several ways of tackling this: going for a longer wheelbase, moving the driver and engine back, or sitting the driver more upright in the cockpit. We opted for something of a compromise route, keeping the driver well reclined and the Judd engine precisely where we wanted it.'

Newey was fortunate in being able to keep the chassis manufacturing process effectively in-house, the carbon-fibre composite chassis and bodywork being produced by March Group PLC's Comtec subsidiary, based at Brackley, a few miles up the Northampton road from Bicester. The rolling-floor wind tunnel located at the same premises was where the 881's profile was shaped.

The result was a sophisticated and aerodynamically quite complicated chassis, a striking feature of which was the distinctive 'waisting' of the monocoque towards the front of the cockpit, producing an ultra-narrow footwell only 25 cm wide at its foremost extremity. 'The size of the driver's feet is now the major criterion in determining the size of this bulkhead,' Newey explained. The front spring/damper units were mounted on this forward bulkhead, activated by pushrods.

With distinctively contoured side pods and water radiator intakes, and a multi-curved diffuser panel, the overall aerodynamic package of the 881 produced considerably more downforce than its predecessor, for no increase in aerodynamic drag. Pushrod suspension was also employed at the rear and a completely new transmission was adopted, which was based on March's CART gearbox, with some new internals produced by Arrow Gears and March, and a revised lubrication system. Three cars were ready for the Brazilian GP season-opener after an epic effort on the part of the factory staff.

The man recruited to drive the second car was a pleasant, gregarious 24-year-old Brazilian who had been a close friend of Ayrton Senna since their childhood karting days at Sao Paulo. Mauricio Gugelmin had come to England in 1981, doing extremely well in Formula Ford and FF2000 before triumphing in the 1985 British F3 Championship, duplicating Senna's achievement of two years earlier. In 1986 and '87 he had contested F3000 with a March and a factory Ralt-Honda respectively, gaining a reputation as a stylish and polished performer. Many people wondered whether Gugelmin was sufficiently aggressive but, as things turned out, he was to complement Capelli superbly.

Ian Phillips: 'Mauricio's big attraction was that he'd been through the British school of motor racing and worked with Dick Bennetts in F3 and F3000 and Ron Tauranac in F3000.

Italian entrepreneur Cesare Gariboldi, seen here between Gugelmin and Capelli, was a crucial catalyst behind the formation of the team. He was sadly killed in a road accident during the winter of 1988/89 and the team's cars for the new season carried the prefix 'CG' before their type number out of respect for his memory. Leyton House March team manager Ian Phillips is on the left.

He was also an experienced test driver, which was extremely important because Ivan had hardly done a day's testing in his life – he'd never been in a team that could afford it. Mr Akagi had a great deal of faith in our decision and was happy to follow our choice.'

At Rio the cars were simply too new and untried, but Capelli's zest produced a splendid ninth on the grid – and a warm handshake from an admiring Carlos Reutemann who had been spectating out on the circuit. Mauricio was a fine 13th, both drivers complaining that their gearchanges began to balk as they heated up, due, it was thought, to the gearbox heat-exchangers failing to cool the oil adequately. Just for this event the 881s were equipped with an additional ⅔-litre oil tank, which could be primed by the driver, specifically to cope with any possible oil surge problems on the fast corners which abound at Rio.

It was a disappointing debut outing for Newey's new design. Ivan's 881 suffered a burst water pipe on the warm-up lap, so he switched to the untried spare, starting from the pit lane. He lasted a mere six laps before the oil light came on (due to an electrical fault), so he called it a day. For future races the oil warning light was removed! Gugelmin's clutch exploded as he left the grid. Phillips's only moment of light relief came when a steward hurried up to their pit and demanded that Capelli be brought in as he'd infringed the starting procedure by swapping cars after the parade lap. Ian had to point out that Ivan had retired several laps earlier.

For Imola the Judd V8s featured additional oil scavenge pumps, but the biggest problem

was nose cones, the 881s losing no fewer than four in as many laps when the fixing bobbin design loading proved inadequate to cope with the downforce generated. Capelli survived a huge spin on the dauntingly fast Tamburello double left-hander after the pits to qualify ninth, but Mauricio was left trailing in a troubled 20th place after a succession of battery problems.

In the race Ivan's gearbox selected two ratios at once as he braked for the Variante Alfa, the 881 spinning off into the sand. Mauricio battled with understeer, overheating and an onboard radio that demonstrated a worrying inclination to fall into his lap under braking to struggle home 15th, two laps down on Senna.

In a further attempt to cool the seriously overheating gearboxes, at Monaco the 881s featured a small conventional gearbox oil radiator. It was another disappointing race. Gugelmin succumbed to electrical failure when lying ninth, while Ivan bumped Alex Caffi's Dallara in the Ste Devote traffic jam on the opening lap, losing a lot of time with a stop to change a rear track rod control arm. He finished tenth, six laps behind, suffering from serious cramp in his right leg and arm, one of the unfortunate by-products of the March's extremely cramped cockpit.

Over the bumps at Mexico City's Magdalena Mixhuca circuit, both drivers expressed the opinion that the car had insufficient front suspension movement, but Ivan squeezed into tenth place on the grid. Gugelmin, hampered by a host of problems the most concerning of which was a broken rear damper mounting, was six places further back. The Brazilian lasted ten laps before an electrical short circuit intervened. Capelli trailed in 16th.

With only a dozen of Judd's 46 Type CV engines on the team's strength, March Racing had insufficient V8s available to go testing as much as the drivers would have liked in the early part of the season, and John's Rugby-based Engine Developments company found itself under pressure to rebuild the engines with the absolute minimum of delay. Prior to the three-race North American tour, the team had made some very promising progress with revised front suspension geometry during tests at Donington Park, but Adrian and the factory staff had insufficient time to fit the new set-up prior to Mexico. Both drivers spent a lot of time grappling with unwanted understeer as a result.

At Montreal's Ile Notre Dame circuit, although Gugelmin retired from the Canadian GP with gearbox trouble, Ivan showed what the 881 could do with a fine fifth behind the all-conquering Senna-Prost McLaren-Honda show, Thierry Boutsen's Benetton B188 and Nelson Piquet's Lotus 100T. It seemed as though the team was on the right track at last.

The mood of optimism received a setback during the following Saturday morning's free practice session at Detroit when Ivan suddenly found his 881 turning sharp left into the pit wall as he exited the waterfront chicane. The cause of the accident could have been a deflating tyre punctured by debris from René Arnoux's Ligier, which had collided with the chicane a few minutes earlier. For a short time it looked very unpleasant indeed as the March's left-front wheel folded back, workers on the pit wall also being showered with debris. Ivan sustained a broken bone in his left foot and, although he later returned to the paddock on crutches, he was clearly out for the rest of the weekend. Mauricio retired with engine trouble while in fifth place, carrying the FOCA onboard camera for the only time in 1988. The meeting had offered little opportunity to test out the spare car, which was fitted with the hotly anticipated new suspension.

Capelli was recovered in time for the French GP at Paul Ricard, where his 881 alone sported the revised front suspension geometry. Ivan qualified tenth, six places ahead of his team-mate, but Mauricio reversed the order in the race as the Marches finished in eighth and ninth positions, the Brazilian running through non-stop as Capelli opted for a tyre change.

Silverstone saw all three cars turned out with the latest suspension configuration together with revised gearbox internals which finally cured the serious overheating problem, and the team spent a couple of days at the Pembrey circuit in South Wales, polishing the chassis set-up in preparation for its home race. From the outset the 881s seemed superbly stable through Silverstone's fast swerves and, despite a spectacular spin at Club, Gugelmin produced the fifth-fastest time, barely a second slower than Prost's fourth-place McLaren MP4/4.

Capelli survived similarly unscathed from a nasty moment at Woodcote when a pin in the left-rear suspension broke, causing his 881 to sit down awkwardly on its haunches while flat in fifth gear. Fortunately he kept control, secure in the knowledge that he had already earned sixth place on the grid.

The race took place in torrential rain and, while Ivan disappointingly retired with a broken valve spring after 34 laps, Mauricio performed flawlessly to bring his 881 home fourth. It

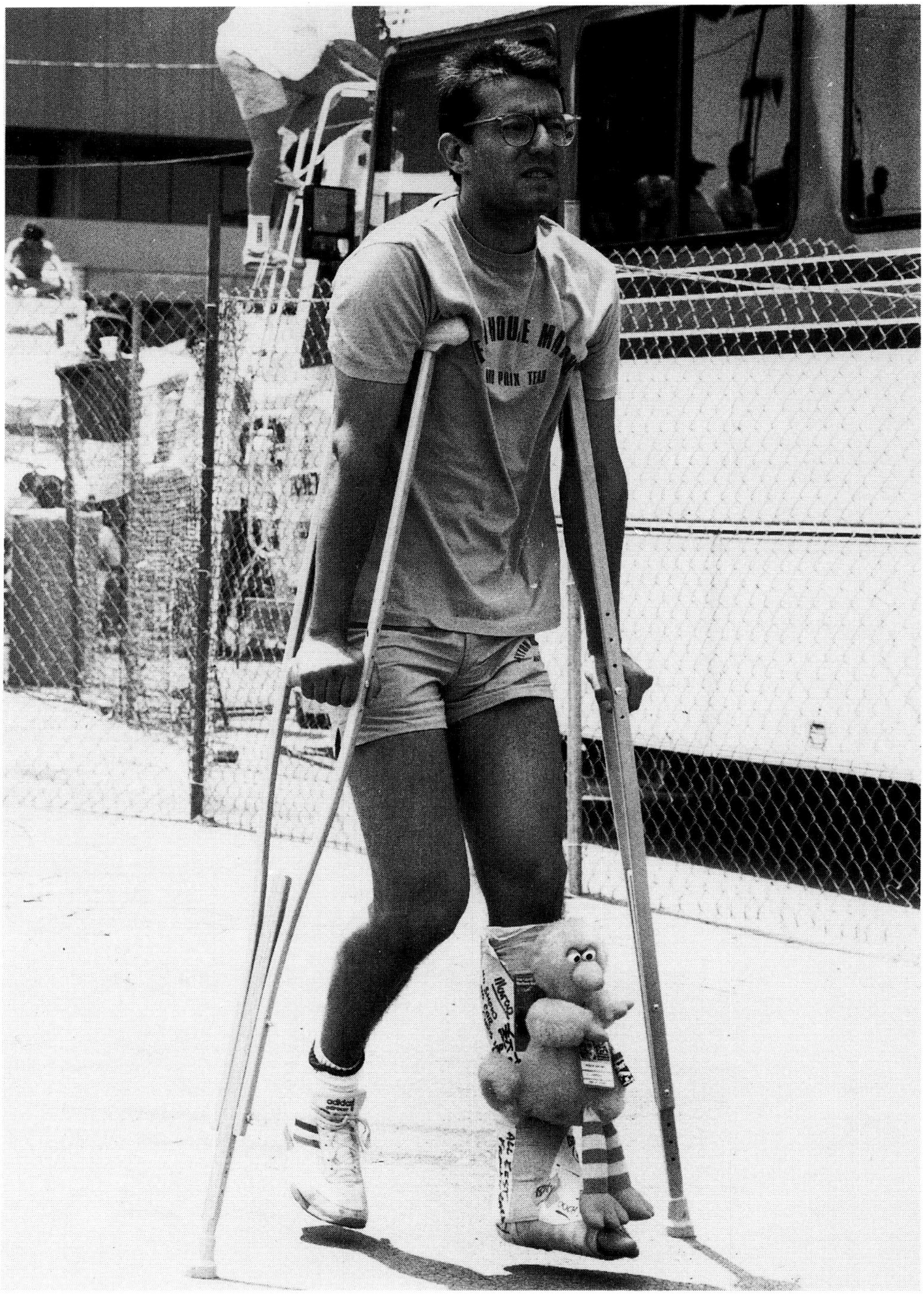

proved to be the start of a promising run. Capelli finished fifth in similarly dank conditions at Hockenheim a fortnight later, but blotted his copybook in Hungary where, after qualifying a magnificent fourth, he mortally over-revved his Judd in the opening-lap sprint. But Mauricio performed splendidly again, bringing his clutchless March home fifth.

The problem of insufficient room in the 881's cockpit was highlighted by retired triple World Champion Jackie Stewart, who sampled the March at Silverstone prior to the Belgian Grand Prix. In Stewart's view, the layout generally reflected that both drivers 'are relatively inexperienced regarding what they should be looking for in terms of cockpit comfort – and indeed operational necessity...I am about the same size as Ivan Capelli and was far from comfortable in the car...The fact of clutch trouble and lack of circulation in Capelli's legs during the 1988 season does not surprise me. The driver has to sit like a half-shut pocket-knife.'

The March 881 monocoque stood up well to Capelli's practice shunt at Detroit in the summer of 1988 (above)***. The popular Italian driver returned to the paddock*** (left) ***after hospital treatment to give us his own interpretation of Long John Silver. That's supposed to be a parrot mounted on his plaster cast...***

Unquestionably, the 881 was too cramped, but it was a point Adrian Newey had firmly taken on board and there would be slightly more foot room provided when it came to designing the 891. Meanwhile the 1988 season continued with the 881s regularly featuring in the results, Capelli finishing fifth on the road at Spa, but eventually inheriting third place when the Benetton-Fords were disqualified for infringing the permissible F1 fuel specifications.

At Monza the Marches qualified 11th and 13th, finishing in fifth and eighth places with Ivan ahead again. Then came the first of two memorable events, the Portuguese GP at Estoril. Capelli qualified third, beaten only by the McLaren-Hondas. Prost waltzed off into the distance almost from the start of the race, but by the end of the opening lap Ivan was third and already showing signs of hustling Ayrton. Hampered by reportedly poor fuel consumption and less-than-perfect handling, Senna increasingly found that Capelli's challenge would not go away.

By lap 20, with Prost now 8.8s ahead, Capelli was clearly sizing up Ayrton's McLaren. As its fuel load lightened, so the 881's handling got even better. At the end of lap 21 Capelli dived out of Senna's slipstream and outbraked him into second place at the end of the start/finish straight.

Thereafter, little by little, he eased closer to Prost. By lap 34 only 1.6s separated the leading McLaren-Honda from the tenaciously driven March-Judd. But that was as close as Ivan would get. Gradually, Alain stretched his advantage to ten seconds at the chequered flag, Capelli easing back to keep his water temperature under control. Mauricio had climbed to fifth when his engine expired, but it had been a glorious day none the less.

A week later at Jerez Capelli found himself boxed in behind an unhelpful Riccardo Patrese's Williams for many laps. It took him until lap 36 to force his way past, but he quickly dealt with Senna for the second successive Sunday and then set off hell for leather after Prost and Mansell at the front of the field. But his engine broke, so March had to be content with Gugelmin's seventh place.

The all-McLaren battle between Prost and Senna for World Championship honours may have dominated attention at Suzuka, but Capelli poked his March into fourth place on the

Aiming for a place at the top. Capelli's 881 tries the outside line as he attempts to out-manoeuvre Riccardo Patrese's obstructive Williams FW12 during the early stages of the 1988 Spanish GP at Jerez. Following are Alessandro Nannini's Benetton B188 and the Ferrari F1/87/88C of Gerhard Berger.

P 84
Agip
Canon
ICI
Mobil
6

grid for the Japanese Grand Prix. Senna stalled on the line, so Ivan completed the first lap behind Prost and Berger, quickly disposing of the Ferrari before moving up onto Alain's gearbox.

With Ivan reeling off a succession of fastest race laps, Alain suddenly realised he was in very real danger of losing the lead, the March continually snapping at his heels. Grappling with a balky gearchange, Alain missed a shift coming out of the tight chicane before the pits and, to the delight of the many Leyton House guests present, Capelli nosed the March into the lead as they crossed the timing line, right in front of the main grandstand. But Prost had the inside line for the next right-hander and reasserted himself. Three laps later Ivan's Judd cut out with electrical trouble and, his disappointment tinged with elation, he abandoned the car in front of the pits. He had made his point.

Gugelmin finished tenth at Suzuka, the Brazilian rounding off his season on a low note at Adelaide, where he was eliminated from the Australian Grand Prix in a collision with Nakajima. Capelli bagged sixth place in this finale to the 1988 season, ending up equal seventh in the World Championship on 15 points along with Alessandro Nannini and Derek Warwick. Gugelmin shared 12th position with Eddie Cheever and Jonathan Palmer on five points apiece. March took a worthy fifth in the Constructors' Championship, equal on 20 points with Williams and Arrows.

March Racing ended the '88 season in a buoyant mood but, sadly, their programme would have to continue without the supportive and popular Cesare Gariboldi. The Italian who did so much to nurture the Leyton House/March alliance in its early days was tragically killed in a road accident over the winter, depriving the close-knit Bicester team of a valued and trusted friend.

In penning the car which Capelli and Gugelmin would drive in 1989 – the type number of which was prefixed by the initials CG in memory of Gariboldi – Newey sought further to enhance the aerodynamic principles established by the 881. Generally smaller than its predecessor, the new car sported larger side pods carrying bigger water radiators for improved cooling, the revised system having been tried on the 881s at the first race of the new season at Rio, where Gugelmin finished an excellent third.

With the new March CG891 not scheduled to make its debut until Monaco, Mauricio Gugelmin was forced to rely on an 881 for the 1989 San Marino Grand Prix at Imola. The old cars were no longer competitive, however.

Chief mechanic Harvey Spencer wears a seriously attentive expression as he listens to the two drivers making a point about the 881.

Power for the CG891 came from the brand new, narrow-angle Judd EV V8, which was made available to March on an exclusive basis in 1989. 'We wanted to reduce the size of the car as much as possible,' explained Newey, 'and the biggest mechanical element in a car is its engine, so I felt that reducing the frontal area of the engine by narrowing its vee-angle was extremely important.' John Judd estimated that fewer than five per cent of the components from the old CV engine had been carried over for use in the new unit. 'A few internal pieces remain the same,' he explained, 'and we employ the same oil pumps. But, apart from that, even where things look similar, they are in fact brand new.' The EV had bigger valves, was lighter and offered a slight power advantage over the previous engine, thanks largely to the fact that it revved higher and breathed better.

For 1989 Judd had originally planned to make a short-stroke version of his 90-degree CV engine, but took on the challenging task of re-engineering the unit with a 76-degree vee in response to Adrian Newey's requirement for a reduced frontal area. The resultant redesign was an extremely complex business.

There were a number of packaging problems which needed to be addressed, such as the positioning of the distributor and alternator, which had previously sat in the middle of the vee. One of the reasons for adopting the latest Magneti Marelli ignition system was that it dispensed with a conventional distributor, allowing the use of eight small coils, each mounted directly above its own spark plug.

The CG891 was built round a familiar carbon fibre composite monocoque and featured pushrod suspension all round. Drive from the Judd EV engine was taken through a new Leyton House March six-speed gearbox, positioned longitudinally, but mounted ahead of the axle rather than behind it. 'We had doubts about building a transverse gearbox,' admits Newey, 'but I wanted the geartrain ahead of the axle to assist the weight distribution and aerodynamics of the car.' That enabled the design to incorporate a distinctively wide, arched diffuser panel beneath the rear wing.

Meanwhile, a deal was done for the sale of the 881 gearbox design to Ligier for incorporation in its new JS33, arranged through Herd's old confederate Max Mosley, the French team's representative within the Formula One Constructors' Association. Herd was rumoured to be keen to take this technical collaboration one step further, feeling that March

LEYTON HOUSE
BP
Marlboro
LEYTON HOUSE
BP
15
15

PERDIGÃO
PERDIGÃO
PERDIGÃO

BP
16

Capelli wrestling his March CG891 through the streets of Phoenix during the inaugural Grand Prix in the Arizona city. He stopped with gearbox problems, one of many retirements in a depressing spiral of bad luck which dominated the team's summer of '89...

could benefit from the use of Ligier's testing arrangements at the new Magny-Cours circuit, a simply splendid facility. However, it was considered that such a technical partnership might well compromise March Racing's overall competitiveness and this proposal was dropped when the finalised deal for Leyton House's acquisition of the F1 team was eventually sealed.

On 30 May 1989 March Racing, along with March Windtunnels and the F3000 operation, passed into the control of Akagi's Emblem BV organisation, a Dutch company specifically established to handle the deal. On that day the March shareholders agreed to the arrangement at an Extraordinary General Meeting.

Ian Phillips rounded off with a harsh critique of March Group and its management in a communiqué issued at the first Phoenix Grand Prix. It read: 'We felt uncomfortable as part of a public company, especially one in total turmoil. There was no management skill of any kind available to us, or any concept of how to do the job properly, and ultimately the contribution demanded of us was entirely unacceptable and detrimental to our work.'

At the time this uncompromising broadside was fired off at March Racing's former colleagues, the CG891 was on the verge of its third race, looking for its first finish. Pressed into service at Monaco, of all places, the new car was forced through the helter-skelter of the three North American races (Mexico, Phoenix and Montreal) before there was sufficient time available for it to be put through a single serious test session.

However, in pre-British GP tyre testing at Silverstone both Capelli and Gugelmin really got to know something about the new car's handling and, into the second half of the '89 season, the team seemed set to regain some of the momentum which had seemingly slipped through its fingers in the first half of the year.

First point for the revitalised team. Ivan Capelli heading for sixth place at Monaco, 1987, in the F3000-derived 871 during the first season of Leyton House involvement.

Shell
Oils
Canon

Mauricio Gugelmin aims for fourth place in the rain-soaked 1988 British Grand Prix at Silverstone, his March 881 pictured ahead of Alessandro Nannini's Benetton B188 and Nigel Mansell's Williams FW12. They finished in reverse order, 2-3-4.

Marlboro
LEYTON march HOUSE
LEYTON HOUSE
LEYTON HOUSE
16
Marlboro

Left: *Great moment. Ivan Capelli's 881 slices inside Ayrton Senna's McLaren-Honda MP4/4 to take second place in the 1988 Portuguese Grand Prix at Estoril. Ivan closed to within three seconds of race winner Alain Prost at one point, holding second place to the finish.*

Capelli with the brand new CG891 during its maiden outing at Monaco, 1989. On course for sixth place, the Italian (above) *suffered an electrical problem and retired just before the finish.*

Home base. The relatively cramped premises of the Leyton House March F1 team at Telford Road, Bicester. The team plans a new purpose-built green-field site for a new headquarters within the next three years.

16
LEYTON HOUSE
LEYTON HOUSE
LEYTON HOUSE
LEYTON HOUSE MARCH
BARCLAY
LEYTON HOUSE

At the start of the 1988 French Grand Prix Mauricio Gugelmin aimed his March CG891 at a gap which suddenly vanished, the ensuing collision with Thierry Boutsen's Williams and Nigel Mansell's Ferrari launching him wildly into the air. Rolling in mid-flight, before landing on the March's roll-over hoop (inset), *the cool Brazilian flicked off the master switch. 'There was nothing else I could do,' he remarked philosophically. He drove the spare March in the restarted race, setting fastest lap to round off an exciting afternoon!*

EAGLE
RHONE-POULENC
LEYTON HOUSE
GOODYEAR
LEYTON HOUSE
GOODYEAR
25
MONEYTRON
LEYTON HOUSE
CARGLASS
37
EAGLE
BP

10
37
33

Below: ***Howdy Holmes at the wheel of the Orbitor during Indianapolis pre-qualification practice in 1980. A revamped version of this car rounded off the season with a third-place finish at Phoenix in the hands of Gary Bettenhausen.***

A.J. Foyt won March its first Indy car race in 1981, albeit a USAC-sanctioned, rain-shortened event at Pocono. But he made the front row at the Brickyard the following year with this 82C (bottom) ***and showed the kids how to drive in the opening stages – after giving his mount some makeshift corrective surgery with the aid of a hammer!***

Left: ***Teo Fabi's Skoal Bandit-sponsored works-backed Forsythe March 83C leads commandingly during the early stages of the 1983 Indy 500. He has just lapped Scott Brayton's 83C, the Eagle 8110 of Steve Chassey and Tony Bettenhausen's 83C.***

Right: ***Two of Penske's 85Cs at the 1985 Indy 500. Al Unser (no. 11) finished fourth, but new recruit Danny Sullivan (no. 5) won after a heart-stopping spin in front of Andretti's Lola.***

Detailed front-end view of the 83C entered by Rick Galles.

5
BOSCH
GOODYEAR
5
PENNZOIL
Miller
AMERICAN
Miller
5
Hertz
11
11 BOSCH
GOODYEAR
11
Miller
AMERICAN
Hertz

CANADIAN TIRE
76
Labatt

Newsweek
KRACO
99 ELECTROLUX
ELECTROLUX
GOODYEAR
EAGLE

Left: *Jacques Villeneuve never scaled the competitive heights of his late brother Gilles, but managed a win at Elkhart Lake in this 85C backed by Gilles's old sponsor, Canadian Tire.*

Some days things don't go right. Michael Andretti (below left) *gave his Kraco 86C this impressive crash test and walked away unhurt.*

Al Unser Junior's Galles Racing March 88C (top) *and* (above) *its Ilmor engine acknowledging the patronage of Chevrolet. The 88C might not have been the car to have, but the Ilmor V8 was most certainly the engine to beat.*

In 1989 the March-Porsche Indy car partnership began to look truly promising, Teo Fabi demonstrating the unquestionable quality of the chassis from the start of the year. Cynics suggested that if it had only had an Ilmor-Chevy engine, the 89P would have been even better...

Section 2: The Indy Cars

Chapter 1

A new challenge

By the end of its first decade, March Engineering was in many ways a distinctly different company to that originally envisaged by the four founding partners. Moreover, with Max Mosley's departure at the end of 1977, of that pioneering quartet only Robin Herd remained. He had always harboured those ambitions to become a success within Formula 1 but, despite the enthusiasm and personal interest he had focused on producing those Williams FW07-clones for John MacDonald's RAM team, they could by no stretch of the imagination be called competitive. Herd's 'unfinished business' in F1 looked as though it would remain just that.

However, approaching the age of 40, Herd, like Mosley, came to appreciate that the business of churning out production cars for the lesser formulae, while profitable enough, retained a rather limited appeal from the engineering standpoint. Herd was anxious that any fresh project should be spiced with a genuine engineering challenge.

The seed of such a new challenge was sown in 1980, when March Engines, the company's Oxford-based special projects consultancy, received an approach to produce a CART chassis for the team owned by plastic-mould manufacturer Sherman Armstrong, a long-time Indianapolis entrant.

Armstrong made it a condition of the deal that John Barnard should provide a major portion of the engineering input. Barnard, who had done a fine job designing Jim Hall's Chaparral 2K, was by this time heavily involved with Ron Dennis in the formation of the McLaren International organisation, so there was no way he could play an active role in such a programme.

What he did manage to do, as he rather cautiously concedes, was to set out a few very basic parameters which provided some fundamental guidance for March Engines on such matters as what sort of aerodynamic package was appropriate. Engineered by Ian Reed and 'Shish' Ahmed, the Orbitor, as the car was called, was built round a March 792-derived chassis and used the ubiquitous Cosworth DFX 2.65-litre turbo V8 as its power unit. Howdy Holmes failed even to complete a qualifying run with the car at Indianapolis, although it certainly showed potential.

Howdy Holmes during a practice run for the 1980 Indy 500 in the Sherman Armstrong-owned Orbitor. With suspension geometry outlined by John Barnard, this one-off special was based loosely round an F2 March 792 monocoque and can be regarded as the pioneering prototype for the firm's Indy involvement.

94
GOODYEAR
GOODYEAR
EAGLE

Three weeks later Holmes drove the Orbitor at Watkins Glen, where it performed quite well despite a braking problem, and a second, tidied-up Mk 2 version – overseen by veteran Indy car preparation wizard George Bignotti – arrived in time for the California 500 at Ontario, only for Holmes to be caught out when a side skirt stuck and crash heavily, breaking a rib. The car was written off, but rose from the ashes at Phoenix, where Gary Bettenhausen rounded off the year with a third place behind Tom Sneva's Phoenix and Mario Andretti's Wildcat in the Miller High Life 150.

The next development came when March received an approach from Bignotti. He visited the team's base with a proposal that March should design four complete corners for his upcoming new machine, but the shrewd Herd, who by now could see certain commercial possibilities, persuaded him that March should build him a complete car. The well-heeled Florida-based Don Whittington, at the time of writing serving a prison sentence for his involvement in a drug-dealing ring, also turned up on the doorstep showing interest in purchasing cars to be raced by himself and his brother Bill, and the next thing everybody knew was that Herd had pledged delivery of several March Indy cars in time for the 1981 Indy 500.

Taken at face value, Herd's assurances may have seemed wildly over-optimistic. But, on the other hand, Indy was in some ways a relatively low-tech affair by the F1 standards of the day and, mindful of how profitable it had been for Williams when Patrick Head's FW07 was metamorphosed into the Longhorn for oil man Bobby Hillin's team, Herd appreciated the potential of this new market. His own RAM March 811 owed its inspiration to the Williams FW07, so it was now reworked to form the Indy car. It also provided the basis of the marque's new Can-Am contender.

Gordon Coppuck, Dave Reeves – now Managing Director of March Engineering – and Ian Reed were entrusted with the task of effectively strengthening the 811 with a thicker-gauge monocoque outer skin to conform to the CART regulations, and the resultant machine retained almost identical inboard coil-spring/dampers, activated by fabricated rocker arms, the pivot points of those at the front being well out in the airstream. The car featured a Weismann transverse gearbox, enabling the rear underbody airflow to be cleaner than that of any existing rival Indy design.

March absolutely hummed with activity for the first three months of 1981 in an effort to get its promised first four 81Cs to the Brickyard in time. According to factory records, chassis 81C/1, less engine and gearbox, was invoiced to owner/driver Don Whittington, 1881 State Road 84, Fort Lauderdale, Florida at $80,000 (plus $38,200 for a Cosworth DFX engine) on 8 April 1981. Nineteen days later, an invoice for $75,000 to Bignotti-Cotter Inc., 130 Roena Street, Indianapolis, Indiana signalled the despatch from Bicester of chassis number two, which was intended for Tom Sneva, while chassis numbers three and four again went to the Whittingtons. In all, nine 81Cs were manufactured and delivered during the course of 1981, bringing revenue of the order of $761,000 into the March coffers.

The 1981 Indy car season saw ground-effect technology exploding across the board, 27 of the 33 contenders for that year's Indy 500 matching that technical description. CART, the splinter-group steered by luminaries such as Roger Penske and Pat Patrick which had broken away from the stuffy USAC establishment in 1978, now effectively ruled the roost everywhere apart from Indianapolis. Thanks to their entrepreneurial efforts, Indy car racing was enjoying better support and promotion, attracting the biggest crowds for more than a decade and more television coverage than ever. A previously moribund series under the unimaginative control of USAC, it was now dramatically revitalised, and against this backdrop of impressive transformation March Engineering made its Indy car debut.

Predictably, Indy car racing suffered what amounted to a rerun of the F1 controversy over aerodynamic side skirts, CART regulations permitting them to make contact with the ground, while USAC stipulated a ban on any skirt which extended below the bottom of the car's chassis. Despite that, and the 48-in. HG boost restriction imposed at the Brickyard, qualifying times for the 1981 '500' proved utterly remarkable, with March's new 81C, out of the box, setting the pace during the second qualifying weekend.

Bill Whittington manhandles himself out of his 81C's cockpit during Indy qualifying, 1981. This shot of the F1-derived chassis shows off the sturdy fabricated front suspension rocker arms with their far-outboard pivot points. One of the Whittington brothers' first chassis soon passed to A.J. Foyt, who would win March's first Indy car victory the following month.

Pole position went to Bobby Unser's Penske PC9B at 200.545 mph, but had it not been for the late delivery of the first Bignotti-Cotter March 81C, Tom Sneva might well have been right at the front. Bignotti had actually managed to get the car out onto the track at the end of the first practice week, but some gearbox damage, caused by the starter pinion repeatedly jamming in the ring gear, forced the team to return to its base to solve the problem. A secondary shaft was fitted down the side of the gearbox for the purpose of coupling an external starter. There was also some experimentation with both a sprag clutch and a straightforward spring-loaded mechanism to take the shaft in and out of mesh. Alan Mertens recalls the whole thing was 'a bit hit and miss' and generally somewhat unreliable.

On the second qualifying weekend they reappeared and the bespectacled Sneva posted a 200.691 mph fastest, only slightly slower than his own all-time Indy qualifying record of 202.156 mph, established three years previously at the wheel of a Penske PC6. Herd attracted a great deal of praise for his company's efforts and Sneva's machine was timed second-quickest only to A.J. Foyt's Coyote when it came to straightline speed. As if to emphasise the new car's quality, Bill Whittington turned an extremely respectable 197.098 mph qualifying average in his 81C.

Come the race itself, Sneva proved every bit as much of a threat as his qualifying performance suggested. Bobby Unser surged into the lead at the start from Johnny Rutherford's Chaparral 2K, Foyt's Coyote and Al Unser's Longhorn 'FW07B'. Carving through the traffic, Sneva made spectacular progress and, with only 14 laps gone, had elbowed his way ahead of Foyt to take third place.

Sneva ran his 15th lap at over 190 mph as he hauled ever closer to Rutherford, while Unser's first pit stop at the end of lap 22 meant that the Chaparral and March were now running in 1-2 formation at the head of the field. By lap 24 Sneva was only a second behind and, as JR spluttered out of fuel, the March 81C surged by to lead on its maiden outing going into Turn One.

Don Whittington, meanwhile, bounced into the wall at Turn Two on lap 43, while Sneva, having led from laps 26 to 32 and again on lap 57, finally pulled off onto the infield inside Turn One as he began his 97th lap. Flames licking round the 81C's rear end betrayed his problem. As he later explained, he had progressively lost his gears, and then his clutch failed, so that was the end of a day's work which netted him $38,200. Bill Whittington made it as far as lap 147 before finally retiring. In the end Bobby Unser won from Mario Andretti's STP Wildcat, the delight of the man from New Mexico somewhat soured by the unfortunate pit lane fire which resulted in his team-mate Rick Mears and Penske crew chief Derrick Walker sustaining painful burns.

The day after the race Unser would be shocked to receive a one-lap penalty for allegedly infringing the rules governing rejoining the race from the pit lane, which resulted in Mario taking the win. One hundred and thirty-eight days later, after an extremely long and complex appeals procedure, Unser was reinstated as the winner. It was a highly unsatisfactory state of affairs.

In the wake of Sneva's superb performance, the March gospel quickly spread through the Indy car world. Having struggled to bring his Coyote into 13th place at Indy, battling with his first experience of ground-effect technology, Foyt decided to switch to a March and purchased one of the Whittingtons' selection of 81Cs, chassis number four having been delivered to the Florida businessmen on 9 May.

Foyt immediately went out to contest the USAC-sanctioned Pocono 500 on 21 June, rain forcing the chequered flag to be shown after only 122 of its 200 laps. At the time Foyt was holding a slim one-second advantage over Geoff Brabham's Penske PC9. With practice also rained out, the draw for grid positions had seen A.J. take pole ahead of Sneva's 81C, which developed gearbox trouble after 70 laps or so, eventually rolling to a halt with a broken throttle cable.

In fact prospects for Brabham looked bright, as Foyt was encountering the first signs of trouble with the Weismann gearbox, his clutch becoming increasingly reluctant to free, making progress out of the pits slower and slower following each fuel stop. Eventually another rain shower saved the day for Foyt, putting the first March Indy car victory into the record books less than a month after the 81C's very first race.

Foyt would later suffer serious elbow injuries in a horrifying 200 mph shunt in the Michigan 500 on 25 July, effectively sidelining him for the rest of the season. That meant that his ex-Whittington 81C seemed destined to lie fallow, but it was snapped up by Mexican Josele Garza, Indianapolis Rookie of the Year at the wheel of a Penske PC7B. Vern Schuppan, third at Indy in a museum-piece McLaren M24, also acquired an 81C, this featuring lightweight Kevlar/carbon-fibre bodywork and a sturdy longitudinal Hewland DGA gearbox rather than the troublesome 'standard kit' Weismann.

That Indy fire notwithstanding, Mears finished up dominating the championship, Penske's 30-year-old driving star maturing to the level which would make him such a formidable contender throughout the decade. But March was piling up orders for 1982, helped by Sneva's continuing fine performances in the Bignotti-Cotter 81C. He led, but failed to finish, in the Michigan 500, eventually won by Pancho Carter's Penske PC7, but won the Tony Bettenhausen 200 at Wisconsin State Fair Park and rounded off the season with a satisfying one-second victory over Bobby Unser's Penske in the Phoenix 150, the last race on the championship trail.

March was now up and running as an Indy car constructor, but the season had not been without its troubles. Bignotti quickly identified weaknesses in the 81C's essentially F1-based running gear and spent much of the year chasing problems through the transmission, also uprating hubs, uprights and constant-velocity joints, all of which were marginal in their standard guise for the strains imposed on them, particularly at Indianapolis.

The Bignotti pit crew bump-start Tom Sneva's gearbox-troubled 81C in the pits at Indy as Gordon Johncock's Wildcat accelerates past him back into the race. Problems with the March transverse Weismann-based gearbox led to Sneva's retirement after he had run among the very fastest.

However, there was no arguing that they had got the job done, of course. Journalist Gordon Kirby, the most highly regarded and perspicacious observer of the Indy car scene, and US correspondent for *Autocourse* for the past decade, summed it up thus: 'The big point about the March 81C was that it had downforce at a time when Indy car technology was in the Dark Ages from the aerodynamic standpoint. As an example, two years earlier, the ground-effect Penske PC7 had set new standards straight out of the box. It established bench-marks that the PC9s were struggling to match several seasons later. In that respect, March timed their Indy car debut perfectly.'

With the price of the 82C pegged at £53,000, deposits were rolling in well before Christmas 1981 and, by the end of January, firm orders for some 15 cars were in the bag. By the time the field lined up for the Kraco Car Stereo 150 which opened the 1982 season at Phoenix on 28 March, eight of the 22 cars on the grid were products of the Bicester factory.

More important, however, than the development of the 82C itself was the evolution of a brand new March-manufactured gearbox to replace the troublesome Weismann transmission which had proved to be the 81C's Achilles' Heel. March took the decision to make its own Indy car transmission, thereby exercising closer scrutiny over the quality of the components involved, shortly before the end of November 1981 and the prototype of the four-speed box was designed by Alan Mertens and Dave Reeves in conjunction with the Indy transmission specialist George Bowers. Flown out to the first race in time to be fitted to Pancho Carter's 82C, the new gearbox performed well. Carter finished sixth and it almost immediately went on offer to all other March customers.

Mears started as he meant to continue, blitzing the opposition at Phoenix with his Penske PC10 to win from Mario Andretti's Wildcat Mk 8B. He repeated the treatment with another win at Atlanta, where Gordon Johncock was second and Danny Sullivan third in the new Forsythe-Brown 82C, thereby registering the best-ever performance by an Indy car rookie up to that point.

Sadly, a March 82C was involved in the most fearful accident seen in Indianapolis history when popular Nebraskan driver Gordon Smiley was killed. Building up speed on his last warm-up lap prior to taking the green flag for his qualifying run, Smiley started to lose control of his Fletcher Racing 82C going into Turn Three, and made the classic Indy error of trying to collect the slide. The car regained adhesion and catapulted him into the wall with a destructive force that virtually atomised the March. Qualifying was suspended for the three hours or so that it took to repair the wall and track surface after the first fatality at the Speedway for nine years.

Smiley's death, along with that of rookie Jim Hickman in August at Milwaukee, triggered efforts to impose some sort of aerodynamic restrictions on Indy car performance for the following season in much the same way as the banning of ground-effect underbodies was intended to reduce cornering forces in F1. But that was for the future, and the Indy 500 went ahead with Mears sustaining Penske's pre-eminence, slamming round at 207.004 mph to grab pole position from team-mate Kevin Cogan (204.082 mph) and the redoubtable A.J. Foyt, now 47 years old, who wheeled his brand new March 82C round at 203.332 mph for his 25th Indy 500 start.

The second row comprised the Wildcat Mk 8Bs of Mario Andretti (203.172 mph) and Gordon Johncock (201.884 mph), together with Don Whittington, who proved he was no softy by elbowing Tom Sneva's Texaco-sponsored 82C back onto the third row with a speed of 201.658 mph. In fact Sneva managed his first lap in the Bignotti 82C at an average of 203.4 mph, but smacked the wall coming out of Turn Two next time round, continuing to finish his run in a remarkable display of tenacity and single-minded commitment. A cursory inspection of the right-rear corner by his mechanics later revealed one and a half inches of toe-in on the rear wheel as well as a badly cracked rim.

In the end 13 March 82Cs and a couple of 81Cs qualified for the Indy 500 grid, and the general consensus of opinion was that there was little to choose between the two cars – or their transverse gearboxes! Foyt and the Whittingtons were still using 1981 Weismann transmissions on their 82Cs, but the Bignotti-Cotter machines of Sneva and his new team-mate Geoff Brabham featured the latest March-made box, which proved relatively trouble-free throughout qualifying, although Sneva expressed concern over its ability to last a race distance.

Further back, Hewland DG300 longitudinal gearboxes were fitted to the 82Cs of Danny Sullivan and talented rookie Bobby Rahal, the bespectacled former Can-Am and IMSA star having made his CART debut at Phoenix a couple of months earlier. Driving for motel chain owner Jim Trueman's team, operated by former Team VDS crew chief Steve Horne, Rahal was destined to become one of the most effective drivers of the decade, and one of the most accomplished March exponents of all in the years that followed. Other March runners of note included former Brabham F1 driver Hector Rebaque, Howdy Holmes, Jerry Sneva (who did his best run with an unlubricated gearbox following a starter pinion failure), the Bobby Unser-managed 82C of Josele Garza, and George Snider, who took over poor Smiley's place in the second Fletcher Racing 82C.

The 1982 Indy 500 was stopped almost before it had started when, coming up to take the green flag, Cogan floored it in second gear, found himself caught out by the way the DFX boost came in, got out of shape, side-swiped Foyt's March and triggered off a multiple shunt which put Andretti's Wildcat straight into the pit wall. Mario was left simmering, impervious to Cogan's emotional explanations as the two men walked away from their damaged cars. 'This is what happens when you have children trying to do a man's job,' he fumed.

Foyt applied a little homespun science to the business of straightening his 82C's bent left-front steering arm, a few brisk taps with a hammer effecting repairs to A.J.'s satisfaction. It might have been just the ticket for a Watson-Offy roadster, but seemed something of a short-term policy to try on a March. Be that as it may, it certainly appeared to do the trick. At the restart Foyt went for it in a big way, his Valvoline/Gilmore-backed March whistling through at the end of the opening lap with a remarkable 1.5s advantage over Mears's Penske. Johncock was third ahead of Sneva, with Bill and Don Whittington making it three 82Cs astern in fourth to sixth places.

Foyt completed that opening lap at a breathtaking 194.342 mph, but by the 20-lap mark, as the leaders picked their way through traffic, Johncock's Wildcat had moved into second place. Two laps later Rick's Penske became the first pacesetter to make a pit stop, followed a lap later by Foyt. By lap 36 Mears had outfumbled the Texan to take a genuine lead and, while Foyt would fleetingly move to the front yet again on lap 64, the Weismann box then became jammed in third gear. Never one to give up easily, A.J. picked up a hammer once again, forcefully applying it to the left-rear wheel in an attempt to free the recalcitrant transmission. In a final act of defiance, before abandoning his efforts to intimidate the March back into action, he ripped off the engine cover and hurled it away!

At the end of the day, the battle for victory proved the closest in Speedway history, Johncock's Wildcat easing out Mears's Penske by a car's length – 0.2s – to score a truly memorable success. Sneva's third place evaporated four laps from the flag when his DFX expired, allowing Pancho Carter up into third, while Al Unser's Longhorn wound up fifth ahead of Don Whittington's 82C, which had suffered a clutch problem and a couple of deflated tyres during the course of the race.

While Mears headed for another championship crown at the wheel of his Penske, Rahal gradually asserted himself as the best of the March 82C performers in his maiden CART season. His car engineered by Lee Dykstra, Bobby proved consistently the fastest rookie during Indy qualifying and only a blown engine late in the race deprived him of a top-six finish at the Brickyard.

His first CART victory came just over a month later at Cleveland, where he beat Mario's Wildcat, and he repeated the success in a 150-mile sprint race at Michigan in September. He finished the year second in the overall points table on 242 to Mears's overwhelming 294. At 29 years old, he had come a long way since guesting at the wheel of a second Wolf WR1 in the 1978 Canadian GP at Montreal.

Two further March 82C victories came courtesy of Tom Sneva, at Milwaukee in August – where he defeated Rahal – and Phoenix again, where he beat Mears commandingly to complete a hat-trick of victories in this end-of-season event. Unfortunately, a shortage of testing put Sneva at loggerheads with Bignotti and it seemed as though they were close to splitting up their partnership by the end of the year, while Geoff Brabham's outings in the team's other 82C were intermittent and similarly unsatisfactory. He was also looking hard for a new position by the end of the summer.

Hector Rebaque managed a somewhat lucky win at Elkhart Lake, where he fended off Al Unser's advances in the Longhorn LR03B. Driving for the Chicago-based Forsythe brothers – who were to make a considerable contribution to March Indy car fortunes throughout 1983 – he fought shy of the ovals after tangling with Foyt in the Michigan 500, but proved more than capable on the road circuits.

The Forsythe team should also be recorded as the outfit which provided the equipment for Al Unser Jnr to make his CART debut, thereby taking credit for helping to launch an outstanding new talent on his journey to the top. Having qualified tenth at Riverside, 'Little Al' clawed his way up to third place in the race before engine problems intervened, although he was still classified fifth at the chequered flag.

For 1983 the CART regulations dispensed with skirts altogether with the intention of achieving a significant reduction in downforce, but preliminary tests of the first March 83C, held at Indianapolis in early November 1982, revealed that to be something of a forlorn hope. With totally revised aerodynamics finalised by Ralph Bellamy working in the wind tunnel at London's Imperial College, the 83C – with its one-piece carbon-fibre underwing – was touted by March as producing a breakthrough similar to that achieved by ground effect.

Mike Mosley ran a lap at 198.1 mph on the 83C's first outing at the Brickyard in near-freezing temperatures, using the car destined for the Kraco Stereo team, so March looked forward confidently to yet another financially rewarding sales bonanza as they started their third season of Indy car racing. A week later, with Ralph Bellamy in attendance, Mosley nudged through the 200 mph barrier, this time using a brand new sister car destined for the Forsythe team.

Interestingly, it was Bellamy's first sight of Indy cars in action. As he told *Autosport* magazine, he was highly impressed. 'There's not much feedback from these guys,' he reported. 'They just say, "It's looser than I like," or "It's pushing," and you balance out the imbalance with wing adjustments.'

Robin Herd outlined lower weight, increased chassis stiffness and more efficient aerodynamics as the fundamental design brief for the new machine. For the first time, carbon-fibre composite materials were employed in the construction process, the upper section of the monocoque being made from this material, while the lower portion and floorpan were crafted in aluminium honeycomb, providing a stiffer, yet at the same time roomier, footbox area.

In line with contemporary trends, the heavy and aerodynamically disruptive suspension rocker arms were replaced with pullrod activation of the inboard spring/damper units, the whole aerodynamic package being tailored round March's own transverse gearbox, which was installed on all machines as an integral part of the rear suspension system. Lightweight Monroe dampers and Cagnola springs – offering more consistency in rate from spring to spring – were fitted immediately behind the gearbox, thereby contributing to a noticeably uncluttered underbody venturi section. As things turned out, most serious March teams would end up using the transverse box only on the ovals, switching to a more reliable Hewland DG300 for the road tracks, which required a slicker, more precise change.

Designed to accept the latest single-pump 'slimline' Cosworth DFX engine, the March 83C was an instant success, with A.J. Foyt, Jim Hall, Jim Trueman, John Paul, Doug Shierson, George Bignotti, Kraco and the Forsythes all remitting $50,000 deposits to Bicester before Christmas 1982. Shortly afterwards Hall, who had switched Johnny Rutherford from the three-year-old John Barnard-designed Chaparral to an 82C the previous summer, cancelled his order and announced his team would be closing its doors.

On Friday, 18 March 1983 March Engineering reached an historically interesting turning-point when the 1000th car emerged from the Murdock Road factory. The 83C was destined for A.J. Foyt, but a little bit of juggling with the records was necessary to obtain this slice of publicity. Ian Phillips was writing press releases and doing some informal PR for the team at the time and admits, 'I think it was really the one thousand and fourth car, so we had to muddle the press release through with a touch of poetic licence...'

While the 83C continued to show an impressive turn of speed throughout winter testing, it was not without its problems. The car suffered a spate of broken rear pullrods, and while March resolved the problem by producing a more sturdy, solid rod – and offering owners a suitable update kit which also improved the geometry slightly – some teams chose to discard the pullrod system altogether, reverting to the 82C's rocker arm layout for the rear end, to give more security in the fastest corners. March also offered update kits to bring customers' 82Cs close to the latest specification, these being available at about half the price of a new car.

Revised Indy car technical regulations were duly imposed for 1983, although rather than make a sudden across-the-board switch to flat-bottomed chassis – as F1 did at the start of the same season – CART and USAC took into account both driver safety and chassis obsolescence by 'raising bodywork/skirts a full inch above the chassis baseline'. That, in conjunction with rear wings being moved forward 7 in. produced cars which felt significantly more comfortable to drive. As Al Unser explained, 'This has managed to reduce the ground effect to the point where the driver's reactions can keep up with what the car is doing – and therefore means the driver has also got to apply his ability to greater use.'

Howdy Holmes was the best-placed March finisher in the opening CART round at Atlanta, ninth in an event which provided Johncock's new Wildcat Mk 9C with a fine triumph over a row of Penskes headed by Al Unser (PC11), John Paul Jnr (PC10) and Peter Halsmer (PC10). Rahal crashed heavily after a pullrod failure, putting the onus on March to get things sorted in time for the Brickyard. When it came to Indianapolis, March was right up there at the sharp end, with Don Whittington lapping at an amazing 205.198 mph in unofficial practice prior to the first qualifying weekend, which was rained out.

Whittington had not been in the cockpit of an open-wheeler since Michigan the previous July and turned in this remarkable performance at the wheel of one of his early 81Cs, uprated with 83C bodywork and rocker arm rear suspension. But a real pointer to impending form came from the ex-Toleman F1 driver and one-time March F2 protégé Teo Fabi, who had been forced to retire his Forsythe 83C from the Atlanta season-opener with yet another rear pullrod malfunction.

With both Herd and Bellamy fussing over his machine, Teo whistled through his rookie driver orientation test with ease and was through the 200 mph barrier within a couple of days. At the other end of the scale, the effectiveness of the March 83C chassis was illustrated graphically by the performance of *Car and Driver* journalist Pat Bedard. Despite not being particularly highly rated, Bedard turned in a 197 mph lap during this practice week.

When it came to official qualifying at the Brickyard, March had everybody beaten. While Penske designer Geoff Ferris and Newman/Haas Lola development engineer Tony Cicale worked frantically to get Mears and Andretti respectively up to speed, it seemed that Mr Herd's wonder car was certainly proving something very special.

Robin himself paced the Indy pit lane throughout the fortnight of qualifying, his face wearing its customary non-committal, comfortable grin. He paid special attention to the Kraco, Interscope and Forsythe entries, but Fabi had switched to Indy car racing largely as a result of Herd's encouragement and when he took the Skoal Bandit-backed Forsythe car out for his qualifying run, the atmosphere in the pit lane was electrifying.

Using more than 10,900 rpm from his Cosworth DFX engine – about 300 rpm fewer than most of his rivals – Teo rattled off an ultra-neat, disciplined four-lap run at an average speed of 207.395 mph. He thus followed Walt Faulkner (1950) as only the second rookie ever to take pole position at Indy, the second non-American after Jimmy Clark.

It was also a performance which put the Forsythe team firmly on the Indy map. Successful businessmen hailing from near Chicago, the Forsythe brothers had first entered Indy car racing two years before with sponsorship for Scott Brayton. Now, for 1983, they had set themselves up as the prestige March runner, that position enhanced by the signing of team manager Barry Green, who had switched from Paul Newman's March Can-Am team to take the job. Initially they had intended to run Chaparral refugee Johnny Rutherford, but when he made a last-minute decision to sign up with Pat Patrick Fabi came into the team as number one rather than JR's partner.

Derek Daly's Wysard Racing 83C contests the 1983 Indy 500. He completed 126 laps before engine problems caused his retirement, but the former Williams F1 driver was classified 19th.

While being enormously satisfied with his own performance, Fabi emphasised that Herd's involvement had been absolutely crucial. 'I think it was very important indeed to have Robin working on the car, because he knows from previous experience just how I like to have the car adjusted. When I stop in the pits and ask for something to be changed, he instantly knows what I mean and makes precisely the right adjustment to produce the required effect.

'It was quite remarkable, really, but during the week prior to qualifying I was working with Ralph Bellamy for the first time, and the whole time I was about 3 mph away from the best time. Then Robin arrived on the day before qualifying and – poof! – we made the big step forward.'

There was at least one March on every row of the grid at Indy, with Mike Mosley's Kraco 83C (205.372 mph) right alongside Fabi, and Tom Sneva on the inside of row two on 203.687 mph. Thanks to his continuing links with Texaco, Sneva had outflanked 65-year-old George Bignotti's attempts to unseat him for 1983 and remained in the team, despite all the grumbling and moaning that had gone on between the two of them the previous autumn. Not that the atmosphere was much improved and it was hardly brightened when Sneva and team-mate Kevin Cogan consumed no fewer than eight engines during practice. A specification change to the team's Mahle pistons seemed to solve the problem and the Sneva/Bignotti partnership would have its reward come race day.

Rahal's TrueSports car was on the outside of row two behind the Eagle 83 of Al Unser Jnr, while the highly rated Danny Ongais and A.J. Foyt were both well down after a succession of problems. Ongais wasted much time practising the turbo 3.4-litre Chevy V6, experiencing major engine problems for his pains, before switching to a DFX-engined 83C to run a lap at just over 202 mph, while A.J. Foyt, who had spent much of the month by his dying father's bedside, qualified at 199.557 mph.

The end of the road for Teo. The diminutive Fabi's works-blessed Forsythe team 83C started the 1983 Indy 500 from pole position and led commandingly in the early stages. Unfortunately, the seal on the neck of the fuel tank ruptured during a pit stop, causing a lake of fuel to seep all over the pit lane. The dejected, helmeted driver can be seen standing just to the right of the stricken car.

From the start of the race it was clear that the March 83Cs would be the masters of Indy, new boy Fabi diving straight into the lead as the green flag was flourished and completing the opening lap with over a second in hand from Mears, Mosley, Rahal and Little Al Unser. Within ten laps he was 5.2s to the good, threading his way through the back-markers with an unobtrusive confidence.

Al Unser Snr timed his first pit stop perfectly when the yellow lights came on after Pat Bedard's 83C clipped the wall at Turn Four, but when the green was given it was Sneva's 83C which began hounding the leading Penske, soon slipping by into the lead. Rahal, Mears and Fabi were all in close touch with the leading group, but when Teo pulled in for fuel after the yellow came out again to signal Roger Mears's departure into the wall disaster struck the Forsythe team.

When the refueller pulled the hose and nozzle away from the March's fuel tank, he was amazed to see fuel spraying from the seals round the neck of the tank filler. It had split away from its sealing O-ring and the leak grew worse by the second. The quick-thinking crew members reached for water buckets as about 15 gallons of methanol spilled across the pit lane, but it was the end of the race for Fabi.

Rahal then had a stint in the lead before Sneva began to assert his authority yet again, and when Bobby stalled his 83C at his next pit stop, thanks to a troublesome clutch, it cost him a lap by the time he had struggled to restart his hot engine. Sneva was fast establishing himself as the dominant performer in the scenario being enacted out on the circuit, although it was clear he would have to work hard to keep Al Unser Snr's Penske PC11 under firm control. With ten laps to go, he dived inside the PC11 as Al was embroiled in a tussle with his son's Eagle and then drove commandingly away to score his first Indy victory – and the first for March Engineering.

Sneva told Gordon Kirby he'd been wondering how long his 83C would last: 'At the start of the month I was obviously extremely excited about our potential, but after the first week of practice I began to get a little concerned about those engine problems. I knew the car was capable of running quick in the race, but I wasn't certain for how long.

'In that respect, we were running very high oil temperature – about 230 degrees – from as early as lap three and I thought it might well be a short day. But it ran high all the way to the finish and, although we had a touch of understeer at the beginning – which was one of the reasons that Fabi was able to run away over those first few laps – we made some adjustments at the first stop and, after that, it was pretty near perfect all the way.'

Tom Sneva's Texaco-backed 83C en route *to March's first Indy 500 victory. The car is outwardly quite similar to the 81C, but note that pullrod front suspension has now been adopted in place of the rocker arm arrangement.*

Bearing in mind the small amount of testing carried out by the Bignotti-Cotter team prior to the race, Sneva agreed that his success represented a pretty good advertisement for the out-

33
TEO FABI
SKOAL
BANDIT
COLONIAL BREAD

GOODYEAR
EAGLE
TEXACO
TEXACO STAR
5
GOODYEAR

INDECK
SKOAL
FABI
33
33
33
GOODYEAR
BANDIT
BOSCH

alex
21
alex

of-the-box capability of the March 83C. But he also counselled firmly against over-confidence in this respect: 'Although we might not be too far off its potential with the way it is in its existing form, we have to recognise that we were probably one of the few teams running an absolutely stock standard 83C. The top teams will all be trying to make modifications to improve the car, so if we lose sight of that, then a standard 83C isn't going to be good enough for very long.'

Two weeks after the 500, the Indy car fraternity was given another reminder of Fabi's enormous talent when he qualified in pole position at Michigan. He led early in the race before clutch problems stymied his efforts and he spun off, leaving John Paul Jnr's Penske PC10 to win from Al Unser's PC11.

At Pocono Fabi was on pole again, leading for much of the race to beat Al Unser Jnr's March by almost a minute. He would win again at Mid Ohio, Laguna Seca and Phoenix to finish in second place in the CART standings on 146 points, 15 behind series winner Al Unser Snr. Interestingly, Unser felt that the Penske PC10B wasn't quite *au point* during the latter part of the year and it was a sign of the prevailing times when team-mate Mears tried a Pennzoil-yellow March 83C the day after he had beaten Rahal's similar car into second place at Michigan in September. Unser fought shy of switching to the March, though, preferring to battle successfully through to the end of the year in the PC10B. The following May he would be March-mounted at the Brickyard...

Sneva's success at Indy, meanwhile, proved something of a fleeting moment of glory. Although his Bignotti-Cotter 83C was first past the chequered flag at Milwaukee, it was disqualified after failing to pass the skirt-height check. Bignotti received the news of his car's exclusion with considerable bad grace, even suggesting that a television cameraman had distorted the March side pod by sitting on it in the crush surrounding the victory celebrations.

Fabi in the Forsythe 83C at speed at Milwaukee, 1983. The Italian finished second in the CART Championship, but he became lukewarm about Indy cars in '84 and tried to dovetail F1 and CART – to no productive effect.

Five weeks later a three-man Court of Appeal accepted Bignotti's contention. SCCA Pro Racing director Burdette Martin, 1961 World Champion Phil Hill and retired Chicago Circuit Judge L. Sheldon Brown found that there was 'sufficient doubt that persons stood or leaned against the car', adding in a lengthy summary that CART 'had a duty to maintain the integrity of the car before it could be inspected'. They further noted that Sneva's 83C had been checked three times previously during the Milwaukee weekend, but some observers considered it a rather surprising verdict, bearing in mind that there was much evidence to suggest the car's side pods were mounted in rubber, encouraging them to 'sag' at high speed. Either way, by the end of the year Sneva and Cogan were both ready to walk, but Bignotti's partner Dan Cotter coaxed the veteran Indy crew chief into semi-retirement for 1984, his place to be effectively taken by ex-F1 team owner Mo Nunn.

Sneva finished the year in fourth place in the CART/PPG Indy Car World Series points table, one place ahead of Rahal. The TrueSports team flirted briefly with the upcoming Chevy V6 and, after crashing his Cosworth-engined 83C very badly during practice at Las Vegas, he had to rely on the GM-propelled machine for the last three races. He failed to finish at either Vegas or Laguna Seca, while a pit lane incident at Phoenix, when a novice's Eagle mowed down three of his mechanics, resulted in Rahal's withdrawal from the final race of the season.

Rahal's Marches, still engineered by Lee Dykstra, were generally regarded as being every bit as well set up as the Forsythe machine – if not better. Further back in the points standings, young Al Unser Jnr had really started to make a name for himself at the wheel of Rick Galles's March 83C, the 21-year-old third-generation star of the famous dynasty from Albuquerque, New Mexico showing all the signs of following in the footsteps of grandfather Louis, Uncle Bobby and father Al. Galles, a third-generation auto dealer and property developer, was also based in Albuquerque and continues to field cars for 'Junior' to this day.

Towards the end of the season Fabi and the Forsythes concluded terms for a continuation of the Italian driver's contract into 1984, the team retaining options on his services for 1985 and '86 as well. Suffused with optimism, the Skoal Bandit-backed team began testing its first 84C well before the end of the year.

Pancho Carter's Johnny Capels-run 82C, seen at Milwaukee in 1983, with driver gesturing his recognition to photographer. The winglets on the leading edge of the side pods were exclusively a Capels development.

In early December the first two March 84Cs were completed and underwent simultaneous tests at Indianapolis in Teo Fabi's hands and at Brands Hatch with Tom Sneva and Jonathan Palmer. Although the 84C bore a strong visual similarity to the car it superseded, Herd and his design staff had produced a totally new machine. One member of that design group was Adrian Newey, the former Fittipaldi aerodynamicist fresh from transforming the 1983 March GTP chassis from 'a lame duck which nobody wanted to have much to do with' into the machine which carried the late Al Holbert to the IMSA title.

One of the most crucial design parameters of the 84C was to make further improvements to safety, particularly in the region of the footbox, and the new monocoque (carbon fibre-topped aluminium honeycomb) was 5-in. shorter than that of the 83C, this being achieved by the use of a taller, shorter fuel cell. The steering rack was repositioned to minimise the possibility of shin damage to the driver in the event of a frontal impact, and the 1-in. wider footwell was further protected by carbon-fibre panels with a 7-in. deeper crushable structure.

Herd presided over a team of six people working in the wind tunnels at London's Imperial College and at Southampton University, creating what was claimed to be the most aerodynamically efficient shape yet produced by the company. To that end, the engine was installed at a three-degree angle, inclined towards the rear in an attempt to improve the airflow beneath the rear of the car. In fact Ralph Bellamy began carrying out the first aerodynamic experiments with the new car's design in mind only a week after Sneva sped to victory in the Indy 500. However, Alan Mertens recalls the engine being canted upwards to reduce driveshaft angularity on the longitudinal transmission, a major problem area at the speedways in particular.

March's official release on the subject claimed that, 'despite the transverse gearbox's success on the 83C, the new aerodynamic package requires a longitudinal transmission...' Newey later remarked, 'They scrapped the transverse box because it just couldn't be made to work properly. It couldn't change gear quickly enough on the road circuits, although it was OK on the ovals where shifting wasn't such a major priority.' In fact the new longitudinal transmission was a very neat package, an elaborate casting incorporating the oil tank, rear air jacks and guides ahead of the rear axle-line in which the coil-spring/dampers would run, well out of the airstream. In addition to developing their own longitudinal box, Ralph Bellamy, Kenny Adams and Dave Williamson were commissioned to do a works-approved Hewland DG300 installation for the 84C.

The new car retained pullrod suspension at the front, but – surprise, surprise – 'advances in aerodynamic knowledge' demanded a return to a rocker arm arrangement at the rear: a clear case of the customers inadvertently carrying out development work for the factory.

The car Palmer tried was the first to be delivered to Mayer Motor Racing, a brand new team established by former McLaren directors Teddy Mayer and Tyler Alexander along with Bill Smith, a partner in McLaren Engines and a New York State Ford dealer who had known Teddy and Tyler since the early 1960s. March was a shareholder in the new company. 'Robin was keen to establish another works-blessed team and we had a very satisfactory relationship with March,' reflects Mayer. 'Howdy Holmes was our second driver and I initially worked on his 84C before switching to run Sneva's car. He could be really finicky and difficult to please but, all things considered, we had a good season. We even came out of it showing a slight profit, which both surprised and pleased March.'

As early as September 1983 the production and sales department at Bicester had made plans to produce 35 Indy cars for the following year. Orders flowed in nicely to start with, but by the end of November trickled to a halt at around 28 cars. The market, it seemed, had dried up.

While the Brands Hatch test took place, Fabi was busy shocking the establishment with his first Indy outing in the Forsythe 84C. Teo managed a 204.6 mph lap in the brand new machine, reporting to team manager Barry Green that it was significantly better than the 83C straight out of the box and especially stable over the bumps. After that splendid flag-waving performance, customer orders for the new car began to pick up once more.

Adrian Newey, meanwhile, settled into his new job as factory-supplied engineer on Rahal's new TrueSports 84C and, while taking responsibility for the front suspension installation, began what amounted to a year-long programme to massage the machine into some sort of sensible shape. On the basis of the results the car would achieve, it was hard to argue that the 84C was anything less than an unqualified, rip-roaring success story, but Newey's comments, made from a purely engineering standpoint, are illuminating.

'An absolute abortion, a horrible racing car', is how the mild-mannered Newey reflected on the 84C some five years later. 'Who designed it? Well, that was one of the problems...nobody did. It just happened. Ralph did the aerodynamics, Alan Mertens the gearbox, me the front suspension installation.

'I started with TrueSports at Phoenix, the first race of the season and the first time I'd ever

Adrian Newey in typically thoughtful pose. His development work on the TrueSports and Kraco Marches, and his design work at Bicester, earned him high regard in the Indy car business.

TEXACO
CHAMPION
HAVOLINE
Tom
HAVOLINE
MOTOR OIL

FORSYTHE RACING

seen an oval track. I really didn't know whether I was coming or going throughout that weekend, but fortunately Steve Horne had things pretty well under control. We started off really badly, but by the end of the season we began to get a handle on the project, although we were still a bit shy of Mario and Little Al in their Lolas. But we slogged away, changing the suspension geometry, doing some revised wing profiles "by eye" and pared it down from around 100 lb to 10 lb overweight.'

Newey's apparently ultra-critical assessment of the 84C was certainly not shared by Dave Reeves, Robin Herd's right-hand man who had joined March at the outset in 1970 as one of five fabricators. Just over a decade later it was largely his effort and enormous application that helped the company transform itself into an almost totally Indy-orientated organisation. He was deeply proud of the company's achievement and, speaking in 1984, made the rather sweeping statement to journalist Ian Phillips that he honestly believed the 84C to be the finest-engineered racing car in the world.

In the 84C's press kit, that was changed to 'the finest commercially available racing car in the world'. But Reeves later firmed up his opinion. 'No, you misunderstand me,' he insisted. 'I mean any racing car, including F1 "one-offs". It might not have the gloss and bullshit of an F1 car. We deem that unnecessary in a production car. But it has everything else, which I challenge anybody else to match in one package.'

Meanwhile, back in the USA, Newey was finding Indy car development a stimulating technical conundrum after being weaned on a diet solely of European road racing. 'People in Europe tend to sneer at the problems of engineering an Indy car,' he remarked. 'But it was a big challenge because you had to develop a chassis which was good round Long Beach and also capable of doing over 200 mph, consistently, at Indianapolis. With four corners, all taken at more or less the same speed, chassis tuning for Indy is a case of tiny adjustments within a very fine margin.'

Tom Sneva (aboard his Mayer Motor Racing 84C) confers with team directors Teddy Mayer (centre) ***and Tyler Alexander, Phoenix, 1984. This was a works-supported effort in which Robin Herd had a financial interest.***

Lightheartedly, he continued, 'By the time you'd set the car up with different springs and shock absorbers on all four corners, one front wing up and one down, it always struck me as they rumbled out of the pit lane that the cars looked as though they'd had the accident already.'

The 1984 season got under way with the first post-F1 Long Beach Grand Prix falling to Mario Andretti's Lola T800 ahead of the 84Cs of Geoff Brabham and Sneva, while 'Terrible Tom' gave Mayer Motor Racing its first victory a fortnight later at Phoenix with Howdy Holmes making it a 1-2 success.

Bobby Rahal set the pace in untimed practice for the Indy 500, popping in a 205.966 mph best, but it was Sneva and Holmes who eventually buttoned up the first two places on the front row with laps in 210.029 and 207.977 mph respectively. With no fewer than 30 Marches in the field, the Nigel Bennett-designed Lola T800 was the only rival that looked like shaking a stick at the Bicester products, the March ranks swollen by the decision of the Penske team to buy 84Cs and shelve their own PC12s for 1984.

'We had to spend a tremendous amount of time and effort in the wind tunnel just to match what March has been doing,' said Bennett, 'because it takes a lot of effort just to register a small improvement.' That the Lola really did have winning potential was underlined when Mario returned a stupendous 212.414 mph during unofficial practice prior to the first qualifying weekend. Generally speaking, the long-tailed T800 was marginally faster than the 84Cs on top speed, Andretti tripping the beam at 222 mph on that quickest lap.

Sneva's pole-position lap was completed with a smaller rear wing than just about anybody else in the pit lane, Holmes opting for a slightly larger one but generally enthusing over the way in which Mayer and his colleagues went about their business. 'The team is fantastic,' he reported. 'They all work hard, but not like maniacs. They're certainly the best outfit I've ever been with.'

Their efforts had not been without problems, however. During qualifying the Mayer Marches started to show signs of losing grease from their left-rear wheel bearings due to leaking seals. If ignored, this could have caused a major across-the-board problem for, while it wasn't too much of a hazard during the brief four-lap qualifying runs, the possibility of a broken driveshaft during the 500-mile blind could by no means be ruled out. With the locked differentials still employed at Indy, a broken driveshaft could be expected to turn a car into the wall. New seals, to a revised specification, were manufactured and made available to every March entrant before the race.

Robin Herd and Forsythe team manager Barry Green crouch on the side pod of Teo Fabi's first 84C during pre-season tests at Laguna Seca.

Completing the front row was Rick Mears's Penske-entered 84C on 207.847 mph, Rick

Indy star. Rick Mears, heading for a brilliant victory in the 1984 Indy 500 in Roger Penske's March 84C. Penske Marches would be first past the chequered flag in two of the next three Indianapolis 500s.

GOODYEAR
Miller
High Life
PENNZOIL 6

confident that he could get to grips with Sneva once the race got under way. Fourth on the grid was the Kraco 84C of the fastest rookie, Michael Andretti (207.805 mph), with Gordon Johncock next up on 207.545 mph and Mario sixth on 207.467 mph, a lone Lola in an ocean of Marches. Apart from Andretti Snr, the only non-March cars to make the grid were Danny Sullivan's Lola T800 and the Eagle 84SB of Kevin Cogan.

Bignotti-Cotter's Mo Nunn was doing a good job presiding over the efforts of his former F1 driver Roberto Guerrero, the genial Colombian having abandoned F1 after a couple of tail-end seasons driving for Ensign during which it became quite clear that his obvious talent was not going to earn him a break with a decent team. With his American wife Katie, he would settle in California and embrace the CART scene with whole-hearted enthusiasm and commitment.

For his first Indy 500 Roberto qualified on the inside of row three at 204.931 mph, surviving a nasty scare when he had to abort his first qualifying run after his 84C's bodywork began to work loose. Further back was another, slightly more celebrated F1 refugee making his Indy debut. Twice World Champion Emerson Fittipaldi suffered a series of new-car problems, but was quickly over the 200 mph mark, impressing everybody in the pit lane with that fluid, controlled style that had helped him to many Grand Prix victories for Lotus and McLaren ten years earlier.

Teo Fabi's Forsythe 84C could only turn a 14th-fastest 203.6 mph, the Italian at the centre of a whirlwind of speculation that he wanted to give up Indy cars in favour of a full season with Bernie Ecclestone's F1 Brabham squad. As it was, Fabi was dovetailing a limited programme of Grands Prix with his Indy car commitments and, as history relates, was doing neither particularly well. Also encountering its fair share of problems was the TrueSports team, Adrian Newey and Bobby Rahal getting rather lost as far as an 'Indy set-up' was concerned and unable to better an 18th-fastest 202.230 mph best.

Controversial win. Tom Sneva's Bignotti-Cotter 84C on its way to victory at Milwaukee in 1984, only to be disqualified for apparently infringing the minimum-ride-height regulations. Later a Court of Appeal would reinstate 'Terrible Tom' to the winner's circle...

The race itself was a remarkable grand slam for Bicester. Neither Lola nor the lone Eagle made it to the chequered flag, so Mr Herd's 84Cs ruled the roost from first to 14th places. When the field was unleashed, Mears cut briskly across Sneva's nose to push the bright-yellow Penske 84C into the lead as the pack blared through Turn One.

The determined Mears ran his first flying lap at almost 201 mph, anxious to make the break, with Sneva second, followed by Michael and Mario Andretti. The younger Andretti was in extremely bullish form and it didn't take him long to ease the Kraco 84C through into second place, after which he began to launch an assault on leader Mears. Also well in the hunt was Al Unser Jnr in the Galles machine, with Guerrero not far behind.

After the first round of fuel stops Mario Andretti took the Lola T800 to the front, sustaining that position through his second fuel halt, which took place during a yellow light period. When the green was given, Mears and Sneva quickly nipped by Mario to resume their private battle for the lead, only to be slowed by a huge shunt when 'motor noter' Pat Bedard's Buick V6-engined 84C smacked the infield wall coming out of Turn Three, comprehensively disassembling itself all over the circuit. This incident also deprived the race of Sullivan's Lola, as Danny ran into the back of Guerrero's March, deranging the T800's front suspension.

When the green came on again it was Fabi's turn to take the lead from Danny Ongais, Unser Jnr, Mears and Sneva. Guerrero was further back now after a precautionary pit stop to check for damage, but still on the same lap as the leading bunch.

A sheared fuel pump drive eventually wrote Fabi out of the equation, while both the Andrettis faded thanks to engine (Mario) and handling (Michael) problems respectively. Into the closing stages and the magnificent Mears really began to stamp his authority on proceedings, although Little Al and Sneva weren't about to let him go unchallenged. The former retired, however, just before two-thirds-distance when a water rail fractured.

Running hard in Rahal's slipstream, Guerrero had a brain-rattling triple spin, but kept his Bignotti-Cotter 84C off the wall, while Mario got tangled up lapping Josele Garza's 84C and retired as a result. During the final yellow light spell, Sneva's 84C suffered the feared wheel bearing failure and, as Mears was unleashed for the run to the flag, the Mayer car came trickling into the pit lane for good.

'All I can say is I'm happy that it happened under a yellow rather than a green,' shrugged Sneva with masterly understatement, 'because a problem like that can do a whole lot of damage when you're running hard.' That was the end of the battle and Mears reeled off the remaining laps to score a two-lap victory over Guerrero, Al Unser Snr, Al Holbert, Michael

Star in the making. Little Al Unser at the wheel of Rick Galles's March 84C.

HAVOLINE
MOTOR OIL
TEXACO STAR 4
GOODYEAR

SILVER BULLET
7
SIMONIZ
VALVOLINE
GALLES
GOODYEAR
Coors LIGHT
DieHard

Andretti and the evergreen A.J. Foyt.

An obviously delighted Mears told Gordon Kirby that throughout the race he'd been concerned about the way in which Sneva and Little Al could whistle through traffic because their 84Cs were fitted with a high-downforce underbody, specially evolved for the shorter tracks, which his Penske machine didn't have. 'I knew I was at a disadvantage from that viewpoint,' he explained, 'so I had to keep cranking some stagger in, cranking in some left-front wing, so that when I was running on my own, the car felt nicely loose. But, on the other hand, I just had to live with that in order to stay with them in traffic.

'They clearly had enough downforce at the front that enabled them to keep the car a little closer balanced. Tom caught me a time or two when we were lapping slower cars and my front end would wipe out [understeer]. I'd have to come off the throttle to prevent the thing from hitting the fence coming off the turns, and Tom would just drive under me. That's where their short-track set-up really helped.'

Tyler Alexander recalls: 'That was real close! When they rolled Mears's car out for the official winner's photo the day after the race, you could hear its wheel bearings clanking away. They'd lasted about 20 laps longer than Sneva's, but were on the point of giving up...'

However, while March certainly dominated the most prestigious race of the year, the sheer volume of cars in the hands of front-running drivers meant that they divided the balance of the winner's laurels. And that could do nothing but help Mario Andretti. His Lola T800 generally displayed better front-end bite than the 84Cs and, although Sneva and Little Al won Milwaukee and Portland respectively in the wake of the Indy 500, Andretti Snr then latched onto a winning streak.

Between the start of July and the end of September the Lola T800 successfully kept March away from the CART winner's circle. Mario triumphed at Meadowlands, Michigan, Road America, Mid Ohio and Michigan again, while 'Sully' took Cleveland, Pocono and Sanair, where Indy winner Mears crashed heavily in the Penske 84C, badly smashing both feet in a shunt which would keep him out of the cockpit until the following year.

March won the last three races of the season, Sneva following Rahal's victories at Phoenix

Michael Andretti in the cockpit of the 'naked' Kraco 84C at Phoenix. The carbon-fibre top/aluminium honeycomb bottom monocoque construction, mandatory for all Indy cars, is well illustrated in this shot.

and Laguna Seca with a win at Las Vegas, but by then it was far too late to prevent Mario taking the championship with 176 points to Sneva's 163, ahead of Bobby R. on 137. With that weight handicap of 100 lb described by Adrian Newey, the March 84C was certainly at a disadvantage compared with the Lola on road circuits and the T800 also benefited from a lower centre of gravity produced by mounting the turbocharger partially within the bellhousing between engine and gearbox.

One thing that did emerge during the year was that the TrueSports 84Cs were fast becoming the 'works-approved' machines and Newey's promotion to the post of chief engineer on the March Indy car project enhanced the Columbus, Ohio-based team's status as spearhead of the factory's effort for 1985. Throughout the season Newey beavered away at improving Rahal's machine, evolving a long-wheelbase variant for the super-speedways, lightening the rear suspension, increasing the rake of the engine and capitalising on the use of a Torsen-Gleason differential similar to that being employed on the F1 McLaren-TAGs. This process of refinement progressed with such unobtrusive subtlety that it took the best part of a year before rival March owners really registered that Rahal was getting a works-backed 'leg-up' over the opposition.

Newey was to take major responsibility for the design of the 85C which, again, was well under way before the end of the previous season. It was quite a job, as he recalls. 'The project wasn't really done in the manner I would have liked because, although it was the first car I'd designed from a clean sheet, I was doing most of it from the US, flying backwards and forwards across the Atlantic while engineering and developing Rahal's 84C.

'I tried to lay down the overall basis for the new car, but some of the things didn't quite happen in the way I wanted. But I did the aerodynamics – using the University of Southampton wind tunnel rather than the one at Imperial College, simply because I felt it was the better of the two and I could also pull the Old Pals Act when it came to getting dates to use it at short notice. I wasn't particularly proud of the car, but it was good enough to get the job done.'

Newey was happy to stay with TrueSports in 1985, getting on well with Jim Trueman and Steve Horne. He also felt he was developing a fine working relationship with Bobby Rahal, a driver for whom he is lavish in his praise to this day. 'Bobby's a fantastic driver and a really good bloke,' he enthuses. 'I think he's probably left it too late to make the switch to F1 now, but I believe, had he done it a few years ago, at the very least he would have been as good as, say, Thierry Boutsen and probably a bit better.

'The best things about him are that he's extremely intelligent, reasonably quick, has a good temperament, provides excellent feedback for the engineer – and doesn't stuff it. Really, he was bloody good.'

Section 2: The Indy Cars

Chapter 2

Keeping the customer happy

The new March 85C represented a major turning-point in March Engineering's Indy car history. While the 84C's lineage could be traced directly back to the F1-derived 81C, the 85C seriously reflected all the accumulated experience of the previous four years as well as a lot of lessons Newey had learned while engineering Rahal's machine.

The fact that the first batch of 85Cs to be delivered were all to road-racing specification reflected Bicester's awareness of the superiority of the Lola T800 away from the speedways. The problem of excess weight was also addressed head-on with the result that the 85C monocoque alone weighed in 20 lb lighter than the older car's and, while still featuring the lower aluminium honeycomb section, the carbon-fibre upper panels now doubled as top bodywork.

For added impact-resistance, the chassis incorporated five main structural bulkheads, on which the suspension pick-up points were mounted for added security. Its design reflected changes in the constructional regulations following the spate of major Indy car accidents the previous year, accidents which had left Rick Mears, Derek Daly and Kevin Cogan, in particular, with extremely serious leg and foot injuries, although the very fact that they survived these shunts at all testified to the progress March had already made in this area over the previous couple of seasons.

The new regulations included a new footbox rule, calling for clutch and brake master cylinders to be positioned within the monocoque behind an additional forward bulkhead. But despite pressure from some quarters for a switch to flat-bottomed chassis regulations, 'venturi' cars remained, although side pod ground clearance was raised a further inch (to 2 in.) for the super-speedways while remaining unchanged for all other events.

The new car's centre of gravity was lowered by reducing the height of the fuel cell and the oil tank was now positioned immediately behind that fuel cell, rather than within the gearbox bellhousing, thereby reducing the wheelbase by another inch and enabling the turbo installation to be lowered by a crucial 5 in. Tests at the Cranfield research centre revealed that the new chassis was torsionally twice as stiff as that of the 84C.

A refined version of the familiar pullrod suspension set-up was employed on the front of the new March, while a narrower-profile top rocker was employed at the rear to activate the inboard spring/dampers. New cast magnesium uprights were employed all round, facilitating better brake cooling, in conjunction with an uprated wheel bearing package.

The transmission was a refined version of that used on the 84C incorporating a new crown wheel design, purpose-made to March specification in the wake of a disappointing number of failures throughout the 1984 season. The slim gearbox casing allowed the width of the crucially important underbody venturis to be increased by 6 in.

For 1985 Newey stayed with TrueSports and would operate in much the same manner, progressively developing Rahal's 85C during the season before incorporating the lessons into the 86C. In their second season together this collaboration started to cause some tremors of dissatisfaction from rival customers, for Newey's obligation was split pretty well 50/50 between TrueSports and the factory and some people felt that Herd was having his cake and eating it by instigating such an arrangement.

Newey is quite straightforward as he reflects on the policy he adopted in 1984: 'The stance I took was that anything developed throughout the season was exclusive to TrueSports, but at the end of the year everything I'd learned would be incorporated into the following year's production car. I would never go so far as to recommend a particular chassis set-up to customers, but the 85C, for example, did benefit from the revised suspension and wings that we produced throughout 1984 on Rahal's car.'

In fact Robin Herd had identified, and exploited, a commercial opportunity to hire a factory engineer to the major teams – for a fairly high price – especially to tend their own cars and, hopefully, enhance their performance beyond that of a standard, off-the-shelf customer car. One team that certainly had no need for a works-supplied engineer was Penske Racing. At the end of 1984 ex-McLaren engineer Alan Jenkins was recruited to the team, which embarked on an intensive off-season programme of car assessment in order to establish its immediate priorities for 1985.

Jenkins: 'We spent the winter on what I can only describe as a mind-boggling trail round the States, testing at just about every circuit you've ever heard of. After the last race of '84 Roger bought the ex-Andretti Lola, and with that, a March 84C, a Penske PC14 and a modified PC12 we tested endlessly. We finally ended up in a paddock somewhere in middle

Penske crew chief Derrick Walker and colleague Earl McMullen look sceptical as Sullivan tells them how his March has been behaving during his first test with the team, at Laguna Seca early in 1985.

America, all sitting round debating what we should do. It came down to plumping for the March, so Roger immediately fired off an order for three 85Cs.'

During the course of the season the Penske Marches would acquire their fair share of home-brewed modifications, including revised bodywork, their own wings, beefed-up rear rocker arms and a headrest fairing to reduce buffeting around the drivers' heads. Jenkins also monitored the progress of TrueSports in order to keep in touch with what the factory was up to.

'It was generally accepted, I think, that one needed different bodywork for the speedways and the road circuits and March obviously liked to foster that impression,' he recalls with a grin. 'It would never have done to let anybody know that you didn't. Anyway, when Rahal turned up at one of the road races with speedway bodywork, and went quite well, we were alerted to this situation. But it was only in the later races that this really filtered through to us.

'In general, though, I think March accepted that customers would do their own development work and we never had any difficulty getting our hands on the necessary drawings to do our own suspension components. Ours were nicer – and cheaper, which always pleased Roger, of course!'

Right: ***Al Unser Snr presses on to fifth place at Long Beach, 1985, in one of the Penske March 85Cs engineered by former McLaren man Alan Jenkins. It was a gentle start to a season which would see Big Al unexpectedly pluck the CART Championship at the last race of the year.***

Danny Sullivan at Long Beach in Penske's 85C. He had a surprise or two up his sleeve for Mario Andretti, come the Brickyard...

Popular Colombian Roberto Guerrero was out of luck at Long Beach in 1985, but would take his Vince Granatelli-run 85C to third place behind Sullivan and Mario Andretti at Indianapolis.

BOSCH
GOODYEAR
PENNZOIL
Miller
AMERICAN
HOLSET
COMPUTERVISION
PENNZOIL
5

Mobil 1
BECKMAN INDUSTRIAL
SHARP
True Value
Master MECHANIC
9

Emerson Fittipaldi really started to get the hang of Indy car racing in 1985. Here his 85C heads for second place behind Mario Andretti's Lola T900 at Long Beach.

Andretti kicked off the 1985 season with another victory at Long Beach, the new Lola T900 clearly set to take up where the previous year's car had left off. But when first unofficial practice for the Indy 500 got under way, it was Rahal's Newey-engineered 85C that set the ball rolling with a lap at 210.970 mph. The previous week Robin Herd had been the honoured recipient of the Duke of Edinburgh's Designer's Prize – the top award for design in British industry – for the March 84C which had dominated Indy so overwhelmingly the previous year.

March remained on top when it came to the final grid line-up at the Brickyard, although the Cosworth DFX brigade had to take a back seat on this occasion. Using a McLaren Engines-prepared stock-block Buick V6 which under USAC (but not CART) regulations was allowed 57 in. of boost in contrast to the 47 in. allocated to the DFX, Pancho Carter bravely took pole position. Despite dramatically blustery conditions, he turned a 212.583 mph lap in his Galles Racing 85C, while Scott Brayton's sister car managed 212.354 mph to line up alongside him. It was the first time a stock-block engine had been on the Indy pole since 1931, ending an eight-year run of domination by the Cosworth DFX.

Completing the front row was a scintillating Rahal on 211.818 mph ahead of Mario's Lola T900 (211.576 mph), leaving the top ten to be completed by a phalanx of 85C-DFXs driven by Emerson Fittipaldi (211.322 mph), Don Whittington (210.991 mph), Al Unser Snr (210.523 mph), Danny Sullivan (210.290 mph), Geoff Brabham (209.215 mph) and Rick Mears (209.796 mph). The previous year's Indy winner, Mears was still effectively recuperating from his Sanair shunt, unable to walk more than a few steps without considerable discomfort, but he was clearly on the mend and demonstrably capable of running at a highly competitive pace. In all, 23 of the race's 33 starters were at the wheel of March 85Cs, but the Lola threat was clearly expanding with Al Unser Jnr, Arie Luyendyk, Jim Crawford, Derek Daly and Tony Bettenhausen all at the wheel of T900s in addition to Mario Andretti.

Track temperatures were already easing towards 115 degrees when the Memorial Day classic got under way, Mario Andretti inwardly convinced that he'd got his best-ever chance of rekindling the distant memory of his 1969 victory. Although Rahal got the jump on the two Buick-engined 85Cs away from the green flag, Andretti was second at the end of the opening lap from Brayton, Fittipaldi, Unser Snr and Carter. When it came to the serious business of racing, the stock blocks were not in the hunt and Carter's Buick coasted into the pits as early as lap six to retire with a broken oil pump.

The first yellow came on at the 15-lap mark when Josele Garza's engine failed, Andretti emerging in the lead after the spate of tactical pit stops which inevitably followed. As the race settled down, Mario began to edge away from Unser Snr (who had already incurred a one-lap penalty for glancing one of his air hoses in the pit lane), Rahal and Fittipaldi, with Guerrero, Brabham, Sullivan and Mears in the next bunch a little further back.

Rahal's hopes of winning were dashed during the first round of fuel stops under the green, when his throttle started to stick. Although his mechanics quickly ripped off the engine cover to lubricate the mechanism, the delay enabled Mario really to pile on the pressure and consolidate a gap. With 150 miles under his belt, he was six seconds ahead of Fittipaldi, while Rahal's challenge was finally blunted after 84 laps when a progressively worsening engine problem heralded his retirement.

Through the spate of pit stops just after half-distance, Mario continued to lead, but some slick work from the Penske crew saw Sullivan's Miller-backed 85C vault up to second place. Suddenly, Andretti had trouble on his hands as Danny began to claw into his advantage. It took 'Sully' a mere six laps to chew through the Lola's four-second advantage and he was now right behind and looking for a way past. On lap 120 he made his move going into Turn One. It was an eye-opening experience for the driver from Louisville, Kentucky!

'Mario's tough, and while you can rely on him he's never going to give you a whole lot of room,' Sullivan told the author over three years later. 'You try a passing manoeuvre on him and you'd better make it count, because he wants to win Indy again real bad.

'On that day, all I did was hurry up my passing move on Mario in the sense that I wasn't certain which lap I was on. When you're running that close behind another car at those sort of speeds, there is a great deal of turbulence, which affects your radio communication with the pits. I couldn't pick up the signals from my pit board either, because the crew were right down at the far end of the pit lane, at a point where I was concentrating on diving out from behind Mario's tail.

'My March was quicker through Turns Three and Four, so I tried running at him a couple

Miller
5
Miller

Heart-stopper! Sullivan's Penske 85C pirouettes wildly amidst a cloud of tyre smoke right in front of Mario's Lola coming off the first turn at Indianapolis. Andretti missed Sullivan, Danny missed the wall – and recovered to win the race!

AL SR.
AL SR.

of times into Turn One and he almost had me over the fence. He later made the remark "I fed him the bait and he took it." Well, I didn't have a whole lot of choice at the time. I didn't want to be down there over the line on the apron, but he just turned sharp left at me.

'OK, so now we're both running side by side, backed off the throttle. As I came off the painted line which delineates the pit exit road round the bottom of Turn One, I felt the car unsettling itself, but figured I could hang onto control. Then it snapped away from me and I thought, "Shit, leading the Indy 500 and I've dropped it." I went round in a cloud of smoke. If I'd been in control, I'd never have dropped it in the first place.'

Sullivan got away with it, spinning round to face in his intended direction after a performance which over-enthusiastic commentators ranked with Jim Clark's 1965 pirouette, but which, in reality, was out of Sullivan's hands. He came straight in to change tyres and certainly learned his lesson.

Only four laps after the end of a lengthy yellow flag period, prompted by Rich Vogler losing control and Tom Sneva crashing in avoidance, Sullivan successfully duplicated the manoeuvre which had previously caused him to come so badly unstuck. This time he moved Mario up the banking and forced him to concede the corner.

Eventually, after another yellow flag, Sullivan's 85C came home the winner by just over three seconds from the infuriated Mario, who made it quite clear that he was desperately disappointed to have been beaten by 'Sully' in the March. Although maturing into an extremely accomplished performer, Sullivan's Aspen image and the manner in which his PR people had massaged him into a media personality grated with some of the Indy Old Guard. It amused the former Tyrrell driver then – and would still amuse him when he finally nailed the CART Championship in 1988.

After Indy, Mario reaffirmed the Lola T900's credentials with wins at Milwaukee and Portland, after which he led the championship standings with 81 points to Sullivan's 47 and Fittipaldi's 35. Over at Penske, however, the curiously unexpected route to the team's seventh Indy car championship in nine years came together as a long-term by-product of Rick Mears's accident at Sanair the previous summer.

Clearly, although Mears had forced himself back into the cockpit remarkably quickly, his shattered feet were going to take considerably longer to mend fully. Realistically, he could not be regarded as a championship contender in a series of which demanding street and road races were now as integral a facet as the super-speedway events.

Penske had therefore recruited the thrusting, bright-eyed and enthusiastic young Sullivan, while at the same time signing 45-year-old Al Unser as a third driver for the three 500-mile classics as well as a back-up driver for the recovering Mears. With Alan Jenkins now tending, and subtly modifying, the Penske team's fleet of six Marches as an adjunct to his main task of designing the new PC15 chassis to accept the upcoming Ilmor V8, Unser Snr's championship challenge gradually picked up momentum as the summer continued.

His third place at Cleveland – his fifth top-five finish in six races – hauled him up to joint second place in the standings, equal with his 23-year-old son, who was demonstrating polished and increasingly mature form in Doug Shierson's 85C. Big Al was then second to Fittipaldi at Michigan, but was an unhappy seventh deputising for Mears at Elkhart Lake, where Jacques Villeneuve put it over Michael Andretti by ten seconds for his sole Indy car victory to date.

Third place behind Mears at Pocono finally thrust Unser Snr into the championship points lead for the first time that season, albeit a mere 5 points clear of the consistent Fittipaldi. But then Little Al took a fourth at Mid Ohio and a third at Sanair, slipping to the head of the points table in front of his father. Al Snr's victory at Phoenix, where Alan Jenkins came up with further-revised front suspension geometry, offering more camber change on his 85C, moved him back ahead of his progeny, who trailed his father across the line to ensure that the battle for the title at the final round of the series would be an all-family affair.

The championship was settled at Tamiami Park in Florida a month later, Al Snr following Sullivan, Rahal and Little Al home to clinch the crown. It was a tribute to Al Snr's dogged persistence and consistency, backed up by Penske's near-flawless standards of race-preparation.

Best of the non-Unsers in the title chase was Bobby Rahal, whose works-supported 85C won three races. TrueSports also raised the spectre of possible Ferrari involvement in CART when team manager Steve Horne made a bold proposal to Maranello that they should produce a turbo V8 which Rahal's team would then use. Bobby actually demonstrated one of

One of the most naturally talented stars on the contemporary Indy car scene, Al Unser Jnr has enjoyed many successes with March. He is pictured with wife Shelley prior to the championship 'shoot out' with his father, Al Snr, for the CART title at Miami in 1985. The tee-shirts reflect their sentiments...

its 85Cs at Fiorano in September, with Adrian Newey in attendance, and Horne pressed hard for the English engineer to join Ferrari to oversee the proposed operation.

'It was an attractive and tempting offer,' recalls Newey, 'but it would have meant splitting my time between Italy and the USA. In the event Ferrari told us that they would not just supply engines, but wanted to do the whole car themselves. Eventually the project came to nothing.' Ironically, Ferrari did build their own Indy V8 and the author recalls Marco Piccinini very self-consciously throwing a sheet over it during a press visit to Maranello in 1986.

In retrospect, it was a reflection of the concern felt by FISA and the F1 constructors at the increasing success of the CART series, and apparently waning interest in F1 in the USA, that they offered the Commendatore a quid pro quo in the form of a 12-cylinder F1 ceiling (rather than the eight-cylinder limit craved by most British teams) if he would only abandon the project. He did, but irony ruled in the end. After Mr Ferrari's death Alfa Romeo appropriated the V8 for its own Indy car efforts, ironically in a March chassis!

Steve Horne's attempts to attract Ferrari into the Indy car arena were symptomatic of the increasing recognition among CART competitors that a full-scale engine war was on the verge of erupting, just as it was in F1. The most immediate threat came from the Ilmor V8, manufactured with Penske backing by former Cosworth engineers Mario Illien and Paul Morgan in Northamptonshire. They had both decided the time was right to leave Cosworth to strike out on their own, opting to tackle the virtual monopoly enjoyed by their former employers with the DFX.

Penske, always with a shrewd eye to giving his team an advantage, undertook to underwrite the project. He was also of the opinion that it would not be too difficult a task to seek out an American corporation keen on financing a potentially Indy-winning engine. As usual, he was right. In the face of a long-established policy that it should not be seen to have a direct involvement in racing, Penske romanced General Motors to such good effect that the Ilmor V8s eventually rolled out of the factory with 'Chevrolet' embossed on their cam covers.

The project to develop the engine kicked off in December 1983 and on 10 August 1985 Rick Mears flew to England to sample the new V8 at the Bruntingthorpe test track, installed in one of the team's March 85Cs. Eight months later, powering the Alan Jenkins-designed Penske PC15, Al Unser Snr would give the Ilmor-Chevy V8 its maiden race outing at Phoenix.

Meanwhile, over at TrueSports, Adrian Newey felt he had probably gone as far as he could. For the second successive season he was faced with the challenge of designing the following year's new car while attempting to engineer Rahal in the field, and he admits that tension began to build up between himself and Steve Horne, who felt he was spending more time in the UK than he ought to. In the end, he transferred, along with the 'works blessing' that went with him, to Kraco, where he would engineer Michael Andretti's almost-successful onslaught on the 1986 CART title.

During the summer of 1985, after lengthy and sometimes acrimonious debate, proposal and counter-proposal, CART finally announced revised technical regulations which were intended to endure from the start of 1986 to the end of 1989. Despite a strenuous campaign by some drivers for flat-bottomed cars, CART decided to stick to ground-effect regulations, reducing the underbody venturi area by 30 per cent with the added stipulation that it would not be permitted to extend beyond the centreline of the rear wheels. There was also a requirement for a 'visibility box' between the bodywork and the rear wing, allowing the driver to see more in his rear-view mirrors.

Side pods were regarded as an integral component in the driver protection package and minimum and maximum widths across the pods were set at 50 in. and 63 in. respectively. For the super-speedways, rear wing dimensions were reduced by 7 in. to a maximum of 56 in., minimum overall length was increased by 4 in. to 184 in. and turbo boost was left at 48 in. It was also announced that the bottom half of the monocoque must be manufactured from aluminium honeycomb – and not carbon fibre – following the style pursued by the last two March designs. This looked like being a major problem for the forthcoming Lotus 96T, which had a tub entirely of carbon fibre and Kevlar, but the project proved stillborn anyway.

In assessing the impact of the new regulations, Adrian Newey reckoned that they would rob the 85C of around 30 per cent of its total downforce if applied to the existing car. Preparing the aerodynamic groundwork for the 86C, he confessed to having clawed back some of that loss, but wasn't specific when it came to figures.

Having won ten of the previous season's 15 races, March concentrated on making its 86C

Al Unser Snr's Penske March 85C took fourth place in the final race of the '85 season at Miami. It was good enough for the 46-year-old veteran to clinch the title.

wesson
NZOIL
5

a better all-round customer car. The constructional layout of the 86C was much the same, retaining the carbon-fibre upper section mated to an aluminium honeycomb lower tub, but to conform with the revised regulations that lower section was extended to form the bottom half of the nosebox. The bathtub itself was manufactured from regulation thicker-core honeycomb and thicker-gauge pre-folded aluminium sheeting, although the rearrangement of the bulkheads ensured that this uprating of material specification carried with it no additional weight penalty.

The car looked distinctively different to its predecessor, the bulbous frontal treatment, a March trademark in previous years, now giving way to a slimmer and more crisp frontal profile. Revised footwell regulations required a slight rearrangement of the pullrod front suspension, but this had been race-proved on Rahal's TrueSports car towards the end of the previous year in its role as the factory-supported March operator.

In order to comply with the 'visibility box' regulation, the rear spring/dampers were now tucked away, mounted horizontally parallel to the gearbox, but retaining rocker arm activation. New cast magnesium uprights were employed, along with new March wheel bearing assemblies, while the steel brake discs were used in conjunction with Alcon calipers, which had also been race-developed on the TrueSports car during 1985.

The Cosworth DFX engine was now canted upwards to the rear at a 2½-degree angle, while an even narrower gearbox casing contained the same internals as on the 85C although, with the oil tank mounted between the fuel cell and the rear bulkhead, the gearbox bell-housing now contained only the oil catch tank, allowing this casting to accommodate the much-lowered turbo installation.

Turned through 90 degrees, the turbo's new position allowed a twin-wastegate configuration and symmetrical exhausts to be used for the first time. However, the way in which the exhausts blended into the top of the underbody diffuser panel caused a degree of controversy when the 86C first rolled out, several rivals suggesting that it was using the effect of the rotating turbines to create additional downforce. However, CART Technical Inspector Kirk Russell gave it the all-clear, so the doubters were left to mumble to themselves.

Although it had been testing since the previous autumn, the official unveiling of the Ilmor 265A V8 came only in February 1986, its debut scheduled for the season-opener at Phoenix installed in the new Penske PC15, which had just been completed. As things turned out, installing a brand new engine in a brand new chassis was not going to prove a particularly productive project.

Although the PC15 would eventually be massaged into halfway respectable form, Al Unser reckoned it was 'lurid' on the super-speedways and for most of the time it took a back seat to the team's fine-handling March 86Cs. Mario Illien would later concede that, wrestling with various inevitable V8 vibration problems, he didn't think running the Ilmor in the PC15 helped Jenkins a great deal 'and I know it certainly didn't help us.' Installed in a trusty 86C, at least there was a chassis baseline by which to cross-reference the engine's performance against a Cosworth DFX.

The Honda V8, of course, wasn't really a Honda at all, despite the fact that it had 'Brabham Honda' on the cam covers. It was, in fact, a straightforward Judd V8, in effect a destroked 2.65-litre turbo version of the F3000 engine he had built previously for Honda, but this time with absolutely no support from the Japanese car maker.

Appropriately, the methanol-burning Judd AV was to be entrusted to Geoff Brabham's care, installed in a Galles team Lola. The Renault and the Ferrari never amounted to anything, but Buick's stock-block Indy special continued and Porsche's long-term plans for 1987 rumbled along in the background. Meanwhile, down in Midland, Texas, Cosworth preparation specialist Franz Weis at VDS Engines developed a short-stroke version of the DFX, mirroring the Northampton firm's own development programme back at headquarters. Kraco and TrueSports were at the head of this particular queue for their March-mounted drivers, Michael Andretti and Bobby Rahal respectively.

For 1986 March continued to have a healthy line-up of competitive runners, aside from Kraco and TrueSports, although Lola was making further inroads into the market with the uprated T86/00. Patrick Racing fielded Fittipaldi and Cogan in March 86Cs and Johnny Rutherford was also worth watching in Alex Morales's machine. And, of course, there was Penske. It promised to be an epic season.

Kevin Cogan opened the year with a good win at Phoenix, followed up by Michael Andretti putting it across the Lola-mounted Al Unser Jnr by a mere 0.2s at Long Beach.

Then it was off to Indy for the month of May with Roberto Moreno catching a lot of attention by running an impressive 205.8 mph rookie test at the Speedway, fractionally quicker than fellow first-timer Jacques Villeneuve, who was obliged to go through the formalities even though he had that 1985 road race victory to his credit.

Into first qualifying and Rick Mears took over, still using Cosworth DFX power in his Penske March. New technical regulations notwithstanding, he hurtled round the Brickyard to establish a new closed-circuit world record of 217.581 mph. Danny Sullivan was alongside on 215.382 mph, with Michael Andretti making it an all-March 86C front row on 214.522 mph. The second row included Rahal on 213.550 mph, Mario Andretti's Lola (212.300 mph) and Al Unser Snr's twitchy Penske PC15-Chevrolet (212.495 mph). With lap speeds creeping up by about 4 mph over the previous year, the new technical regulations were adjudged a qualified success, although the way in which Indy lap speeds would accelerate through to 1989 would continue to cause concern.

Testing at Laguna Seca early in 1986 for the Kraco team. On the right Newey and Michael Andretti confer with the rest of the crew, while the 86C stands waiting.

The new 86C seemed to be a more effective oval track car than the Lola, Gordon Kirby noting in *Autosport* that 'most Marches were able to take a smoother, higher arc through the four corners than even the best-handling Lolas, and the best of the Marches were very clearly superior to the best Lolas.' It did not, however, enjoy a trouble-free first few races. Ever since winter testing, the new cars had been suffering a variety of breakages, ranging from underbodies coming away to the lower rear wishbone pulling out of its pick-up point, a problem from which even Michael Andretti's Kraco car was not immune, suffering two such failures.

There was also some concern that the driveshafts wouldn't last the distance in the face of

Michael Andretti splashes through the rain during qualifying at Portland, 1985. Father Mario won the race for Lola.

the hot air blasted at them from the 86C's standard exhaust system, although this was one area where the Penske cars were not affected, their DFXs being equipped with Holset turbochargers installed beneath the tail of the engine cover with higher-mounted exhausts on either side. However, although Alan Jenkins and Geoff Ferris had followed the usual Penske formula of producing their own suspension components and bodywork modifications, Sullivan still fell victim to a rear wishbone pulling out on the first day of practice. Structural failures on the Penske cars were rare occurrences.

Robin Herd retrospectively paints a charmingly soft-focus picture of life as an Indy constructor, but while the $150,000 price tag of the 86C might well have been one of the cheapest passports to success at Indy, these suspension failures early in the car's life were seen by many customers as an irritating example of the way in which they were left to carry out the Bicester company's development testing. In that respect, they were annoyingly reminiscent of the rear pullrod failures which had beleaguered the 83C and forced many owners to revert to rocker arm rear suspension on their own initiative. The general feeling in CART circles was that the 86C was a good off-the-shelf racer, but would benefit from a reasonable amount of 'home refinement' to bring it up to the build-quality of the rival Lola brand.

That said, there was no faulting the 86C's track performance, as Indianapolis proved yet again. Delayed for the first time in its history by rain until the Saturday following its scheduled date, the 500 took place in perfect conditions under clear blue skies. Trying to regain his position on the parade lap after being late away from the grid, Tom Sneva wiped his March into the wall after getting a little too enthusiastic on cold tyres, then a smoke-bomb was let off in the infield close to Turn Three, and these two incidents caused the race to suffer a further slight delay.

When the pack was unleashed on the green flag, Michael Andretti reminded everybody whose son he is with an aggressive chop across in front of the two Penske 86Cs on his left, sweeping into Turn One clearly in the lead. Immediately he began to ease away from Mears, Cogan, Sullivan and Rahal, leaving father Mario in trouble almost from the outset with a Lola chassis that felt less than perfect. After sparkbox problems delayed the Newman/Haas Lola early on, Mario called it a day, rather than slog on at the back of the field.

With 40 laps completed, Mears had clawed back to within a second of the Kraco March and, when Andretti Jnr dived in for his third fuel stop, Mears followed him in and emerged in the lead thanks to some slick work by the Penske pit crew. Running alone and no longer having to worry about the turbulence caused by the other March in front of him, Rick now began to pound off on his own, leaving Michael to fend off the increasingly single-minded challenge of Rahal.

With Andretti making a quick stop for new tyres and more fuel under the next brief yellow light, Rahal moved up into second place and, on lap 82, managed to ease through into the lead. At half-distance he had almost six seconds in hand over Mears, with Cogan and Unser Jnr next up. Englishman Jim Crawford, the former Lotus F1 driver, had meanwhile attracted a great deal of favourable comment with his splendid performance in one of the stock-block Buick-engined 86Cs, hauling it up to ninth place before the V6 ran up the white flag after 70 laps.

It was turning into a hectic 500-mile sprint, with at least three contenders well in the frame for most of the way. Michael Andretti's early show at the front of the field eventually lost its fine cutting edge thanks to a fading clutch which was making his return to the circuit after pit stops an excruciatingly slow procedure.

Rahal made a well-judged tyre stop under the yellow just before the 140-lap mark and was now set fair for a strong run to the finish. He had another lucky break on lap 165, when the yellow came on after Moreno stalled on the circuit, so when the pack was unleashed for the last 30 laps it was Mears, Cogan and Rahal at the head of the field.

Mears got badly balked lapping Randy Lanier's 86C, allowing both Cogan and Rahal to jump through into first and second places. With ten laps left to run Cogan was three seconds ahead. It began to look like the end of Rahal's efforts to score that long-dreamed-of Indy win for Jim Trueman, by now very frail and close to losing a manful battle against cancer. But Bobby could see that Cogan's 86C was sliding around a lot now, its tyres clearly in a worse state than those on the TrueSports March.

Going into lap 199, his fuel warning light blinking ominously on the instrument panel, Rahal hauled onto Cogan's tail and thrust through into the lead going into Turn One. 'You can't trust those warning lights. They're wrong most of the time,' he told Gordon Kirby

Bobby Rahal's TrueSports 86C, featuring plenty of suspension and aerodynamic modifications evolved by Adrian Newey, heads for victory at Laguna Seca in 1986.

Bud
VALVOLINE
J.R.T.
Bud
3
HORTON
GOODYEAR
sleep cheap!

Emerson Fittipaldi led for much of the distance at Portland in 1987 in the Patrick Racing March 87C-Chevrolet, only to retire with engine trouble. Three weeks later at Cleveland, however, he would confirm the potential of the new V8 with a fine victory.

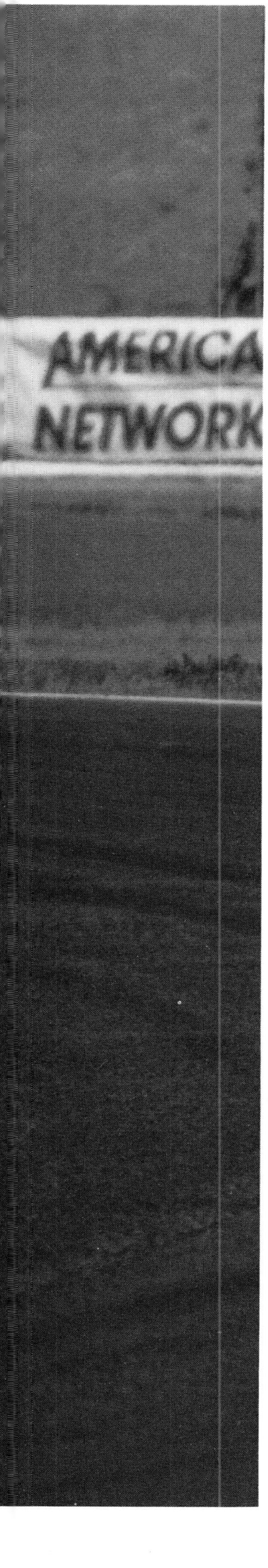

after the race. 'I just wound up the boost and yelled, "Don't leave me now baby!" all the way round that final lap. Out of Turn Four for the last time, I wasn't even looking for the chequered flag. Only when I saw our crew going nuts on the pit wall did I know we'd done it.'

Cogan, Mears and Roberto Guerrero made it a March 1-2-3-4, with Little Al's Lola the first of the thinly spread non-Bicester brigade to make it to the finish. Michael Andretti faded to sixth, while poor Sullivan was a distant ninth, utterly bewildered by the way in which his Penske 86C was plagued by terminal understeer almost from the start.

For TrueSports, of course, it was a more than usually emotional moment. Despite his frail condition, Jim Trueman paid a personal tribute to Rahal's efforts at the post-race press conference and accompanied him on the victory lap. Eleven days later, the man who had founded the Red Roof Inns motel chain, and backed Rahal long before they graduated to Indy cars together, passed away.

Michael Andretti came back to score his second win at Milwaukee, following that up by taking second place behind his father at Portland. This put him into a commanding position in the championship table, 13 points ahead of Tom Sneva, and it seemed as though he might be on the verge of leading all the way to the title. But the Kraco team was beset by a spate of mid-season engine failures on its self-prepared DFXs and those, allied to a dash of over-energetic motoring on Michael's part, meant that the following eight races netted him only a couple of second places (to Sullivan at Cleveland and Rahal at Michigan).

For all that, Andretti Jnr led 11 of the season's 17 races and over a quarter of the laps raced during 1986, although not until the penultimate round at Phoenix did he get back into the winner's circle. By then Rahal was virtually unassailable at the head of the championship table and Michael had to settle for the runner-up spot.

Ironically, Herd had hitched Adrian Newey's fortunes to Michael Andretti's star just as TrueSports burst through to take the CART title. It is interesting to hear Adrian's views on the Kraco driver, who was clearly a slightly different proposition to work with from Rahal: 'He hadn't got Bobby's feel for the car by any means. He wasn't as good as his father in this respect. But Michael had never worked with an engineer before and he was quick, eager and willing to try anything. If I'd suggested to him that we'd put the back wheels on the front and then asked him to run flat-out through Turn Three at Indy, he'd have done it.'

By the start of the 1987 season March had reached a remarkable production landmark when the 200th Indy car, chassis 87C-22, rolled off the Bicester 'production line' destined for Interscope Racing. The 87C was a joint Alan Mertens/Robin Herd design, Adrian Newey having left March to join the short-lived FORCE F1 operation. When that withdrew at the end of 1986, he switched to engineering Mario Andretti's Newman/Haas Lola T87/00 Indy car for the first half of the following season.

There is a distinct touch of *déjà-vu* when one reads the publicity blurb surrounding the 87C's specification. 'Retains the best elements of the old, married to innovation and advance in areas open to development,' was the theme of the new car's design rationale, and it was also pointed out that the 87C was not a totally new car, retaining the basic concept of the 1986 machine. However, the monocoque, manufactured now by the company's Brackley-based subsidiary Comtec, had been rearranged to create a lower centre of gravity, stiffer and stronger internal bulkheads were employed and three different suspension configurations, catering for road circuit, super-speedway and short oval tracks, were also available.

The entire rear end of the 87C was redesigned with a lower engine installation and an entirely new gearbox with a magnesium casing for improved rigidity with no added weight. Disappointingly, perhaps, March lost the custom of the CART Champions, TrueSports opting for Lola chassis in 1987, but by the same token, following a frustrating season with the Lola T86/00s, Rick Galles opted for March 87Cs in which to install his Judd/Honda engines, while Doug Shierson also made the switch from Lola to March for Al Unser Jnr.

At the start of the year, of course, it was confidently expected that March would face its most challenging ever Indy car season, for Porsche had arrived on the scene with its own engine and chassis and the upcoming Penske PC16-Chevrolet was sure to be a contender. In fact these two machines were disastrous failures and Penske would win another Indy 500 with its faithful March 86Cs, beating the latest Bicester car into second place.

The Ilmor-Chevrolet V8 would now be seen powering three different chassis, namely Penske, Lola (Mario Andretti) and March (Patrick Racing for Emerson Fittipaldi and Kevin Cogan), the last-named now utilising the engineering skills of the respected Lee Dykstra.

EWELL
GOODYEAR

Other changes on the CART scene included Goodyear preparing to use radial tyres for the first time at Indianapolis, Akron now confident that it had surmounted the major delamination problems which had led to the 1985 Michigan 500 being postponed after a succession of failures which required the scrapping of a complete production batch of covers.

The season opened with Mario Andretti scoring yet another Long Beach triumph, while the March 87C had its first visit to the victory circle at Phoenix, where Roberto Guerrero scored an enormously popular maiden Indy car victory, the Colombian now entered by Vince (son of Andy) Granatelli, who had bought out Dan Cotter's operation at the end of the previous season.

Mario took pole at Indy at a breathtaking 215.390 mph, not as fast as Mears's record 1986 speed, but quick enough to keep the March and Penske brigade wondering what on earth they had to do. Rahal was next up with 213.316 mph, reflecting the fact that none of the Lola teams was having much difficulty adapting their cars to work on Goodyear's radials. However, the March 87C wasn't in the same street in this respect, many drivers reporting that their new cars didn't respond precisely to chassis adjustment, and working out a decent set-up was clearly a major problem.

Over at Penske Racing, meanwhile, it was clear that the new PC16 was going to be little more than an also-ran and, to compound the problem, new team signatory Danny Ongais crashed one of the cars very heavily during the first week of practice, receiving a glancing blow to the head from a wayward front wheel. Before first qualifying Roger Penske took a dramatic policy decision, hauling out a Chevy-engined 86C which Mears had used towards the end of the previous season and with which he had established a closed-course record of 233 mph at Michigan over the winter. It was being prepared as a museum-piece at the team's Reading, Pennsylvania base, but was rushed to the Speedway in time for first qualifying. Clearly developing more downforce than the new 87C, it allowed Rick to barnstorm his way round to grab third place on the front row at 211.467 mph.

Thus encouraged, a second 86C was built up for Sullivan, this being one of the Cosworth-engined cars reworked to accept a Chevrolet engine. The next drama arose when the track medical authorities made it clear that Ongais would not be given the OK to drive in that year's event, so Penske did a deal with Al Unser Snr, who had been wandering round in the role of spectator for the first week of practice. He had already declined the offer of a ride in the March-Buick after Jim Crawford broke both his legs in a practice accident, and had been wondering whether any other opportunity might come his way. Now it had. And how!

Unser managed 23rd place on the grid with a 207.423 mph lap, his 86C still using Cosworth DFX power, while the best of the 87Cs was Guerrero at 210.680 mph in the middle of row two, flanked by the Lolas of A.J. Foyt, preparing for his 30th outing at the Speedway on 210.935 mph, and Dick Simon (209.960 mph). On the third row were a trio of 87Cs in the hands of Arie Luyendyk, Johnny Rutherford and Michael Andretti, the last-named admitting that he only really 'began to make sense' of his new March during the second week of practice.

From the start of the race, nobody seemed to be in the same street as Mario Andretti. His involvement in the race was a pretty straightforward story. Apart from a handful of laps following fuel stops, Mario utterly dominated proceedings.

Mears and Rahal led the pursuit at the end of lap one, by which time the yellow lights were already on after Josele Garza became involved in a first-corner tangle with Pancho Carter. But when the green flag was given after five laps, Andretti Snr piled on the pressure and began turning regular laps in the 204 mph bracket. With 20 laps completed the order was Andretti Snr, Mears, Guerrero, Rahal, Simon, Rutherford and Andretti Jnr.

Luyendyk then came into the reckoning, pulling up to second place by lap 35, by which time Michael Andretti's Kraco 87C had coasted slowly into the pits with a broken driveshaft constant-velocity joint, a brief fire breaking out before he called it a day. Guerrero, Sullivan and Mears were still on the same lap as Mario's Lola, with Sneva, Gordon Johncock, Fabrizio Barbazza, Rutherford and Simon a lap down. At this point Al Unser Snr's Penske 86C-Cosworth was a further lap behind, 13th overall.

The opening phase of the race hadn't been good for Big Al. Only just missing the wayward Garza at the first turn – 'It sure scared me ... I thought he was going to hit my left-rear' – he was lapped by Mario as early as lap 17 and then lost more time when he stalled his engine at his first fuel stop.

Stepping into the Penske team at the last moment to drive a year-old March 86C, Al Unser Snr claimed a dramatic victory in the 1987 Indy 500.

'I think the biggest problem we suffered in the early stages of the race was getting used to

Roberto Guerrero scoring the first win of his Indy car career at Phoenix, 1987, at the wheel of Vince Granatelli's 87C. Later that year he would crash badly while tyre testing at Indianapolis, sustaining serious head injuries from which, thankfully, he has completely recovered. In 1989 he signed to drive for the Johnny Capels-operated March-Alfa Indy car programme.

STP
VALVOLINE
True Value
4
True Value
STP
BOSCH
STP
BOSCH

the turbulence and knowing the car, because I hadn't run it on the track very much,' explained Unser Snr. 'I was probably being very easy on myself and the car so as I wouldn't make a mistake. I think that's why I lost so much ground in the early stages. I should have been a lot more aggressive and I wasn't. But the turbulence was bad back there and the car bounced around quite a bit.'

Electrical failure put Rick Mears out after 75 laps, shortly before team-mate Sullivan emerged unscathed from a huge spin at Turn Four in the surviving Chevy-engined March 86C. Just after half-distance Mario was still nursing a confident five-second lead over Guerrero and Sullivan, but Al Unser had the Penske March-Cosworth up to fourth ahead of Luyendyk and Sneva. Then came disaster.

On lap 130 Tony Bettenhausen's March 86C shed its right-front wheel, which was immediately collected by Guerrero's 87C. Mercifully, the wayward component bounced off the nose of the Granatelli car, missing its driver's helmet, but it arced over the protective fence and hit a spectator sitting in the very top row of the grandstands. He died a few hours later in hospital and the consequent legal action, in which March was joined as a defendant, had still to be settled as this book went to press.

Roberto headed straight for the pits, losing over a lap having his car checked and a new nose cone fitted. That allowed Sullivan to move into second place, but he soon came in for fuel, allowing the Colombian to regain the position. Danny rejoined in fourth place behind Big Al, who was close behind the Granatelli March, but when Mario raised his lap speed back into the 200 mph bracket, only Roberto could match him and Unser Snr began to drop away.

With only 40 laps to go, Mario had over a lap on the field, but on lap 177 – only 23 to run – the Newman/Haas Lola slowed suddenly and coasted into the pits. The Ilmor-Chevy V8 had suffered a major electrical malfunction. The sparkbox and wastegate were changed, but it was effectively all over.

Guerrero was now 42 seconds ahead of Big Al's Penske 86C and, with one more stop to go, seemed *en route* to victory. Roberto made that last pit stop at the end of lap 182. The clutch was very hot and he was worried about stalling the engine. Down came the Granatelli March from its air jacks – and Roberto's worst nightmare was realised. The engine died.

By the time he accelerated back onto the circuit, Al Unser Snr was just racing past to put a whole lap on the 87C. It was heart-breaking for the South American, who had been the only driver on the same planet as Mario, but a fairy-tale ending for the man who hadn't had a drive – any drive – at the start of the month of May.

Despite another yellow light period for Mario's struggling Lola, eight laps from the finish, Guerrero couldn't get back on terms with the Penske March. But he fought like a tiger all the way to the line, 86C heading 87C past the chequered flag by a mere 4.5s. Unser's victory, which netted him $526,762, was his fourth, Al having previously triumphed in 1970, '71 and '78. Added to brother Bobby's victories in 1968, '75 and '81, it meant that the family's tally now stood at seven Indianapolis wins.

Two laps down, in a splendid third place, was Fabrizio Barbazza's Arciero team 87C, with the cars of Al Unser Jnr and Gary Bettenhausen sustaining Bicester's stranglehold on the Indy winner's circle. Unser was generous in praising his rivals, acknowledging just how well Mario Andretti and Guerrero had performed: 'Mario had us covered, let's not kid ourselves. He ran off and left us there and there wasn't anything I could do with him. Guerrero was going to be a battle for me, I guarantee you. He could out-run me and I knew if he didn't have any problems, I wouldn't be able to handle him. I could stay with him and that's about all.'

Unser's success decided Roger Penske on an unequivocal course of action. He scrapped the PC16 project, fired Alan Jenkins, concentrated on the March 86C-Chevys for the rest of the season – and hired Nigel Bennett to design the 1988 Penske PC17. Nigel had been responsible for pencilling Mario's Lola and Penske had seen enough of that to be convinced that the former Firestone tyre engineer had a pretty clear idea of what was required of an Indy car design.

Michael Andretti proved that he could get the best out of a March 87C-Cosworth package, winning at Milwaukee in the aftermath of Indianapolis, but Rahal grabbed victory at Portland and Meadowlands with his Lola, moving into a championship points advantage he was never to relinquish. He would consolidate that lead with a succession of consistent performances, including further victories at Laguna Seca and Tamiami Park. TrueSports was as

Alan Mertens, a long-time member of the March design team, engineered the Galles Racing 88C of Al Unser Jnr as the Albuquerque driver fought against the prevailing Lola tide throughout 1988.

professional as ever, being the only organisation to operate a separate test team, and their Franz Weis-prepared DFXs were generally more reliable than the works-supplied V8s used by Kraco. In fact Michael Andretti's title hopes foundered largely because of mechanical unreliability consequent on developing Cosworth's new electronic fuel system.

A lucky win at Mid Ohio for Guerrero kept the talented Colombian within striking distance of the championship, but the balance of his season was wiped out when he crashed during tyre testing at Indianapolis. A left-rear suspension breakage on his March 87C propelled him into the wall and he sustained serious head injuries as the right-front whiplashed back, catching his helmet a heavy blow. The prospects looked bleak to start with, but he regained consciousness fully within three weeks and was soon out of hospital, on the road to complete recovery and looking forward to a racing return in 1988.

March really dropped the ball when it came to the 88C, of which a project run of 25 cars was envisaged. Throughout the previous season there had been more than a few sideways glances as Kraco experimented with stiffer monocoques and frequent changes to suspension layout and geometry, their efforts overseen by factory-supplied engineer Peter Gibbons, with whom Michael developed a fine working relationship. It was quite clear that many privateers did not regard the 87C as the bargain of the age and, even before Alan Mertens and Herd got down to producing the ultra-compact 88C, the damage had been done and customers began to desert.

Nasty moment. Michael Andretti finds that Turn One at Phoenix is not flat-out in a March 88C. He crashed the Kraco car heavily in this pre-season test. He would later follow the prevailing tide and switch to a Lola.

It wasn't the technical competence of March Engineering that was being called into question. Anybody scanning the recent history of Indy car racing could see at a glance that a succession of extremely competent, well-engineered off-the-shelf racing cars had been produced over a four-year period. Although Herd would subsequently blame much of the responsibility for March's fading Indy star on the amount of management time demanded by the resurgent F1 programme, many people identified signs of Robin becoming over-confident and taking the company's pre-eminent position for granted. The irony was, of course, that its domination depended largely on paying customers – not a works team as such – so once one of the key teams decided to desert, the ripple-effect was almost inevitable. By trying to serve, in effect, too many masters, March had stifled the goose that laid the golden egg.

At the start of January 1988 the wraps came off the first 88C, destined for Al Holbert's Porsche Indy operation for the eventual purpose of evaluating the new German V8 free from the performance constraints of the dreadful 2708 CART chassis, which had suffered two dismal outings at the end of the previous season in the hands of Holbert himself and Al Unser Snr. Yet, almost simultaneously, March announced that, because of reduced demand, its Indy car production line was having to shed 14 employees. The recent collapse of the US dollar obviously aggravated the situation, but it wasn't preventing team after team from beating a path to Lola's factory in Huntingdon.

March stressed in its literature that the 88C was spawned as the result of no fewer than 708 wind tunnel tests carried out during the previous season and that it developed 13 per cent more downforce with an 8 per cent reduction in drag. Its design process had also utilised March's Applicon CAD/CAM system, which certainly helped produce a significantly smaller monocoque, while a slight reduction in the inclination of the engine/transmission unit was claimed to have lessened pitch sensitivity and contributed to a more stable centre of pressure. Pullrod suspension was retained at the front, but for the first time pushrod activation made an appearance at the rear.

At this point in the year, Shierson, Kraco, Rick Galles, Pat Patrick and Johnny Capels all had firm orders in for 88Cs. There still seemed a chance that Bicester might turn the prevailing tide, but it was going to be a long shot.

Lola's T88/00 and the brilliant Penske PC17 proved, almost from the outset, more than the 88C could handle. In fact, had it not been for Rick Galles's and Al Unser Jnr's stoic season-long efforts with their Ilmor-engined 88C, March would never have got a sniff of the winner's circle. Although Mario and Guerrero opened the year with a fine Lola 1-2 at Phoenix, Little Al then proceeded to lap Bobby Rahal's TrueSports Lola-Judd at Long Beach and went into the Indy 500 equal second in the championship points table.

Indy, of course, proved the vital stumble for March. Michael Andretti and Kraco were still effectively the works-backed operation, but Michael was feeling a little irked after the team's first car had been written off in a pre-season Phoenix test, again when the rear suspension broke. By the time he got to Indy he'd massaged the chassis into halfway reasonable form but, after a spate of engine failures, could only qualify tenth, some 9 mph off Rick Mears's breathtaking 219.198 mph pole winner in Nigel Bennett's new Penske PC17.

In fact it was a sign of the times when the trio of Chevy-engined PC17s – Mears, Sullivan and Big Al Unser – lined up together on the front row, Mario Andretti hanging on in fourth place with Little Al's 88C fifth. Of Junior's efforts, Alan Mertens commented, 'The kid's a hero. He carried that car today.' Appreciating the seriousness of the situation, Robin Herd got Adrian Newey – by then well into his first season with the Leyton House-backed F1 team – to pay a flying visit to the Speedway to brief individual teams on the correct use of some new chassis and suspension components. Basically, the 88C had too much drag and its drivers had to reduce downforce significantly, thereby making the cars nervous to handle, if they were to match Penske and Lola for straightline speed. Newey remembers the visit as 'a bit of a waste of time – there wasn't much that could be done in three days to a car I knew very little about.'

The race itself could hardly stall the further inevitable loss of customers. Emerson Fittipaldi kept the faith and hauled his 88C-Chevy into second place, a mere seven seconds behind Rick Mears's Penske, but that didn't prevent Patrick Racing from switching to Lola chassis in the weeks that followed. The same applied to Michael Andretti, who finished fourth for Kraco, while Shierson also reverted to Lola for Raul Boesel. Teo Fabi continued to trail round in the Porsche-engined 88C, learning about the rather average German V8's

Quaker State
8
WITH QSX
GOODYEAR
BOSCH
8
BOSCH
Quaker State
PORSCHE

Teo Fabi in the March 88C-Porsche at Laguna Seca towards the end of the 1988 season. This project received a major setback when its driving force, Al Holbert, pictured above (left) *in conversation with respected Indy car journalist Gordon Kirby, died in an air crash in September 1988. However, the team continued in 1989 with a brand new March chassis and, at the time of writing, mid-season, Fabi is showing the March 89P-Porsche to be a formidable combination.*

Valvoline
VALVOLINE
STROH
GALLES
Foot-Joy
RED LION INNS
VALVOLINE
3
STROH
Raychem
RED LION INNS
BOSCH
GALLES

Gallant trier. Little Al Unser kept the March flag fluttering with some determined drives in this Ilmor-engined Galles 88C, although Alan Mertens had developed it into more of a 'Galles' than a March by the end of the 1988 season.

performance, but he was never likely to be a threat. Otherwise, within a month of the 1988 Indy 500, only Little Al and the Galles team remained loyal to Bicester, and they had their reservations.

Much of the credit for keeping Al Junior in play during 1988 must go to Alan Mertens, who was under pressure from the March management to assume the direction of a planned new in-house engineering consultancy, but successfully resisted a proposal that was not to his taste at all. By the end of 1988 he had split from March to establish, with Galles's backing, Galmer Engineering, which would act as the team's R&D subsidiary, based a stone's throw from the March factory.

'We did an enormous amount to our 88C,' he recalls, 'to the point that it was more a "Galles" than a March by the end of the year. We carried out a lot of structural changes, revised the front and rear suspension geometry and altered the relationship between the wing positions and the aerodynamic underbody tunnels. But Junior did a really brilliant job for us. He never ceases to amaze me. He quickly found out what the problems were, came to terms with them and just drove faster and faster all year. He is so keen and committed – a brilliant driver really...'

So Penske and Lola carved up the lion's share of the remaining race wins, but Little Al took the Galles March to victory on the Toronto street circuit, at Meadowlands and at Tamiami Park, emphasising his emergence as probably the most impressive long-term driving talent on the Indy car scene. At the end of the day he lost the battle for the 1988 CART title to Danny Sullivan, a driver with less God-given flair, but certainly equipped with superior hardware.

As far as the Indy car future is concerned at the time of writing, March's Bicester factory spent most of the winter 1988/89 producing its new 89P chassis exclusively for Porsche. It was touted as a logical development of the 88C, incorporating some rear suspension changes made by Alan Mertens while engineering the Galles car in 1988, but also including a brand new pushrod front suspension set-up. In fact it was much more than that, being an aerodynamically excellent design overseen by Gordon Coppuck which proved just how good a chassis March could produce when it really tried. Simultaneously, at Ralt's old Weybridge base, the company successfully completed an independent contract to develop an Indy car for Alfa Romeo. Sadly, this project's chief designer, Maurice Phillippe, was to die suddenly a couple of weeks before the 89CE's encouraging race debut at Detroit on 18 June in the hands of Roberto Guerrero.

Whether March has a future as a commercial manufacturer of Indy cars remains to be seen. The company has fallen from the high wire in other formulae on previous occasions, but with the single Porsche-engined car the only contemporary March on the grid for the 1989 Indianapolis 500, the collapse of its Indy car market has probably marked the biggest reversal of fortunes in its 20-year history.

Built at the Ralt base in Weybridge, the March 89CE-Alfa was designed by Maurice Phillippe, whose tragic and premature death occurred on 5 June. A fortnight later Guerrero drove this machine into eighth place on its maiden outing in the first CART Detroit Grand Prix.

PPG
CART
21
TURBO
GARRETT
MARCH
GOODYEAR

21
MAGNETI
MARELLI
digital
VALVOLINE
MARCH

Appendix 1

The production cars

When the fledgling March Engineering produced the lone type 693 Formula 3 'special' back in the summer of 1969, nobody involved in the project could have imagined that over the next 20 years almost 1500 racing cars would roll through the doors of the Bicester factory. If there was one thing that March could do well, it was building and selling racing cars on a commercial basis, particularly for the junior single-seater formulae.

In the 1960s it was popularly believed that tubular spaceframe chassis were most suitable for production racing cars because they were so easy to maintain and repair. The 693 prototype had been constructed round a square-tube frame and in 1970 the first generation of off-the-peg March single-seaters for paying customers followed that lead. Yet it has to be said that March very nearly destroyed its reputation almost before the end of that first year, for the F2, F3 and FF machines were not in the same league as the opposition. It was hard to make a case for buying a March 702 or 703 when Brabham's BT30 and BT28 had superior handling and came from a company with a proven record of building customer racing cars that were easy to operate.

Both Formulae 2 and 3 represented potentially profitable commercial markets and March launched its assault in the former by initiating an arrangement with Malcolm Guthrie Racing to operate a semi-works team. Malcolm, the son of the former BOAC Chairman Sir Giles Guthrie, had the financial wherewithal to underpin a great enthusiasm for motor racing, his lavish transporter and Lamborghini Espada road car attracting a great deal of admiration at the time. The previous season Guthrie had driven his own F2 Brabham BT30, finishing as high as fourth in the Monza Lottery, and by the end of the following year he probably wished that he'd kept it.

Ronnie Peterson raced – and crashed – the other Guthrie 702 alongside the team's owner throughout 1970, and although the spaceframe machine was massaged into halfway respectable form by the end of the year Robin Herd appreciated that something better would be needed for 1971. Shortly after 702 privateer Xavier Perrot won a non-title F2 race at the Nürburgring the day the German GP took place at Hockenheim, the first of the 712 monocoques was completed back at Bicester. This was to be probably the most significant customer machine March ever built for, with various specification uprates over the years, it lasted through much of the decade as the basis of a wide range of single-seaters.

Meanwhile, in F3, the March 703 was having a similarly unspectacular time, the Petonyer-backed, Andrew Marriott-managed semi-works machines of Ian Ashley and Tom Walkinshaw proving a real handful. Privateer Dave Morgan generally got his 703 working rather better than the factory-blessed entries on the British scene, his sponsorship from the Adelphi Staff Bureau being the indirect cause of the author almost receiving a very serious smack in the face from Walkinshaw on one occasion. After the Petonyer cars had been outclassed for the umpteenth time by Morgan's 703, I wrote jocularly in *Motoring News,* 'isn't it about time Andrew Marriott went down to the Adelphi Staff Bureau to see if they've got any racing drivers on their books?'

Understandably, I suppose, the dour Walkinshaw suffered something of a sense of humour failure and very nearly clocked me one in the Mallory Park paddock the following weekend. However, there was no improvement in the works cars' performance and then Tom hurt his ankles badly in a big shunt at Brands Hatch towards the end of the summer, his place in the team being briefly taken by Colin Vandervell, the son of the Vanwall team founder, G.A. 'Tony' Vandervell. Ashley, who now flies corporate jets in the USA, crashed so frequently in those days that his extrovert driving antics barely attracted any comment...

After selling only six of those gormless 702s in 1970, the 712M (for 'monocoque') really struck a chord the following year. The factory's effort was spearheaded by Ronnie Peterson, who successfully raced to the European F2 Championship, beating off challenges from François Cevert's Elf-backed Tecno, the Automovil Club Argentina's Brabham BT30 driven by Carlos Reutemann and the works-assisted BT36s of Rondel Racing, operated by Ron Dennis and Neil Trundle, now respectively Managing Director and Chief Mechanic of McLaren International. Frank Williams also operated a fleet of 712Ms, inadvertently helping with the factory's development programme when his cars' monocoques began cracking up round the footwell while contesting early-season F2 races in far-away Colombia.

March generally enjoyed good relationships with its customers, helping out in the field as much as possible, although there were occasionally moments when tensions ran high between factory and non-works racing teams. One such celebrated episode came at Sao Paulo's Interlagos circuit late in the year, during the South American F2 tour, when Ronnie Peterson's mechanic, Keith Leighton, almost got himself lynched.

March customer Wilson Fittipaldi, elder brother of double World Champion Emerson, came to the starting line in front of his home crowd with a starter motor problem and did not switch off his engine, knowing that it would prove impossible to restart. Leighton, keen that Ronnie's rivals should not be given any undue assistance, leaned into the cockpit and flicked off Fittipaldi's ignition switch. Wilson, a big, tall lad, shot out of the cockpit like a fire cracker and was only just restrained from pummelling the nonplussed March mechanic into the ground!

On the British F3 scene Roger Williamson gave added credibility to March efforts by winning the Lombard Championship in the first year of the 'airbox restrictor' 1600 cc F3 regulations. James Hunt was also a leading F3 exponent in 1971, totalling his spaceframe 713S – F3 customers still had a choice of chassis construction – during a pre-season testing shunt at Goodwood. The future World Champion over-drove dramatically on occasion to keep up, as he would do again in 1972 when he handled the works STP-liveried side-radiator 723, which was notoriously deficient in straightline speed. But there was absolutely no doubting James's sheer commitment, and when Alan Rees saw the way he was manhandling the 723 through Silverstone's Stowe Corner he became utterly convinced of Hunt's long-term potential.

By the start of 1972 Formula 2 was an extremely important commercial market for March Engineering, so there was obvious disappointment when the new Surtees TS10, driven by Mike Hailwood, beat the Bicester machines to the European Championship. Ronnie wasn't eligible, of course, as he was now a graded F1 driver and team-mate Niki Lauda's outings in the series were sporadic as his catastrophic F1 programme took precedence. Niki won the British F2 title, however, based on the results of five domestic F2 races (at Mallory Park, Oulton Park, Thruxton, Crystal Palace and Oulton Park again).

March had made a foray into Formula Ford during 1970 and '71, using an adaptation of the 703 spaceframer, but while Ian Taylor scored a spectacular last-lap victory in the 1970 Hockenheim round of the prestigious Johnsons Euro-Trophy that was about as far as March's achievement went in this particular sphere. By 1972 March concluded that the more senior single-seater formulae were far more profitable and that FF1600 should be left to the specialists, of which there were many.

The 1972 season also saw Xavier Perrot, now retired from circuit racing, take a 722 to victory in the European Hillclimb Championship, while the British Formula Atlantic title fell to American Bill Gubelman's similar car. March also produced some 20 versions of the 722 for the US domestic equivalent, Formula B, and Chuck Sarich became the first driver to win a USA-based championship behind the wheel of one of Robin Herd's products.

On the British F3 scene March was eclipsed by GRD and Ensign in 1972, although the relative lack of success of the 723 did little damage to customer demand the following year and Bicester increased its sales to 26 units in this category in 1973. Tony Brise clinched the Lombard and Forward Trust titles in 1973, while Ian Taylor took the John Player title.

In F2 the team's prospects were dramatically revitalised by a tie-up with BMW for engine supply and Jean-Pierre Jarier grabbed back the European title from Surtees's grasp. A good number of very competitive privateers got their hands on 732-BMWs, the most notable being Roger Williamson (who won the Monza Lottery in Tom Wheatcroft's car a few weeks before he was killed at Zandvoort), Vittorio Brambilla and Colin Vandervell, the last-named dovetailing F2 with the British F/Atlantic series, which he won. March had also succeeded in tapping the Japanese F2 market, victory in that country's national championship falling to Motaharu Kurosawa.

In 1974 that hard-headed Derby businessman Brian Henton won March two British F3 titles, while Tom Pryce scored the marque's first victory in the Monaco F3 classic. Patrick Depailler saw to it that March F2 fortunes were well looked after, the Frenchman clinching the European Championship, while Jim Crawford followed in Vandervell's wheel tracks by winning the British F/Atlantic series.

Not everything in the garden was to be totally rosy, however, and in 1976/77 the company encountered very difficult times indeed. March fell off the high wire in F2, one of its crucially important markets, and the 772 in particular was a highly unsuccessful machine – only eight were sold, as opposed to 19 762s. This underlined the harsh commercial message that a customer-orientated racing car manufacturer is only as good as its last championship.

There were other problems which compounded the company's difficulties. In the early days its sales manager had been a cheery Kiwi by the name of Bill Stone, who also raced his own 708 Formula Ford machine. After he moved on, March sales were channelled through AMFP Euroracing, a Silverstone-based operation founded by Martino Finotto, Paolo Pavanello (later to run the works Alfa F1 cars) and former racer Sandro Angeliri. The deal was that they bought all customer cars from March and then sold them on, but the business went very badly wrong when Angeliri got offside with the law and later jumped bail, fleeing the country.

This was all happening in the background just at the time when all the 772s had been sold to Angeliri – and March had produced the F/Atlantic-based 772P which very nearly won the 1977 International Trophy in the hands of Patrick Neve. This was a rather uncomfortable state of affairs for the factory, as the new car's arrival on the scene made sales of the existing 772 virtually impossible. Thankfully, by the end of the year the BMW-engined 782 prototype had made its race debut in the hands of Bruno Giacomelli and the following year's production was sold out, 29 cars eventually being completed. Giacomelli clinched the 1978 European F2 title, March's first success in this category in four years.

Meanwhile exciting developments had been taking place on the opposite side of the Atlantic. In 1976 a new French-Canadian star by the name of Gilles Villeneuve had popped up to win the North American F/Atlantic title at the wheel of a March fielded by the former works F1 mechanic Ray Wardell, one of the stalwarts from the early days. The following year Villeneuve would repeat that achievement, after which his career path headed, onwards and upwards, into F1.

The 1978 and '79 seasons were extremely good for March, the company producing more than 100 cars for the first time during the latter year, but one only has to glance through the production figures in the separate appendix in this book to see how the March star faded in 1980 and '81. Herd is suitably modest on the matter, but the sole surviving March founder dug deep into his personal resources to keep the company afloat at this time. The financial problems involved in sustaining sales in the European categories prompted March to capitalise on its introduction to the Indy car market every bit as much as Robin's enthusiasm for a fresh technical challenge.

From a numerical standpoint 1981 was pretty bad, only 62 customer cars being sold. Although this number was down to 47 the following year, the 1982 total included 20 extremely expensive Indy cars which helped haul March Engineering back into the black. In fact, like many companies, March had been living on bank overdraft facilities all the way through the 1970s and, when the account finally went into credit in 1982, Herd autographed the bank statement and sent it to the manager as a souvenir!

Having successfully survived the financial hurdles of the early 1980s, March sought to diversify and expand its off-track activities as the decade wore on. Comtec, specialising in the development of strong and lightweight composites material, became operational in mid-1986, while Aerotec opened its own wind tunnel facility in 1987. Confident that the group had the engineering potential to expand beyond mere motor racing horizons, the March management structure was reorganised in 1986, with Herd taking the position of Executive Chairman in addition to retaining his post as Technical Director. Further recognition of his efforts came in the Queen's New Year's Honours at the start of '87 when Robin was awarded the CBE for his outstanding engineering achievements through the company. It was a sweet moment indeed.

With the group's turnover now approaching $20 million, the decision was taken to seek a listing on the London Stock Exchange's Unlisted Securities Market. Handled by Barclays de Zoette Wedd, the company was duly floated in May 1987, and for a while the 5p shares soared towards the £1.50 mark. But there was trouble on the horizon. March's plummeting Indy car sales were having a serious adverse effect on the company's profitability and, by the end of 1988, March was staring a £4,495,099 trading loss squarely in the face. In the inevitable circular to investors it was stated that 'shareholders are entitled to know how this very serious situation came about.'

By this stage the March Group was made up of four constituent entities: March Engineering, which designed and manufactured customer racing cars; March Windtunnel, offering aerodynamic consultancy and wind tunnel facilities; Comtec; and March Racing, the latter operating the Leyton House-backed Grand Prix team. It had also acquired the share capital of Ron Tauranac's Ralt organisation, guaranteeing the group a continuing strong production base for the manufacture of customer racing cars both for F3 and for Indy, if that market should pick up again in the future.

I quote from the report: 'The concentration on F1 also precluded top management attention being given to the remainder of the group and the quality and performance of the principal products, especially those manufactured by March Engineering, suffered severely as a consequence.

'March Engineering was by far the largest contributor to these results, with a loss before taxation of approximately £3.5 million. For four years, from 1983 to 1986, March Engineering dominated the CART series, the American equivalent of F1, with its famous Indy cars. The company was also the leading constructor in both European and Japanese F3000 events. In the early part of 1988, however, a deterioration in the performance and reliability of the cars affected drivers' confidence and team owners' sponsorship prospects. As a consequence, March Engineering lost its pre-eminence in the markets for its two primary products. The consequent dramatic reduction in volume raised unit costs and prevented the recovery of overheads. At the same time it adversely affected the sale of spare parts and made substantial stock write-offs necessary. In the year to 31st October 1988, write-offs and bad debts amounted to £2.1 million.'

By this stage three directors – Charles Towns, Malcolm Shaw and Lachlan Shackleton-Fergus, all of whom had been recruited for their 'big business' management know-how – were either removed or invited to resign from the board. The business of building and selling racing cars was not a predictable affair which necessarily responded to the conventional touch of professional business management techniques, as they found to their disappointment.

In addition it was explained that the contribution to operating March Racing's F1 challenge exceeded sponsorship income and that neither Comtec nor March Engineering Projects Ltd, which was established to exploit the group's prototype engineering skills, proved profitable. The suggestion that March Racing was a drain on March Engineering's resources is fiercely rebutted by the F1 team, although those 'down the road' at Engineering's factory recall frequent visits from Leyton House personnel during 1988 with requests to help out with various urgent tasks connected with the Grand Prix build programme.

At the end of 1988 Leyton House boss Akira Akagi began negotiations with March Group with a view to his purchasing all the ordinary share capital not already owned by Herd or himself. On 13 February 1989, at the request of the company, dealings in the ordinary shares were suspended. The following day it was announced that the discussions with Akagi had been terminated and that the board was pursuing alternative proposals for the restructuring of the group with a view to retaining its independence.

Depending on whom one talked to at this somewhat confused time, differing versions were heard of precisely why the negotiations had collapsed. Akagi's financial advisers were said to have suggested he should withdraw the offer. Some March old hands believed he thought he could get the group for less than the originally discussed figure. Others speculated that he was less than happy with Herd's continued connection with the restructured company.

Either way, March made its own arrangements to refinance the group and, in a decision ratified by shareholders at an Extraordinary General Meeting of the company held on 30 May 1989, agreed to sell just March Racing, March Windtunnel and the F3000 operation to Akagi, who was also licensed to use the March name for a period of ten years in respect of F1 and F3000 activities.

The net consideration for this deal was £6.25 million and included the acquisition of Akagi's entire holding in March Group PLC. Further finance was raised by a rights issue of shares, generating £2.8 million for the company, which should comfortably assure its future. On completion of these proposals, Roger D. Young was installed as Chief Executive of March Group. Formerly Chief Executive of the London operations of the Swiss bank, Bank Julius Baer, it was confidently hoped that his industrial and financial experience would set March Group PLC on a secure road to a profitable future after an extremely difficult couple of years.

Appendix 2
Race results
Formula 1

KEY TO ABBREVIATIONS

Ret	Retired
DNQ	Did not qualify
UNC	Not classified
DIS	Disqualified
DNS	Did not start

(Capital letters denote World Championship qualifying rounds.)

1970

7 March, SOUTH AFRICAN GP, Kyalami

J. Stewart	701/2	3rd
J. Servoz-Gavin	701/4	Ret:engine
C. Amon	701/1	Ret:overheating
J. Siffert	701/5	10th
M. Andretti	701/3	Ret:overheating

22 March, Race of Champions, Brands Hatch

J. Stewart	701/2	1st
C. Amon	701/1	Ret:engine

19 April, SPANISH GP, Járama

J. Stewart	701/2	1st
J. Servoz-Gavin	701/7	5th
C. Amon	701/1	Ret:engine
J. Siffert	701/5	DNQ
M. Andretti	701/3	3rd

26 April, International Trophy, Silverstone

J. Stewart	701/2	2nd
C. Amon	701/1	1st

10 May, MONACO GP, Monte Carlo

J. Stewart	701/2	Ret:engine
J. Servoz-Gavin	701/7	DNQ
C. Amon	701/1	Ret:suspension
J. Siffert	701/5	8th
R. Peterson	701/8	7th

7 June, BELGIAN GP, Spa-Francorchamps

J. Stewart	701/2	Ret:engine
C. Amon	701/1	2nd
J. Siffert	701/5	10th
R. Peterson	701/8	UNC

21 June, DUTCH GP, Zandvoort

J. Stewart	701/2	2nd
F. Cevert	701/7	Ret:engine
C. Amon	701/1	Ret:clutch
J. Siffert	701/5	Ret:engine
R. Peterson	701/8	9th

5 July, FRENCH GP, Clermont-Ferrand

J. Stewart	701/4	9th
F. Cevert	701/7	11th
C. Amon	701/1	2nd
J. Siffert	701/5	Ret:accident
R. Peterson	701/8	Ret:transmission

19 July, BRITISH GP, Brands Hatch

J. Stewart	701/4	Ret:clutch line
F. Cevert	701/7	7th
C. Amon	701/1	5th
J. Siffert	701/5	Ret:suspension
M. Andretti	701/3	Ret:suspension
R. Peterson	701/8	9th

2 August, GERMAN GP, Hockenheim

J. Stewart	701/4	Ret:engine
F. Cevert	701/7	7th
C. Amon	701/1	Ret:engine
J. Siffert	701/5	8th
M. Andretti	701/3	Ret:gear selector
R. Peterson	701/8	Ret:engine
H. Hahne	701/10	DNQ

16 August, AUSTRIAN GP, Österreichring

J. Stewart	701/4	Ret:fuel-line
F. Cevert	701/7	Ret:engine
C. Amon	701/1	8th
J. Siffert	701/5	9th
M. Andretti	701/3	Ret:accident

6 September, ITALIAN GP, Monza

J. Stewart	701/4	2nd
F. Cevert	701/7	6th
C. Amon	701/1	7th
J. Siffert	701/5	Ret:engine
R. Peterson	701/8	Ret:engine

20 September, CANADIAN GP, St Jovite

F. Cevert	701/7	9th
C. Amon	701/1	3rd
J. Siffert	701/5	Ret:engine
R. Peterson	701/8	UNC

4 October, UNITED STATES GP, Watkins Glen

F. Cevert	701/7	Ret:lost wheel
C. Amon	701/1	5th
J. Siffert	701/5	9th
R. Peterson	701/8	11th

25 October, MEXICAN GP, Mexico City

F. Cevert	701/7	Ret:engine
C. Amon	701/1	4th
J. Siffert	701/5	Ret:engine

1971

24 January, Argentinian GP, Buenos Aires

H. Pescarolo	701/6	2nd
D. Bell	701/1	Ret:engine
J. Siffert	701/5	Ret:suspension

6 March, SOUTH AFRICAN GP, Kyalami

R. Peterson	711/2	10th
A. Soler-Roig	711/4	Ret:engine
A. de Adamich	711/1	13th
H. Pescarolo	701/6	11th
J. Love	701/9	Ret:transmission

21 March, Race of Champions, Brands Hatch

R. Peterson	711/3	Ret:brakeshaft
R. Allen	701/6	6th
M. Beuttler	701/11	Ret:metering unit

28 March, Questor GP, Ontario Motor Speedway, California

R. Peterson	711/2	13th
H. Pescarolo	711/3	Ret:suspension
D. Bell	701/6	Ret:suspension
J. Cannon	701/3	11th

9 April, Rothmans Trophy, Oulton Park

A. Rollinson	701/1	5th
M. Beuttler	701/11	Ret:broken bracket

18 April, SPANISH GP, Montjuich Park

R. Peterson	711/2	Ret:ignition
A. Soler-Roig	711/4	Ret:fuel-line
A. de Adamich	711/1	Ret:transmission
H. Pescarolo	711/3	Ret:wing/engine

8 May, International Trophy, Silverstone

R. Peterson	711/1	Ret:accident
H. Pescarolo	711/3	5th
M. Beuttler	701/11	7th

23 May, MONACO GP, Monte Carlo

R. Peterson	711/2	2nd
N. Galli	711/1	DNQ
A. Soler-Roig	711/4	DNQ
S. Barber	711/5	DNQ
H. Pescarolo	711/3	8th

13 June, Rindt Memorial Trophy, Hockenheim

R. Peterson	711/2	2nd
N. Galli	711/1	5th
A. Soler-Roig	711/4	8th
X. Perrot	701/5	UNC
M. Beuttler	701/11	Ret:gearbox
R. Allen	701/6	Ret:fuel leak
S. Barber	711/5	6th

20 June, DUTCH GP, Zandvoort

R. Peterson	711/2	4th
N. Galli	711/1	Ret:accident
A. Soler-Roig	711/4	Ret:engine
H. Pescarolo	711/3	UNC
S. Barber	711/5	UNC

4 July, FRENCH GP, Paul Ricard

R. Peterson	711/6	Ret:engine
A. de Adamich	711/1	Ret:engine
A. Soler-Roig	711/4	Ret:fuel pump
H. Pescarolo	711/3	Ret:gearbox
F. Mazet	701/5	13th
J. Max	701/6	UNC

17 July, BRITISH GP, Silverstone

R. Peterson	711/6	2nd
A. de Adamich	711/1	UNC
N. Galli	711/4	11th
H. Pescarolo	711/3	4th
M. Beuttler	711/2	Ret:engine

1 August, GERMAN GP, Nürburgring

R. Peterson	711/6	5th
N. Galli	711/4	12th
A. de Adamich	711/1	Ret:fuel injection
H. Pescarolo	711/3	Ret:suspension
M. Beuttler	711/2	DIS

15 August, AUSTRIAN GP, Österreichring

R. Peterson	711/6	8th
N. Galli	711/4	12th
N. Lauda	711/1	Ret:handling
H. Pescarolo	711/3	6th
M. Beuttler	711/2	UNC

21 August, Gold Cup, Oulton Park

J.-P. Jarier	701/10	8th
H. Pescarolo	711/3	Ret:accident
T. Trimmer	701/6	Ret:accident
M. Beuttler	701/11	Ret:engine

5 September, ITALIAN GP, Monza

R. Peterson	711/6	2nd
N. Galli	711/4	Ret:electrics
A. de Adamich	711/1	Ret:engine
H. Pescarolo	711/3	Ret:suspension
M. Beuttler	711/2	Ret:engine
J.-P. Jarier	701/10	UNC

19 September, CANADIAN GP, Mosport Park

R. Peterson	711/6	2nd
N. Galli	711/4	UNC
M. Beuttler	711/1	UNC
H. Pescarolo	711/3	DNS
S. Barber	711/5	Ret:engine

3 October, UNITED STATES GP, Watkins Glen

R. Peterson	711/6	3rd
N. Galli	711/4	Ret:broken wheel
H. Pescarolo	711/3	Ret:engine
S. Barber	711/5	UNC

24 October, John Player Trophy, Brands Hatch

R. Peterson	711/6	10th
H. Pescarolo	711/3	Ret:accident

1972

23 January, ARGENTINIAN GP, Buenos Aires

R. Peterson	721/1	6th
N. Lauda	721/2	11th
H. Pescarolo	721/3	8th

4 March, SOUTH AFRICAN GP, Kyalami

R. Peterson	721/1	5th
N. Lauda	721/2	7th
H. Pescarolo	721/3	11th
C. Pace	711/3	17th
R. Stommelen	721/4	13th

19 March, Race of Champions, Brands Hatch

R. Peterson	721X/1	12th
M. Beuttler	721/2	Ret:fuel pressure

30 March, Brazilian GP, Interlagos

R. Peterson	721/1	2nd
L. Bueno	721/2	6th
H. Pescarolo	721/3	Ret:throttle jam
C. Pace	711/3	Ret:throttle jam

23 April, International Trophy, Silverstone

H. Pescarolo	721/3	Ret:overheating

1 May, SPANISH GP, Járama

R. Peterson	721X/2	Ret:fuel leak
N. Lauda	721X/1	Ret:throttle
H. Pescarolo	721/3	11th
C. Pace	711/3	6th
M. Beuttler	721G/1	DNQ
R. Stommelen	721/4	Ret:accident

14 May, MONACO GP, Monte Carlo

R. Peterson	721X/2	11th
N. Lauda	721X/1	16th
H. Pescarolo	721/3	Ret:accident
C. Pace	711/3	17th
M. Beuttler	721G/1	13th
R. Stommelen	721/4	10th

29 May, Gold Cup, Oulton Park

R. Peterson	721X/2	Ret:collision

4 June, BELGIAN GP, Nivelles-Baulers

R. Peterson	721X/2	9th
N. Lauda	721X/1	12th
H. Pescarolo	721/3	UNC
C. Pace	711/3	5th
M. Beuttler	721G/1	Ret:driveshaft
R. Stommelen	721/4	11th

18 June, Gran Premio Republica Italiana, Vallelunga

N. Lauda	721/2	DNS
H. Pescarolo	711/3	Ret:suspension
M. Beuttler	721G/1	4th

2 July, FRENCH GP, Clermont-Ferrand

R. Peterson	721G/3	5th
N. Lauda	721G/2	Ret:driveshaft
H. Pescarolo	721/3	DNS
C. Pace	711/3	Ret:engine
M. Beuttler	721G/1	Ret:out of fuel
R. Stommelen	721/4	16th

15 July, BRITISH GP, Brands Hatch

R. Peterson	721G/3	7th
N. Lauda	721G/4	9th
C. Pace	711/3	Ret:differential
M. Beuttler	721G/1	13th
R. Stommelen	721/4	10th

30 July, GERMAN GP, Nürburgring

R. Peterson	721G/3	3rd
N. Lauda	721G/4	Ret:oil tank split
H. Pescarolo	721/3	Ret:accident
C. Pace	711/3	UNC
M. Beuttler	721G/1	8th
R. Stommelen	721/4	Ret:electrical

13 August, AUSTRIAN GP, Österreichring

R. Peterson	721G/3	12th
N. Lauda	721G/4	10th
H. Pescarolo	721/3	DNS
C. Pace	711/3	UNC
R. Stommelen	721/4	UNC
M. Beuttler	721G/1	Ret:metering unit

10 September, ITALIAN GP, Monza

R. Peterson	721G/3	9th
N. Lauda	721G/4	13th
H. Pescarolo	721/3	DNQ
C. Pace	711/3	Ret:accident
M. Beuttler	721G/1	10th

24 September, CANADIAN GP, Mosport Park

R. Peterson	721G/3	DIS
N. Lauda	721G/4	DIS
H. Pescarolo	721/3	13th
C. Pace	711/3	9th
M. Beuttler	721G/1	UNC
S. Barber	711/5	UNC

8 October, UNITED STATES GP, Watkins Glen

R. Peterson	721G/3	4th
N. Lauda	721G/4	19th
H. Pescarolo	721/3	14th
C. Pace	711/3	Ret:fuel injection
M. Beuttler	721G/1	13th
S. Barber	711/5	16th

22 October, John Player Challenge Trophy, Brands Hatch

R. Peterson	721G/3	8th
M. Beuttler	721G/1	15th
H. Pescarolo	721/3	Ret:steering
J. Watson	721/4	6th

1973

28 January, ARGENTINIAN GP, Buenos Aires		
J.-P. Jarier	721G/4	UNC
M. Beuttler	721G/2	Ret:suspension
11 February, BRAZILIAN GP, Interlagos		
J.-P. Jarier	721G/4	Ret:transmission
M. Beuttler	721G/2	Ret:engine
3 March, SOUTH AFRICAN GP, Kyalami		
J.-P. Jarier	721G/4	UNC
M. Beuttler	721G/2	UNC
29 April, SPANISH GP, Montjuich Park		
H. Pescarolo	731/4	8th
M. Beuttler	731/2	7th
20 May, BELGIAN GP, Zolder		
J.-P. Jarier	731/4	Ret:accident
M. Beuttler	731/2	Ret:accident
3 June, MONACO GP, Monte Carlo		
J.-P. Jarier	731/4	Ret:gearbox
M. Beuttler	731/2	Ret:engine
J. Hunt	731/3	9th
D. Purley	731/1	Ret:fuel system
17 June, SWEDISH GP, Anderstorp		
J.-P. Jarier	731/4	Ret:throttle cable
M. Beuttler	731/2	8th
R. Wisell	731/1	DNS
1 July, FRENCH GP, Paul Ricard		
J.-P. Jarier	731/4	Ret:driveshaft
R. Wisell	731/2	Ret:engine
J. Hunt	731/3	6th
14 July, BRITISH GP, Silverstone		
R. Williamson	731/4	Ret:accident
M. Beuttler	731/2	11th
J. Hunt	731/3	4th
D. Purley	731/1	DNS
29 July, DUTCH GP, Zandvoort		
R. Williamson	731/4	Ret:accident
M. Beuttler	731/2	Ret:electrics
J. Hunt	731/3	3rd
D. Purley	731/1	Ret:withdrew
5 August, GERMAN GP, Nürburgring		
M. Beuttler	731/2	16th
D. Purley	731/1	15th
19 August, AUSTRIAN GP, Österreichring		
J.-P. Jarier	731/1	Ret:engine
J. Hunt	731/3	Ret:metering unit
M. Beuttler	731/2	Ret:damaged oil-cooler
9 September, ITALIAN GP, Monza		
M. Beuttler	731/2	Ret:gear lever
J. Hunt	731/3	DNS
D. Purley	731/1	9th
23 September, CANADIAN GP, Mosport Park		
J.-P. Jarier	731/1	UNC
M. Beuttler	731/2	Ret:engine
J. Hunt	731/3	7th
7 October, UNITED STATES GP, Watkins Glen		
J.-P. Jarier	731/1	11th
J. Hunt	731/3	2nd
M. Beuttler	731/2	10th

1974

13 January, ARGENTINIAN GP, Buenos Aires		
H.-J. Stuck	741/1	Ret:clutch
H. Ganley	741/2	8th
27 January, BRAZILIAN GP, Interlagos		
H.-J. Stuck	741/1	Ret:driveshaft
H. Ganley	741/2	Ret:ignition switch
3 February, GP Presidenta Medici, Brasilia		
H.-J. Stuck	741/1	Ret:wing broke
H. Ganley	741/2	6th
30 March, SOUTH AFRICAN GP, Kyalami		
H.-J. Stuck	741/1	5th
V. Brambilla	741/2	10th
7 April, International Trophy, Silverstone		
N. Takahara	741/2	11th
28 April, SPANISH GP, Járama		
H.-J. Stuck	741/1	4th
V. Brambilla	741/2	DNS
12 May, BELGIAN GP, Nivelles-Baulers		
H.-J. Stuck	741/1	Ret:clutch
V. Brambilla	741/2	9th
26 May, MONACO GP, Monte Carlo		
H.-J. Stuck	741/1	Ret:accident
V. Brambilla	741/2	Ret:accident
9 June, SWEDISH GP, Anderstorp		
R. Wisell	741/1	Ret:suspension
V. Brambilla	741/2	10th
23 June, DUTCH GP, Zandvoort		
H.-J. Stuck	741/1	Ret:accident
V. Brambilla	741/2	10th
7 July, FRENCH GP, Dijon-Prenois		
H.-J. Stuck	741/1	DNQ
V. Brambilla	741/2	11th
20 July, BRITISH GP, Brands Hatch		
H.-J. Stuck	741/1	Ret:accident
V. Brambilla	741/2	Ret:fuel pressure
M. Wilds	731/3	DNQ
4 August, GERMAN GP, Nürburgring		
H.-J. Stuck	741/1	7th
V. Brambilla	741/2	13th
18 August, AUSTRIAN GP, Österreichring		
H.-J. Stuck	741/1	11th
V. Brambilla	741/2	6th
8 September, ITALIAN GP, Monza		
H.-J. Stuck	741/1	Ret:chassis breakage
V. Brambilla	741/2	Ret:accident
22 September, CANADIAN GP, Mosport Park		
H.-J. Stuck	741/1	Ret:engine
V. Brambilla	741/2	DNQ
6 October, UNITED STATES GP, Watkins Glen		
H.-J. Stuck	741/1	DNQ
V. Brambilla	741/2	Ret:metering unit

1975

12 January, ARGENTINIAN GP, Buenos Aires

V. Brambilla	741/2	9th

26 January, BRAZILIAN GP, Interlagos

V. Brambilla	741/2	Ret:engine

1 March, SOUTH AFRICAN GP, Kyalami

V. Brambilla	751/1	Ret:oil leak
L. Lombardi	741/2	Ret:fuel pressure

16 March, Race of Champions, Brands Hatch

L. Lombardi	751/2	Ret:handling

12 April, International Trophy, Silverstone

L. Lombardi	751/2	12th

27 April, SPANISH GP, Montjuich Park

V. Brambilla	751/3	5th
L. Lombardi	751/2	6th

11 May, MONACO GP, Monte Carlo

V. Brambilla	751/3	Ret:accident
L. Lombardi	751/2	DNQ

25 May, BELGIAN GP, Zolder

V. Brambilla	751/3	Ret:brakes
L. Lombardi	751/2	Ret:engine

8 June, SWEDISH GP, Anderstorp

V. Brambilla	751/3	Ret:driveshaft
L. Lombardi	751/2	Ret:metering unit

22 June, DUTCH GP, Zandvoort

V. Brambilla	751/3	Ret:collision
L. Lombardi	751/2	14th

6 July, FRENCH GP, Paul Ricard

V. Brambilla	751/3	Ret:damper
L. Lombardi	751/2	18th

19 July, BRITISH GP, Silverstone

V. Brambilla	751/3	6th
H.-J. Stuck	751/2	Ret:accident
L. Lombardi	751/1	Ret:ignition
M. Donohue	751/4	5th

3 August, GERMAN GP, Nürburgring

V. Brambilla	751/3	Ret:suspension
H.-J. Stuck	751/2	Ret:engine
L. Lombardi	751/1	7th
M. Donohue	751/4	Ret:puncture

17 August, AUSTRIAN GP, Österreichring

V. Brambilla	751/3	1st
H.-J. Stuck	751/2	Ret:accident
L. Lombardi	751/1	17th
M. Donohue	751/4	DNS

24 August, Swiss GP, Dijon-Prenois

V. Brambilla	751/3	11th

7 September, ITALIAN GP, Monza

V. Brambilla	751/3	Ret:clutch
H.-J. Stuck	751/2	Ret:accident damage
L. Lombardi	751/1	Ret:accident

5 October, UNITED STATES GP, Watkins Glen

V. Brambilla	751/3	7th
H.-J. Stuck	751/2	8th

1976

25 January, BRAZILIAN GP, Interlagos

V. Brambilla	761/1	Ret:oil leak
H.-J. Stuck	761/2	4th
L. Lombardi	761/3	14th

6 March, SOUTH AFRICAN GP, Kyalami

V. Brambilla	761/1	8th
H.-J. Stuck	761/2	12th
R. Peterson	761/3	Ret:collision

14 March, Race of Champions, Brands Hatch

V. Brambilla	761/1	4th

28 March, UNITED STATES GP WEST, Long Beach, California

V. Brambilla	761/1	Ret:collision
H.-J. Stuck	761/2	Ret:collision
R. Peterson	761/3	10th

11 April, International Trophy, Silverstone

V. Brambilla	761/1	2nd

2 May, SPANISH GP, Járama

V. Brambilla	761/1	Ret:accident
H.-J. Stuck	761/2	Ret:gearbox
R. Peterson	761/3	Ret:transmission
A. Merzario	761/4	Ret:gear linkage

16 May, BELGIAN GP, Zolder

V. Brambilla	761/1	Ret:driveshaft
H.-J. Stuck	761/2	Ret:suspension
R. Peterson	761/3	Ret:accident
A. Merzario	761/4	Ret:engine

30 May, MONACO GP, Monte Carlo

V. Brambilla	761/1	Ret:suspension
H.-J. Stuck	761/2	4th
R. Peterson	761/3	Ret:accident
A. Merzario	761/4	DNQ

13 June, SWEDISH GP, Anderstorp

V. Brambilla	761/1	10th
H.-J. Stuck	761/2	Ret:engine
R. Peterson	761/3	7th
A. Merzario	761/4	14th

4 July, FRENCH GP, Paul Ricard

V. Brambilla	761/1	Ret:engine
H.-J. Stuck	761/2	7th
R. Peterson	761/3	19th
A. Merzario	761/4	9th

18 July, BRITISH GP, Brands Hatch

V. Brambilla	761/1	Ret:suspension
H.-J. Stuck	761/2	Ret:accident
R. Peterson	761/3	Ret:fuel pressure
A. Merzario	761/4	Ret:engine

1 August, GERMAN GP, Nürburgring

V. Brambilla	761/1	Ret:accident
H.-J. Stuck	761/2	Ret:clutch
R. Peterson	761/3	Ret:accident
A. Merzario	761/4	Ret:brakes

15 August, AUSTRIAN GP, Österreichring

V. Brambilla	761/1	Ret:accident
H.-J. Stuck	761/2	Ret:fuel pressure
R. Peterson	761/6	6th

29 August, DUTCH GP, Zandvoort

V. Brambilla	761/1	6th
H.-J. Stuck	761/2	Ret:engine
R. Peterson	761/6	Ret:engine

12 September, ITALIAN GP, Monza

V. Brambilla	761/1	7th
H.-J. Stuck	761/2	Ret:accident
R. Peterson	761/6	1st

3 October, CANADIAN GP, Mosport Park

V. Brambilla	761/1	14th
H.-J. Stuck	761/2	Ret:handling
R. Peterson	761/6	9th

10 October, UNITED STATES GP, Watkins Glen

V. Brambilla	761/1	Ret:burst tyre
H.-J. Stuck	761/2	5th
R. Peterson	761/6	Ret:chassis breakage

24 October, JAPANESE GP, Fuji

V. Brambilla	761/1	Ret:engine
H.-J. Stuck	761/2	Ret:electrics
R. Peterson	761/6	Ret:engine cut out

1977

9 January, ARGENTINIAN GP, Buenos Aires

I. Scheckter	761B/1	Ret:battery
A. Ribeiro	761B/2	Ret:gear lever

23 January, BRAZILIAN GP, Interlagos

I. Scheckter	761B/1	Ret:transmission
A. Ribeiro	761B/2	Ret:engine

5 March, SOUTH AFRICAN GP, Kyalami

H.-J. Stuck	761B/1	Ret:engine
A. Ribeiro	761B/2	Ret:engine
B. Lunger	761/2	14th

20 March, Race of Champions, Brands Hatch

B. Hayje	761B/3	7th
A. Ribeiro	761B/2	Ret:electrics
B. Henton	761/T	4th

3 April, UNITED STATES GP WEST, Long Beach, California

B. Henton	761B/1	10th
A. Ribeiro	761B/3	Ret:gearbox
B. Lunger	761/2	Ret:collision

8 May, SPANISH GP, Járama

I. Scheckter	761B/1	11th
A. Ribeiro	761B/3	DNQ
B. Lunger	761/2	10th
B. Henton	761/T	DNQ
B. Hayje	761/3	DNQ
A. Merzario	761B/2	Ret:suspension

22 May, MONACO GP, Monte Carlo

I. Scheckter	761B/1	DNQ
A. Ribeiro	761B/3	DNQ
B. Hayje	761/3	DNQ
A. Merzario	761B/2	DNQ

5 June, BELGIAN GP, Zolder

I. Scheckter	761B/1	Ret:accident
A. Ribeiro	761B/3	DNQ
P. Neve	761/7	10th
B. Hayje	761/3	15th
A. Merzario	761B/2	14th
B. de Dryver	761/T	DNQ

19 June, SWEDISH GP, Anderstorp

I. Scheckter	761B/1	Ret:driveshaft
A. Ribeiro	761B/3	DNQ
B. Hayje	761/3	DNQ
M. Kozarowitsky	761/8	DNQ

3 July, FRENCH GP, Dijon-Prenois

I. Scheckter	761B/1	UNC
A. Ribeiro	761B/3	DNQ
B. Hayje	761/3	DNQ
A. Merzario	761B/2	Ret:gearbox

16 July, BRITISH GP, Silverstone

I. Scheckter	761B/1	Ret:accident
A. Ribeiro	761B/3	DNQ
P. Neve	761/7	10th
M. Kozarowitsky	761/8	DNQ
A. Sutcliffe	761/3	DNQ
B. Henton	761/T	DNQ
A. Merzario	761B/2	Ret:driveshaft

31 July, GERMAN GP, Hockenheim

I. Scheckter	761B/1	Ret:clutch
A. Ribeiro	761B/3	8th
P. Neve	761/7	DNQ
A. Merzario	761B/2	DNQ

14 August, AUSTRIAN GP, Österreichring

I. Scheckter	761B/1	Ret:accident
A. Ribeiro	761B/3	DNQ
P. Neve	761/7	9th
A. Merzario	761B/2	Ret:gear linkage
B. Henton	761/T	DNQ

28 August, DUTCH GP, Zandvoort

I. Scheckter	771/2	10th
A. Ribeiro	761B/3	11th
P. Neve	761/7	DNQ
A. Merzario	761B/2	DNQ
B. Hayje	761/3	DNQ
M. Bleekemolen	761/8	DNQ

11 September, ITALIAN GP, Monza

I. Scheckter	771/2	Ret:transmission
A. Ribeiro	761B/3	DNQ
P. Neve	761/7	7th

2 October, UNITED STATES GP, Watkins Glen

I. Scheckter	771/2	Ret:accident
A. Ribeiro	761B/3	15th
P. Neve	761/7	18th

9 October, CANADIAN GP, Mosport Park

I. Scheckter	771/2	Ret:engine
A. Ribeiro	761B/3	8th
P. Neve	761/7	Ret:engine

23 October, JAPANESE GP, Fuji

I. Scheckter	771/2	DNS
A. Ribeiro	761B/3	12th

1981

7 February, South African GP, Kyalami		
D. Daly	811/02	11th
E. Salazar	811/03	Ret:gearbox
15 March, UNITED STATES GP WEST, Long Beach, California		
D. Daly	811/02	DNQ
E. Salazar	811/03	DNQ
29 March, BRAZILIAN GP, Rio		
D. Daly	811/02	DNQ
E. Salazar	811/03	DNQ
12 April, ARGENTINIAN GP, Buenos Aires		
D. Daly	811/01	DNQ
E. Salazar	811/03	DNQ
3 May, SAN MARINO GP, Imola		
D. Daly	811/01	DNQ
E. Salazar	811/03	Ret:oil pressure
17 May, BELGIAN GP, Zolder		
D. Daly	811/05	DNQ
E. Salazar	811/04	DNQ
31 May, MONACO GP, Monte Carlo		
D. Daly	811/05	DNQ
E. Salazar	811/04	DNQ
21 June, SPANISH GP, Járama		
D. Daly	811/04	16th
E. Salazar	811/03	14th
5 July, FRENCH GP, Dijon-Prenois		
D. Daly	811/04	Ret:engine
E. Salazar	811/03	Ret:suspension
18 July, BRITISH GP, Silverstone		
D. Daly	811/06	7th
E. Salazar	811/03	DNQ
2 August, GERMAN GP, Hockenheim		
D. Daly	811/06	Ret:tie rod
16 August, AUSTRIAN GP, Österreichring		
D. Daly	811/06	11th
30 August, DUTCH GP, Zandvoort		
D. Daly	811/06	Ret:suspension
13 September, ITALIAN GP, Monza		
D. Daly	811/06	Ret:gearbox
27 September, CANADIAN GP, Montreal		
D. Daly	811/06	8th
17 October, LAS VEGAS GP, Las Vegas, Nevada		
D. Daly	811/06	DNQ

1982

23 January, SOUTH AFRICAN GP, Kyalami		
J. Mass	821/08	12th
R. Boesel	821/07	15th
21 March, BRAZILIAN GP, Rio		
J. Mass	821/08	10th
R. Boesel	821/09	Ret:puncture
4 April, UNITED STATES GP WEST, Long Beach, California		
J. Mass	821/08	8th
R. Boesel	821/09	9th
9 May, BELGIAN GP, Zolder		
J. Mass	821/08	Ret:engine
R. Boesel	821/09	8th
E. de Villota	821/07	DNQ
23 May, MONACO GP, Monte Carlo		
J. Mass	821/08	DNQ
R. Boesel	821/09	DNQ
E. de Villota	821/07	DNQ
6 June, UNITED STATES GP, Detroit, Michigan		
J. Mass	821/08	7th
R. Boesel	821/09	Ret:accident
E. de Villota	821/07	DNQ
13 June, CANADIAN GP, Montreal		
J. Mass	821/08	11th
R. Boesel	821/09	Ret:engine
E. de Villota	821/07	DNQ
3 July, DUTCH GP, Zandvoort		
J. Mass	821/11	Ret:engine
R. Boesel	821/10	Ret:engine
E. de Villota	821/07	DNQ
18 July, BRITISH GP, Brands Hatch		
J. Mass	821/11	10th
R. Boesel	821/10	DNQ
25 July, FRENCH GP, Paul Ricard		
J. Mass	821/10	Ret:accident
R. Boesel	821/10	DNQ
8 August, GERMAN GP, Hockenheim		
R. Keegan	821/11	DNQ
R. Boesel	821/10	Ret:puncture
15 August, AUSTRIAN GP, Österreichring		
R. Keegan	821/11	Ret:bent steering arm
R. Boesel	821/10	DNQ
29 August, SWISS GP, Dijon-Prenois		
R. Keegan	821/11	Ret:spun off
R. Boesel	821/10	Ret:oil leak
12 September, ITALIAN GP, Monza		
R. Keegan	821/11	DNQ
R. Boesel	821/10	DNQ
25 September, LAS VEGAS GP, Las Vegas, Nevada		
R. Keegan	821/07	12th
R. Boesel	821/11	13th

1987

12 April, BRAZILIAN GP, Rio		
I. Capelli	87P/1	DNS
3 May, SAN MARINO GP, Imola		
I. Capelli	871/1	Ret:ignition
17 May, BELGIAN GP, Spa-Francorchamps		
I. Capelli	871/1	Ret:engine
31 May, MONACO GP, Monte Carlo		
I. Capelli	871/1	6th
21 June, UNITED STATES GP, Detroit, Michigan		
I. Capelli	871/1	Ret:broken battery
5 July, FRENCH GP, Paul Ricard		
I. Capelli	871/1	Ret:engine
12 July, BRITISH GP, Silverstone		
I. Capelli	871/1	Ret:gearbox
26 July, GERMAN GP, Hockenheim		
I. Capelli	871/3	Ret:electrics
9 August, HUNGARIAN GP, Hungaroring		
I. Capelli	871/1	10th
16 August, AUSTRIAN GP, Österreichring		
I. Capelli	871/3	11th
6 September, ITALIAN GP, Monza		
I. Capelli	871/1	13th
20 September, PORTUGUESE GP, Estoril		
I. Capelli	871/1	9th
27 September, SPANISH GP, Jerez		
I. Capelli	871/1	12th
18 October, MEXICAN GP, Mexico City		
I. Capelli	871/1	Ret:engine
1 November, JAPANESE GP, Suzuka		
I. Capelli	871/1	Ret:accident
15 November, AUSTRALIAN GP, Adelaide		
I. Capelli	871/1	Ret:spun off

1988

3 April, BRAZILIAN GP, Rio		
M. Gugelmin	881/2	Ret:clutch
I. Capelli	881/3	Ret:faulty warning light
1 May, SAN MARINO GP, Imola		
M. Gugelmin	881/2	15th
I. Capelli	881/3	Ret:gearbox
15 May, MONACO GP, Monte Carlo		
M. Gugelmin	881/2	Ret:electrics
I. Capelli	881/3	10th
29 May, MEXICAN GP, Mexico City		
M. Gugelmin	881/2	Ret:electrical
I. Capelli	881/3	16th
12 June, CANADIAN GP, Montreal		
M. Gugelmin	881/2	Ret:gearbox
I. Capelli	881/3	5th
19 June, UNITED STATES GP, Detroit, Michigan		
M. Gugelmin	881/2	Ret:engine
I. Capelli	881/3	DNS
3 July, FRENCH GP, Paul Ricard		
M. Gugelmin	881/2	8th
I. Capelli	881/3	9th
10 July, BRITISH GP, Silverstone		
M. Gugelmin	881/2	4th
I. Capelli	881/3	Ret:engine
24 July, GERMAN GP, Hockenheim		
M. Gugelmin	881/2	8th
I. Capelli	881/3	5th
7 August, HUNGARIAN GP, Hungaroring		
M. Gugelmin	881/2	5th
I. Capelli	881/3	Ret:engine
28 August, BELGIAN GP, Spa-Francorchamps		
M. Gugelmin	881/2	Ret:spun off
I. Capelli	881/5	3rd
11 September, ITALIAN GP, Monza		
M. Gugelmin	881/2	8th
I. Capelli	881/5	5th
25 September, PORTUGUESE GP, Estoril		
M. Gugelmin	881/2	Ret:engine
I. Capelli	881/5	2nd
2 October, SPANISH GP, Jerez		
M. Gugelmin	881/2	7th
I. Capelli	881/5	Ret:engine
30 October, JAPANESE GP, Suzuka		
M. Gugelmin	881/3	10th
I. Capelli	881/5	Ret:electrics
13 November, AUSTRALIAN GP, Adelaide		
M. Gugelmin	881/2	Ret:collision
I. Capelli	881/5	6th

1989

26 March, BRAZILIAN GP, Rio		
M. Gugelmin	881/6	3rd
I. Capelli	881/5	Ret:suspension
23 April, SAN MARINO GP, Imola		
M. Gugelmin	881/6	Ret:gearbox
I. Capelli	881/5	Ret:accident
7 May, MONACO GP, Monte Carlo		
M. Gugelmin	881/6	Ret:engine
I. Capelli	CG891/2	Ret:electrics
28 May, MEXICAN GP, Mexico City		
M. Gugelmin	CG891/3	DNQ
I. Capelli	CG891/3	Ret:c/v joint
4 June, UNITED STATES GP, Phoenix, Arizona		
M. Gugelmin	CG891/3	DIS
I. Capelli	CG891/2	Ret:transmission
18 June, CANADIAN GP, Montreal		
M. Gugelmin	CG891/2	Ret:electrics
I. Capelli	CG891/3	Ret:accident
9 July, FRENCH GP, Paul Ricard		
M. Gugelmin	CG891/3	UNC
I. Capelli	CG891/4	Ret:engine

Indy cars

Top-12 race finishes only; Cosworth-DFX engines used unless stated otherwise.

1981

21 June, Pocono, Pennsylvania		
A.J. Foyt	81C	1st
5 September, Milwaukee, Wisconsin		
T. Sneva	81C	1st
31 October, Phoenix, Arizona		
T. Sneva	81C	1st

1982

28 March, Phoenix, Arizona		
D. Carter	82C	6th
T. Sneva	81C	7th
H. Haywood	82C	10th
T. Bettenhausen	82C	12th
1 May, Atlanta, Georgia		
D. Sullivan	82C	3rd
J. Hickman	81C	7th
G. Smiley	81C	9th
D. Carter	82C	10th
30 May, Indianapolis 500, Indianapolis Motor Speedway, Indiana		
D. Carter	82C	3rd
T. Sneva	82C	4th
D. Whittington	81C	6th
J. Hickman	81C	7th
H. Holmes	82C	10th
B. Rahal	82C	11th
13 June, Milwaukee, Wisconsin		
A.J. Foyt	82C	2nd
T. Sneva	82C	4th
J. Parsons	82C	6th
G. Brabham	82C	7th
J. Garza	81C	8th
H. Holmes	82C	10th
4 July, Cleveland, Ohio		
B. Rahal	82C	1st
G. Brabham	82C	6th
18 July, Michigan International Speedway		
B. Rahal	82C	3rd
G. Brabham	82C	7th
M. Mosley	82C	8th
J. Hickman	82C	9th
T. Bettenhausen	82C	10th
H. Holmes	82C	11th
1 August, Milwaukee, Wisconsin		
T. Sneva	82C	1st
B. Rahal	82C	2nd
H. Holmes	82C	4th
D. Carter	82C	6th
M. Mosley	82C	7th
J. Garza	82C	8th
G. Brabham	82C	10th
15 August, Pocono, Pennsylvania		
B. Rahal	82C	3rd
G. Brabham	82C	4th
T. Bettenhausen	82C	5th
J. Parsons	82C	7th
29 August, Riverside, California		
T. Sneva	82C	2nd
J. Rutherford	82C	3rd
A. Unser Jnr	82C	5th
19 September, Elkhart Lake, Wisconsin		
H. Rebaque	82C	1st
B. Rahal	82C	3rd
T. Bettenhausen	82C	7th
T. Sneva	82C	9th
H. Holmes	82C	10th
D. Carter	82C	11th
J. Rutherford	82C	12th
26 September, Michigan International Speedway		
B. Rahal	82C	1st
G. Brabham	82C	3rd
T. Bettenhausen	82C	4th
H. Holmes	82C	5th
M. Mosley	82C	7th
6 November, Phoenix, Arizona		
T. Sneva	82C	1st
B. Rahal	82C	5th
T. Bettenhausen	82C	6th
G. Bettenhausen	82C	9th
H. Holmes	82C	10th
D. Carter	82C	11th
M. Mosley	82C	12th

1983

17 April, Atlanta, Georgia		
H. Holmes	83C	9th
T. Bettenhausen	82C	10th
29 May, Indianapolis 500, Indianapolis Motor Speedway, Indiana		
T. Sneva	83C	1st
K. Cogan	83C	5th
H. Holmes	83C	6th
D. Carter	83C	7th
S. Brayton	83C	9th
12 June, Milwaukee, Wisconsin		
T. Sneva	83C	1st
T. Fabi	83C	4th
M. Mosley	82C	5th
B. Rahal	83C	6th
H. Holmes	83C	7th
T. Bettenhausen	83C	10th
3 July, Cleveland, Ohio		
T. Fabi	83C	3rd
M. Mosley	83C	4th
T. Sneva	83C	5th
D. Carter	82C	8th
D. Wilson	83C	10th
H. Holmes	83C	12th
17 July, Michigan International Speedway		
B. Rahal	83C	5th
D. Carter	82C	6th
D. Ferguson	81C	11th
S. Brayton	83C	12th
31 July, Elkhart Lake, Wisconsin		
D. Carter	82C	7th
14 August, Pocono, Pennsylvania		
T. Fabi	83C	1st
A. Unser Jnr	83C	2nd
M. Mosley	83C	4th
B. Rahal	83C	5th
D. Carter	82C	6th
T. Bettenhausen	83C	10th
28 August, Riverside, California		
B. Rahal	83C	1st
T. Fabi	83C	2nd
T. Sneva	83C	5th
D. Carter	82C	7th
T. Bettenhausen	83C	8th
D. Ongais	83C	10th
11 September, Mid Ohio		
T. Fabi	83C	1st
B. Rahal	83C	3rd
H. Holmes	83C	8th
D. Carter	82C	10th
18 September, Michigan International Speedway		
B. Rahal	83C	2nd
T. Fabi	83C	3rd
H. Holmes	83C	8th
T. Bettenhausen	83C	9th
M. Mosley	83C	11th
9 October, Las Vegas, Nevada		
D. Carter	82C	6th
B. Rahal	83C	9th
23 October, Laguna Seca, California		
T. Fabi	83C	1st
H. Holmes	83C	5th
B. Rahal	83C	7th
30 October, Phoenix, Arizona		
T. Fabi	83C	1st
T. Sneva	83C	3rd
K. Cogan	83C	6th
Mike Andretti	83C	9th
D. Carter	82C	11th
T. Bettenhausen	83C	12th

1984

1 April, Long Beach, California		
G. Brabham	84C	2nd
T. Sneva	84C	3rd
E. Fittipaldi	83C	5th
J. Villeneuve	83C	6th
D. Daly	84C	7th
Mike Andretti	84C	10th
15 April, Phoenix, Arizona		
T. Sneva	84C	1st
H. Holmes	84C	2nd
Mike Andretti	84C	3rd
D. Simon	84C	4th
D. Ongais	84C	5th
B. Rahal	84C	7th
G. Johncock	84C	10th
E. Fittipaldi	83C	12th
27 May, Indianapolis 500, Indianapolis Motor Speedway, Indiana		
R. Mears	84C	1st
R. Guerrero	84C	2nd
A. Unser	84C	3rd
A. Holbert	84C	4th
Mike Andretti	84C	5th
A.J. Foyt	84C	6th
B. Rahal	84C	7th
H. Johnson	84C	8th
D. Ongais	84C	9th
J. Garza	84C	10th
G. Snider	84C	11th
D. Firestone	82/83C	12th
3 June, Milwaukee, Wisconsin		
T. Sneva	84C	1st
R. Mears	84C	2nd
A. Unser Jnr	84C	3rd
Mike Andretti	84C	4th
A. Unser	84C	5th
G. Johncock	84C	6th
H. Holmes	84C	7th
D. Ongais	84C	10th
T. Fabi	84C	12th

17 June, Portland, Oregon

A. Unser Jnr	84C	1st
G. Brabham	84C	2nd
T. Fabi	84C	3rd
D. Daly	84C	4th
T. Sneva	84C	5th
J. Villeneuve	83C	6th
J. Garza	84C	7th
G. Johncock	84C	9th
R. Mears	84C	10th
D. Ongais	84C	11th
Mike Andretti	84C	12th

1 July, Meadowlands, New York

G. Brabham	84C	3rd
A. Unser Jnr	84C	4th
A. Holbert	84C	5th
T. Sneva	84C	6th
E. Fittipaldi	84C	7th
A. Unser	84C	8th
C. Ganassi	84C	9th
R. Mears	84C	10th
B. Rahal	84C	11th
G. Johncock	84C	12th

8 July, Cleveland, Ohio

C. Ganassi	84C	2nd
Mike Andretti	84C	3rd
R. Mears	84C	4th
R. Guerrero	84C	5th
D. Daly	84C	6th
A. Holbert	84C	7th
G. Brabham	84C	8th
J. Villeneuve	84C	9th
A. Unser	84C	10th
S. Brayton	84C	11th
H. Holmes	84C	12th

15 July, Michigan International Speedway

T. Sneva	84C	2nd
R. Mears	84C	3rd
G. Johncock	84C	4th
R. Guerrero	84C	5th
D. Carter	84C	6th
J. Rutherford	84C	7th
K. Cogan	84C	8th
G. Brabham	84C	9th
J. Garza	84C	11th
D. Simon	84C	12th

5 August, Elkhart Lake, Wisconsin

B. Rahal	84C	2nd
A. Unser	84C	3rd
R. Mears	84C	4th
G. Brabham	84C	5th
J. Paul Jnr	84C	6th
J. Garza	84C	7th
A. Luyendyk	84C	8th
G. Johncock	84C	9th
K. Cogan	84C	10th
R. Guerrero	84C	11th
S. Brayton	84C	12th

19 August, Pocono, Pennsylvania

R. Mears	84C	2nd
B. Rahal	84C	3rd
T. Sneva	84C	4th
D. Ongais	84C	5th
S. Brayton	84C	6th
D. Carter	84C	7th
A. Unser	84C	8th
H. Holmes	84C	9th
G. Bettenhausen	84C	10th
G. Johncock	84C	11th
D. Simon	84C	12th

2 September, Mid Ohio

B. Rahal	84C	2nd
E. Fittipaldi	84C	4th
R. Mears	84C	5th
H. Holmes	84C	6th
T. Sneva	84C	7th
A. Unser	84C	8th
J. Paul Jnr	84C	9th
G. Johncock	84C	10th
J. Garza	84C	11th
S. Brayton	84C	12th

9 September, Sanair, Quebec, Canada

B. Rahal	84C	2nd
Mike Andretti	84C	3rd
J. Garza	84C	4th
J. Rutherford	84C	5th
A. Unser Jnr	84C	6th
J. Villeneuve	84C	8th
H. Holmes	84C	9th
S. Brayton	84C	11th
D. Simon	84C	12th

22/23 September, Michigan International Speedway

T. Sneva	84C	2nd
D. Ongais	84C	3rd
A. Unser	84C	4th
B. Rahal	84C	5th
A. Unser Jnr	84C	6th
Mike Andretti	84C	7th
H. Holmes	84C	8th
J. Garza	84C	10th
G. Brabham	84C	11th
E. Fittipaldi	84C	12th

14 October, Phoenix, Arizona

B. Rahal	84C	1st
A. Unser Jnr	84C	2nd
Mike Andretti	84C	3rd
T. Sneva	84C	4th
D. Ongais	84C	5th
D. Carter	84C	7th
J. Garza	84C	8th
J. Villeneuve	84C	9th
J. Rutherford	84C	11th

21 October, Laguna Seca, California

B. Rahal	84C	1st
Mike Andretti	84C	3rd
A. Unser Jnr	84C	4th
G. Brabham	84C	5th
A. Unser	84C	6th
R. Guerrero	84C	7th
B. Giacomelli	84C	8th
T. Sneva	84C	10th
J. Paul Jnr	84C	11th

11 November, Las Vegas, Nevada

T. Sneva	84C	1st
J. Paul Jnr	84C	3rd
A. Unser Jnr	84C	4th
G. Brabham	84C	5th
R. Guerrero	84C	6th
B. Rahal	84C	7th
S. Brayton	84C	8th

1985

14 April, Long Beach, California

E. Fittipaldi	85C	2nd
D. Sullivan	85C	3rd
A. Unser	85C	5th
G. Brabham	85C	6th
J. Villeneuve	85C	7th
J. Rutherford	85C	10th
S. Brayton	85C	11th

26 May, Indianapolis 500, Indianapolis Motor Speedway, Indiana

D. Sullivan	85C	1st
R. Guerrero	85C	3rd
A. Unser	85C	4th
J. Parsons	85C	5th
J. Rutherford	85C	6th
Mike Andretti	85C	8th
K. Cogan	85C	11th

2 June, Milwaukee, Wisconsin

R. Mears	85C	3rd
D. Sullivan	85C	4th
D. Carter	85C	5th
R. Guerrero	85C	6th
J. Garza	85C	7th
E. Fittipaldi	85C	8th
B. Rahal	85C	9th
G. Brabham	85C	12th

16 June, Portland, Oregon

E. Fittipaldi	85C	3rd
A. Unser	85C	4th
K. Cogan	85C	5th
S. Brayton	85C	6th
M. Roe	85C	7th
P. Halsmer	85C	8th
J. Rutherford	85C	9th
B. Giacomelli	85C	10th
R. Boesel	85C	11th
J. Garza	85C	12th

30 June, Meadowlands, New York

E. Fittipaldi	85C	2nd
A. Unser	85C	3rd
Mike Andretti	85C	4th
B. Giacomelli	85C	5th
T. Sneva	85C	6th
K. Cogan	85C	7th
R. Boesel	85C	11th
J. Lammers	85C	12th

7 July, Cleveland, Ohio

G. Brabham	85C	2nd
A. Unser	85C	3rd
J. Villeneuve	85C	4th
J. Garza	85C	6th
Mike Andretti	85C	7th
E. Fittipaldi	85C	8th
K. Cogan	85C	9th
B. Giacomelli	85C	10th
R. Boesel	85C	12th

28 July, Michigan International Speedway

E. Fittipaldi	85C	1st
A. Unser	85C	2nd
J. Rutherford	85C	4th
B. Rahal	85C	6th
K. Cogan	85C	7th
S. Brayton	85C-Buick	8th
S. Chassey	85C-Chevrolet	12th

4 August, Elkhart Lake, Wisconsin

J. Villeneuve	85C	1st
Mike Andretti	85C	2nd
B. Rahal	85C	4th
E. Fittipaldi	85C	5th
A. Unser	85C	7th
R. Boesel	85C	8th
H. Johnson	85C	12th

18 August, Pocono, Pennsylvania

R. Mears	85C	1st
A. Unser	85C	3rd
B. Rahal	85C	4th
D. Sullivan	85C	5th
E. Fittipaldi	85C	6th
D. Simon	85C	10th
S. Chassey	85C-Chevrolet	11th
D. Carter	85C	12th

1 September, Mid Ohio

B. Rahal	85C	1st
D. Sullivan	85C	2nd
J. Villeneuve	85C	3rd
B. Giacomelli	85C	6th
E. Fittipaldi	85C	8th
J. Garza	85C	11th
S. Chassey	85C-Chevrolet	12th

8 September, Sanair, Quebec, Canada

J. Rutherford	85C	1st
D. Carter	85C	2nd
G. Brabham	85C	4th
D. Sullivan	85C	5th
J. Garza	85C	6th
K. Cogan	85C	9th

22 September, Michigan International Speedway

B. Rahal	85C	1st
R. Mears	85C	2nd
K. Cogan	85C	4th
J. Garza	85C	6th
D. Ongais	85C	7th
D. Sullivan	85C	8th
J. Rutherford	85C	9th
D. Carter	85C	10th
P. Halsmer	85C	11th
A. Unser	85C	12th

6 October, Laguna Seca, California

B. Rahal	85C	1st
A. Unser	85C	2nd
R. Guerrero	85C	4th
B. Giacomelli	85C	6th
J. Garza	85C	7th
D. Sullivan	85C	8th
Mike Andretti	85C	9th
R. Keegan	85C	12th

13 October, Phoenix, Arizona

A. Unser	85C	1st
D. Sullivan	85C	4th
Mike Andretti	85C	5th
B. Rahal	85C	6th
D. Carter	85C	7th
E. Fittipaldi	85C	8th
J. Garza	85C	10th
S. Chassey	85C-Chevrolet	11th
G. Brabham	85C	12th

9 November, Tamiami Park, Florida

D. Sullivan	85C	1st
B. Rahal	85C	2nd
A. Unser	85C	4th
R. Moreno	85C	5th
D. Ongais	85C	6th
B. Whittington	85C	8th
J. Garza	85C	9th
R. Keegan	85C	10th
D. Dobson	85C	11th

1986

6 April, Phoenix, Arizona

K. Cogan	86C	1st
T. Sneva	86C	2nd
E. Fittipaldi	86C	3rd
D. Sullivan	86C	4th
J. Rutherford	86C	5th
R. Guerrero	86C	8th
R. Lanier	86C	11th

13 April, Long Beach, California

Mike Andretti	86C	1st
T. Sneva	86C	4th
J. Garza	85C	7th
J. Villeneuve	86C	8th
J. Rutherford	86C	9th
D. Sullivan	86C	11th
D. Dobson	85C	12th

1 June, Indianapolis 500,
Indianapolis Motor Speedway, Indiana

B. Rahal	86C	1st
K. Cogan	86C	2nd
R. Mears	86C	3rd
R. Guerrero	86C	4th
Mike Andretti	86C	6th
E. Fittipaldi	86C	7th
J. Rutherford	86C	8th
D. Sullivan	86C	9th
R. Lanier	86C	10th
G. Bettenhausen	85C	11th

8 June, Milwaukee, Wisconsin

Mike Andretti	86C	1st
T. Sneva	86C	2nd
R. Mears	86C	3rd
J. Rutherford	86C	4th
B. Rahal	86C	6th
J. Garza	86C	7th
E. Pimm	86C	10th
D. Sullivan	86C	11th

15 June, Portland, Oregon

Mike Andretti	86C	2nd
T. Sneva	86C	4th
J. Villeneuve	86C	5th
E. Pimm	86C	6th
R. Lanier	86C	9th
M. Nish	86C	10th

29 June, Meadowlands, New York

D. Sullivan	86C	1st
E. Fittipaldi	86C	2nd
B. Rahal	86C	3rd
R. Guerrero	86C	4th
J. Villeneuve	86C	5th
R. Lanier	86C	6th
J. Rutherford	86C	7th
J. Garza	86C	8th
D. Dobson	86C	11th
E. Pimm	86C	12th

6 July, Cleveland, Ohio

D. Sullivan	86C	1st
Mike Andretti	86C	2nd
R. Mears	86C	4th
T. Sneva	86C	5th
J. Garza	86C	7th
R. Lanier	86C	9th
J. Rutherford	86C	10th
R. Miaskiewicz	85C	11th

20 July, Toronto, Ontario, Canada

B. Rahal	86C	1st
D. Sullivan	86C	2nd
K. Cogan	86C	5th
A. Luyendyk	86C	6th
R. Mears	86C	8th
T. Sneva	86C	9th
J. Rutherford	86C	10th
J. Morton	86C	12th

2 August, Michigan International Speedway

J. Rutherford	86C	1st
J. Garza	86C	2nd

17 August, Pocono, Pennsylvania

K. Cogan	86C	2nd
A. J. Foyt	86C	4th
J. Garza	86C	7th
R. Mears	86C	8th
S. Swindell	86C	9th

31 August, Mid Ohio

B. Rahal	86C	1st
R. Guerrero	86C	2nd
D. Sullivan	86C	3rd
K. Cogan	86C	4th
D. Daly	86C	6th
J. Rutherford	86C	8th
Mike Andretti	86C	10th
J. Villeneuve	86C	11th

7 September, Sanair, Quebec, Canada

B. Rahal	86C	1st
E. Fittipaldi	86C	3rd
K. Cogan	86C	4th
D. Sullivan	86C	5th
Mike Andretti	86C	6th
J. Parsons	86C	7th
D. Daly	86C	10th

28 September, Michigan International Speedway

B. Rahal	86C	1st
Mike Andretti	86C	2nd
E. Fittipaldi	86C	3rd
K. Cogan	86C	4th
E. Pimm	86C	7th
R. Mears	86C-Ilmor/Chevy	8th
J. Rutherford	86C	9th
D. Sullivan	86C	12th

4 October, Elkhart Lake, Wisconsin

E. Fittipaldi	86C	1st
Mike Andretti	86C	2nd
R. Mears	86C-Ilmor/Chevy	3rd
R. Guerrero	86C	4th
B. Rahal	86C	5th
D. Sullivan	86C	6th
J. Villeneuve	86C	10th

12 October, Laguna Seca, California

B. Rahal	86C	1st
D. Sullivan	86C	2nd
Mike Andretti	86C	3rd
R. Guerrero	86C	5th
E. Fittipaldi	86C	7th
K. Cogan	86C	9th
E. Pimm	86C	11th
J. Rutherford	86C	12th

19 October, Phoenix, Arizona

Mike Andretti	86C	1st
D. Sullivan	86C	2nd
B. Rahal	86C	3rd
E. Fittipaldi	86C	5th
E. Pimm	86C	7th

9 November, Tamiami Park, Florida

R. Guerrero	86C	2nd
K. Cogan	86C	4th
J. Villeneuve	86C	6th
B. Rahal	86C	8th
E. Pimm	86C	10th
J. Rutherford	86C	12th

1987

5 April, Long Beach, California

A. Unser Jnr	87C	2nd
T. Sneva	87C	3rd
Mike Andretti	87C	4th
J. Garza	87C	5th
C. Robinson	86C	6th
R. Lewis	86C	8th
J. MacPherson	87C	10th
T. Bettenhausen	86C	11th

12 April, Phoenix, Arizona

R. Guerrero	87C	1st
A. Luyendyk	87C	3rd
Mike Andretti	87C	4th
J. Garza	87C	6th
G. Brabham	87C-Judd/Honda	8th
J. Rutherford	87C	9th
F. Barbazza	87C	12th

24 May, Indianapolis 500,
Indianapolis Motor Speedway, Indiana

A. Unser	86C	1st
R. Guerrero	87C	2nd
F. Barbazza	87C	3rd
A. Unser Jnr	87C	4th
G. Bettenhausen	86C	5th
S. Fox	86C	7th
J. MacPherson	87C-Judd/Honda	8th
T. Bettenhausen	86C	10th
J. Rutherford	87C	11th

31 May, Milwaukee, Wisconsin

Mike Andretti	87C	1st
B. Rahal	87C	2nd
A. Luyendyk	87C	4th
A. Unser Jnr	87C	5th
E. Fittipaldi	87C-Ilmor/Chevy	7th
J. MacPherson	87C-Judd/Honda	8th
D. Sullivan	86C-Ilmor/Chevy	11th
G. Brabham	87C-Judd/Honda	12th

14 June, Portland, Oregon

Mike Andretti	87C	2nd
F. Barbazza	87C	4th
S. Brayton	87C	5th
J. Garza	87C	6th
J. Rutherford	87C	7th
R. Lewis	87C	8th
G. Brabham	87C-Judd/Honda	9th

28 June, Meadowlands, New York

E. Fittipaldi	87C-Ilmor/Chevy	3rd
G. Brabham	87C-Judd/Honda	4th
Mike Andretti	87C	5th
A. Luyendyk	87C	6th
T. Sneva	86C-Buick	7th
A. Unser Jnr	87C	8th
S. Brayton	87C	10th
J. Rutherford	87C	11th
K. Cogan	87C-Ilmor/Chevy	12th

5 July, Cleveland, Ohio

E. Fittipaldi	87C-Ilmor/Chevy	1st
A. Unser Jnr	87C	3rd
D. Sullivan	86C-Ilmor/Chevy	4th
R. Guerrero	87C	5th
Mike Andretti	87C	6th
T. Sneva	87C	8th
J. Rutherford	87C	9th
R. Lewis	87C	12th

19 July, Toronto, Ontario, Canada

E. Fittipaldi	87C-Ilmor/Chevy	1st
D. Sullivan	86C-Ilmor/Chevy	2nd
R. Guerrero	87C	4th
Mike Andretti	87C	5th
T. Sneva	87C	6th
A. Luyendyk	87C	7th
S. Goodyear	87C	8th
R. Lewis	87C	9th
F. Barbazza	87C	10th
R. Miaskiewicz	86C	12th

2 August, Michigan International Speedway

Mike Andretti	87C	1st
A. Unser	86C	2nd
D. Sullivan	86C-Ilmor/Chevy	4th
A. Luyendyk	87C	5th
F. Barbazza	87C	6th
E. Fittipaldi	87C-Ilmor/Chevy	7th
G. Brabham	87C-Judd/Honda	8th
D. Jones	86C	10th
T. Bettenhausen	86C	11th
J. Garza	87C	12th

16 August, Pocono, Pennsylvania

R. Mears	86C-Ilmor/Chevy	1st
G. Brabham	87C-Judd/Honda	2nd
R. Guerrero	87C	3rd
A. Luyendyk	87C	4th
D. Carter	87C	6th
Mike Andretti	87C	8th
K. Cogan	87C-Ilmor/Chevy	9th
J. Garza	87C	11th

30 August, Elkhart Lake, Wisconsin

G. Brabham	87C-Judd/Honda	2nd
A. Unser Jnr	87C	3rd
A. Luyendyk	87C	4th
D. Sullivan	86C-Ilmor/Chevy	5th
J. Andretti	87C	6th
R. Guerrero	87C	7th
F. Barbazza	87C	8th
R. Mears	86C-Ilmor/Chevy	9th

6 September, Mid Ohio

R. Guerrero	87C	1st
D. Sullivan	86C-Ilmor/Chevy	3rd
R. Mears	86C-Ilmor/Chevy	4th
K. Cogan	87C-Ilmor/Chevy	5th
E. Fittipaldi	87C-Ilmor/Chevy	6th
G. Brabham	87C-Judd/Honda	7th
J. Garza	87C	8th
J. Andretti	87C	10th
A. Luyendyk	87C	11th
J. Rutherford	87C	12th

20 September, Nazareth, Pennsylvania

Mike Andretti	87C	1st
R. Mears	86C-Ilmor/Chevy	3rd
A. Luyendyk	87C	4th
K. Cogan	87C-Ilmor/Chevy	5th
A. Unser Jnr	87C	6th
J. Garza	87C	8th
J. MacPherson	87C	9th
A. Unser	87C	10th
G. Brabham	87C-Judd/Honda	11th
J. Andretti	87C	12th

11 October, Laguna Seca, California

D. Sullivan	86C-Ilmor/Chevy	2nd
R. Mears	86C-Ilmor/Chevy	3rd
A. Unser Jnr	87C	4th
G. Brabham	87C-Judd/Honda	5th
A. Luyendyk	87C	6th
J. Andretti	87C	7th
J. Garza	87C	8th
J. MacPherson	87C	9th
S. Goodyear	87C	11th
D. Carter	87C	12th

31 October, Tamiami Park, Florida

D. Sullivan	86C-Ilmor/Chevy	2nd
R. Boesel	87C	3rd
E. Fittipaldi	87C-Ilmor/Chevy	4th
A. Unser Jnr	87C	5th
R. Mears	86C-Ilmor/Chevy	6th
Mike Andretti	87C	7th

1 November, Tamiami Park, Florida

Mike Andretti	87C	1st
A. Unser Jnr	87C	2nd
G. Brabham	87C-Judd/Honda	3rd
R. Mears	86C-Ilmor/Chevy	5th
R. Boesel	87C	6th
J. Andretti	87C	8th

1988

10 April, Phoenix, Arizona

Mike Andretti	88C	3rd
R. Boesel	88C	5th
T. Fabi	88C-Porsche	7th
K. Cogan	87C	8th
H. Holmes	88C	10th
B. Vukovich	87C	11th
S. Atchison	86C	12th

17 April, Long Beach, California

A. Unser Jnr	88C-Ilmor/Chevy	1st
K. Cogan	87C	3rd
R. Boesel	88C	4th
R. Moran	87C	6th
Mike Andretti	88C	7th
S. Atchison	86C	9th

29 May, Indianapolis 500,
Indianapolis Motor Speedway, Indiana

E. Fittipaldi	88C-Ilmor/Chevy	2nd
Mike Andretti	88C	4th
P. Krueger	88C	8th
K. Cogan	88C	11th
H. Holmes	88C	12th

5 June, Milwaukee, Wisconsin

E. Fittipaldi	88C-Ilmor/Chevy	3rd
R. Boesel	88C	4th
Mike Andretti	88C	7th
H. Holmes	88C	8th
T. Fabi	88C-Porsche	9th

19 June, Portland, Oregon

E. Fittipaldi	88C-Ilmor/Chevy	3rd
A. Unser Jnr	88C-Ilmor/Chevy	4th
T. Fabi	88C-Porsche	7th
J. Jones	88C	8th
Mike Andretti	88C	11th

3 July, Cleveland, Ohio

A. Unser Jnr	88C-Ilmor/Chevy	4th
J. Jones	88C	7th
K. Cogan	88C	10th
S. Atchison	86C	12th

17 July, Toronto, Ontario, Canada

A. Unser Jnr	88C-Ilmor/Chevy	1st
Mike Andretti	88C	3rd
J. Jones	88C	7th
T. Fabi	88C-Porsche	10th
H. Holmes	88C	11th
R. Moran	87C	12th

24 July, Meadowlands, New York

A. Unser Jnr	88C-Ilmor/Chevy	1st
Mike Andretti	88C	6th
J. Jones	88C	7th
T. Bettenhausen	88C	8th

7 August, Michigan International Speedway

P. Krueger	86C	5th
J. Jones	88C	8th
S. Atchison	86C	10th

21 August, Pocono, Pennsylvania

A. Unser Jnr	88C-Ilmor/Chevy	2nd
R. Guerrero	88C	3rd
H. Holmes	88C	7th
J. Jones	88C	8th
B. Vukovich	88C	9th
R. Vogler	88C	11th
S. Atchison	88C	12th

4 September, Mid Ohio

A. Unser Jnr	88C-Ilmor/Chevy	4th
J. Jones	88C	7th
T. Fabi	88C-Porsche	8th
E. Pimm	87C	12th

11 September, Elkhart Lake, Wisconsin

A. Unser Jnr	88C-Ilmor/Chevy	7th
T. Fabi	88C-Porsche	8th
H. Holmes	88C	11th

25 September, Nazareth, Pennsylvania

T. Fabi	88C-Porsche	4th
R. Guerrero	87C	6th
J. Jones	88C	11th

16 October, Laguna Seca, California

A. Unser Jnr	88C-Ilmor/Chevy	6th
K. Cogan	88C	9th
T. Fabi	88C-Porsche	10th

5 November, Tamiami Park, Florida

A. Unser Jnr	88C-Ilmor/Chevy	4th

6 November, Tamiami Park, Florida

A. Unser Jnr	88C-Ilmor/Chevy	1st
K. Cogan	88C	4th
B. Jourdain	86C	6th
H. Holmes	88C	8th
S. Atchison	86C	9th

1989

9 April, Phoenix, Arizona

T. Fabi	89P-Porsche	6th
K. Cogan	88C	10th

16 April, Long Beach, California

T. Sneva	86C-Buick	10th

28 May, Indianapolis 500,
Indianapolis Motor Speedway, Indiana

R. Vogler	88C	8th

4 June, Milwaukee, Wisconsin

T. Fabi	89P-Porsche	3rd

18 June, Detroit, Michigan

T. Fabi	89P-Porsche	4th
R. Guerrero	89CE-Alfa Romeo	8th

25 June, Portland, Oregon

T. Fabi	89P-Porsche	4th

2 July, Cleveland, Ohio

T. Fabi	89P-Porsche	4th
K. Cogan	88C	11th

Appendix 3
Cars manufactured by type

Year	Type	Description	No. made	Total overall
1969				
	693	Formula 3	1	1
1970				
	701	Formula 1	10	10
	702	Formula 2	6	6
	703	Formula 3	16	17
	705	Formula B (Atlantic)	5	5
	707	Group 7 Can-Am sports	3	3
	708	Formula Ford 1600	8	8
	709	Formula Ford USA	2	10
		Total 1970	50	51
1971				
	711	Formula 1	7	17
	712M	Formula 2 (monocoque)	20	26
	713M	Formula 3 (monocoque)	11	28
	713S	Formula 3 (spaceframe)	9	37
	717	Group 7 Can-Am sports	1	4
	718	Formula Ford 1600	4	14
	719	Formula Ford USA	3	17
	71B	Formula Atlantic/B USA	13	18
		Total 1971	68	119
1972				
	721	Formula 1	4	21
	721G	Formula 1 (based on F2)	6	27
	721X	Formula 1 (mid-gearbox)	2	29
	722	Formula 2	20	46
	722	Formula Atlantic	4	22
	722	Formula B USA	20	42
	723	Formula 3	20	57
	722A	Formula 5000	1	1
	729	Formula Ford USA	6	23
		Total 1972	83	202
1973				
	731	Formula 1	5	34
	732	Formula 2	14	60
	733	Formula 3	26	83
	73A	Formula 5000	6	7
	73B	Formula Atlantic/B	22	64
	73S	Group 5 2-litre sports	19	19
		Total 1973	92	294

Year	Type	Description	No. made	Total overall
1974				
	741	Formula 1	2	36
	742	Formula 2	30	90
	743	Formula 3	29	112
	74A	Formula 5000	2	9
	74B	Formula Atlantic/B	13	77
	74S	Group 5 2-litre sports	11	30
		Total 1974	87	381
1975				
	751	Formula 1	5	41
	752	Formula 2	25	115
	753	Formula 3	22	134
	75A	Formula 5000	1	10
	75B	Formula Atlantic/B	12	89
	75R	Formula Renault	8	8
	75S	Group 5 2-litre sports	5	35
		Total 1975	78	459
1976				
	761	Formula 1	6	47
	762	Formula 2	19	134
	763	Formula 3	16	150
	76A	Formula 5000	2	12
	76B	Formula Atlantic/B	20	109
	76S	Group 5 2-litre sports	2	37
	76S	Group 5 3-litre sports	1	38
		Total 1976	66	525
1977				
	771	Formula 1	2	49
	761B	Formula 1 (updated 761)	2	51
	2-4-0	Formula 1 (4 rear wheels added to 761)	0	
	772	Formula 2	8	142
	772P	Formula 2 (Atlantic-based)	2	144
	773	Formula 3	18	168
	77B	Formula Atlantic/B	29	138
		Total 1977	61	586

Year	Type	Description	No. made	Total overall
1978				
	781	Formula 1	2	53
	782	Formula 2	29	173
	772	Formula 2 (Hillclimb)	1	174
	783	Formula 3/Super Vee	31	199
	78B	Formula Atlantic/B	19	157
	77B	Formula Atlantic/B	1	158
		Total 1978	83	669
1979				
	792	Formula 2	32	206
	793	Formula 3	25	224
	79C	Formula 3 (based on 792)	1	225
	79B	Formula Atlantic/B	23	181
	79A	Formula B (based on 792)	3	184
	79V	Formula Super Vee	21	21
		Total 1979	105	774
1980				
	802	Formula 2	25	231
	803	Formula 3	27	252
	80A	Formula Atlantic/B	25	209
	80V	Formula Super Vee	16	37
		Total 1980	93	867
1981				
	811	Formula 1	6	59
	812	Formula 2	11	242
	813	Formula 3	12	264
	81H	Hillclimb	1	1
	81A	Formula B (USA-spec)	9	218
	81A	Formula Atlantic/Pacific	5	223
	81S	Sports 2000	5	5
	81P	GTP	1	1
	81C	Indianapolis	9	9
	817	Can-Am Group 7 sports	3	7
		Total 1981	62	929
1982				
	822	Formula 2	13	255
	82A	Formula Atlantic/B	5	228
	82C	Indianapolis	20	29
	82G	Group C & GTP	4	5
	82S	Sports 2000	5	10
		Total 1982	47	976

Year	Type	Description	No. made	Total overall
1983				
	832	Formula 2	25	280
	822	Formula 2	1	281
	83C	Indianapolis	21	50
	83G	Group C & GTP	5	10
	83S	Sports 2000	8	18
		Total 1983	60	1036
1984				
	842	Formula 2	20	301
	84C	Indianapolis	47	97
	84G	Group C & GTP	7	17
	84S	Sports 2000	3	21
		Total 1984	77	1113
1985				
	85J	Formula 2 (for Japan)	11	312
	85C	Indianapolis	44	141
	85B	Formula 3000	16	16
	85G	Group C & GTP	10	27
	85O	Oldsmobile record car	2	2
		Total 1985	83	1196
1986				
	86J	Formula 2 (for Japan)	15	327
	86C	Indianapolis	38	179
	86B	Formula 3000	19	35
	86G	Group C & GTP	11	38
	86A	ARS	20	20
		Total 1986	103	1299
1987				
	871	Formula 1	3	62
	87P	Formula 1 (F3000-based)	1	63
	87C	Indianapolis	33	212
	87B	Formula 3000	37	72
	87G	Group C & GTP	3	41
		Total 1987	77	1376
1988				
	881	Formula 1	4	67
	88C	Indianapolis	20	232
	88B	Formula 3000	22	94
	88GC	Grand Champion	8	8
	88G	Group C & GTP	1	42
	86A	ARS	4	24
		Total 1988	59	1435

Total number of cars manufactured by formula

Formula 2	327
Formula 3	264
Indianapolis	232
Formula Atlantic/B	228
Formula 3000	94
Formula 1	67
Group C & GTP	42
Group 5 2/3-litre sports	38
Super Vee	37
ARS	24
Formula Ford	23
Sports 2000	21
Formula 5000	12
Formula Renault	8
Grand Champion	8
Can-Am	7
Oldsmobile record car	2
Hillclimb	1
Total	1435